ADJUSTMENT CRISIS in the THIRD WORLD

Richard E. Feinberg and
Valeriana Kallab, Editors

Contributors:

Albert Fishlow
Tony Killick
Graham Bird
Jennifer Sharpley
Mary Sutton
Stanley Please
Joan M. Nelson
Colin I. Bradford, Jr.
Riordan Roett
Lance Taylor
DeLisle Worrell

Transaction Books
New Brunswick (USA) and London (UK)

Copyright © 1984 by Overseas Development Council, Washington, D.C.

All rights reserved under International and Pan-American Copyright Conventions.
No part of this book may be reproduced or transmitted in any form or by any means,
electronic or mechanical, including photocopy, recording, or any information storage and retrieval system, without prior permission in writing from the publisher. All
inquiries should be addressed to Transaction Books, Rutgers—The State University,
New Brunswick, New Jersey 08903.

Library of Congress Catalog Number: 84-8690
ISBN: 0-87855-988-4 (paper)
Printed in the United States of America

Library of Congress Cataloging in Publication Data
Main entry under title:

Adjustment crisis in the Third World.

    1. Developing countries—Economic policy—Addresses, essays,
lectures. 2. Developing countries—Foreign economic relations—
Addresses, essays, lectures. 3. Debts, External—Developing coun-
tries—Addresses, essays, lectures. 4. International Monetary
Fund—Addresses, essays, lectures. 5. World Bank—Addresses, es-
says, lectures. I. Feinberg, Richard E. II. Kallab, Valeriana.
HC59.7.A733   1984   337'.09172'4   84-8690
ISBN 0-87855-988-4 (pbk.)

Adjustment Crisis in the Third World

Acknowledgments

Series Editors and Project Directors:
Richard E. Feinberg
Valeriana Kallab

Associate Editor:
Linda Starke

In the course of the preparation of this first volume in the Overseas Development Council's new series, *U.S.-Third World Policy Perspectives*, many individuals have in different ways earned the admiration and gratitude of their ODC colleagues. The editors especially want to highlight and express personal thanks for the roles played by John W. Sewell, ODC president, and John P. Lewis, ODC senior advisor and chairman of the Program Advisory Committee, both of whom contributed importantly to the substantive planning of this volume and the series and provided valuable comments and criticisms along the way; with characteristic grace and good sportsmanship, they chose to act as consulting editors "in the wings."

Members of the ODC Board and Program Advisory Committee called attention to various aspects of the adjustment crisis in the Third World that merited analysis and policy advice in this volume, helped to identify and persuade the experts who could contribute to this effort, and commented on manuscript drafts. ODC visiting fellows Ernest H. Preeg and Joan M. Nelson provided valuable comments on several manuscripts. The editors also wish to express the Council's gratitude and their personal thanks to the authors for their dedication, patience, and humor in the development and shaping of their presentations, whereby they made the project interesting and enjoyable for all involved.

Special recognition and thanks for their respective roles in the preparation of *Adjustment Crisis in the Third World* go to project associate editor Linda Starke; to Philip Murphy and Carol Cramer for editorial assistance; and to Rosemarie Philips, Nellie Rimkus, Moira AE McQuillen, and Louise A. Fleischman for valuable administrative contributions in laying the groundwork for the series and this volume. Special thanks for skillfully applying new techniques to the production of this volume go to Robin E. Ward and Marguerite Turner.

Scott Bramson of Transaction Books and Steve Wetzler of Mid-Atlantic Photo Composition deserve thanks for their contributions, respectively, to promotion and distribution of the series and to production planning and execution. The series design of the *U.S.-Third World Policy Perspectives* series is the work of John Kaljee of Artwork Unlimited, to whom the Council and the editors are especially grateful for the preparation of this first volume. Credit and thanks for printing this book go to Wayne C. Penley, Sr., and Thomas Hicks of Victor Graphics.

The Overseas Development Council gratefully acknowledges the help of the Ford, William and Flora Hewlett, and Rockefeller Foundations, whose financial support contributes to the preparation of this series.

Contents

Preface ix

Overview: The Adjustment Imperative and U.S. Policy
Richard E. Feinberg 3

    Chronic Crisis 5
    U.S. Interests 11
    Future Action 15

Summaries of Recommendations 19

1. The Debt Crisis: Round Two Ahead?
Albert Fishlow 31

    A Liquidity Crisis? 38
    A Closer Look at the Assumptions 40
    The Politics of Adjustment and Default 46
    The Present Policy Mold 49
    Radical Proposals for Restructuring Debt 53
    A More Feasible Alternative 55

2. The IMF: Case for a Change in Emphasis
Tony Killick, Graham Bird, Jennifer Sharpley, and Mary Sutton ... 59

    The Case for Change in IMF Conditionality 61
    A "Real-Economy" Strategy: Adjustment With Growth 64
    Implications for IMF Practices and Policies 68
    Possible Sources of Additional Financing 73
    The Case for Change in Developing-Country Policies 76
    Conclusion 80

3. The World Bank: Lending for Structural Adjustment
Stanley Please 83

    Structural Adjustment Lending 87
    Constraints on the Program 89
    Qualitative Evaluation 93
    Public Expenditures 96

4. The Politics of Stabilization
Joan M. Nelson 99

    Determinants of Political Sustainability 101
    Political Sustainability: What Governments Can Do 108
    Political Sustainability: What Outsiders Can Do 114

5. **The NICs: Confronting U.S. "Autonomy"**
   Colin I. Bradford, Jr. 119

   Outward-Oriented Growth Strategies: Some Cautions 121
   Global Shifts in Industrial Structure 126
   The Global Policy Stalemate 129
   Conclusions 136

6. **Brazil's Debt Crisis**
   Riordan Roett 139

   The Situation in Brazil 140
   The Political Impact of the Crisis 141
   U.S. Policy Choices 143
   Conclusion 145

7. **Mexico's Adjustment in the 1980s:**
   Look Back Before Leaping Ahead
   Lance Taylor 147

   Price Rationalization and the Exchange Rate 148
   Ineffectiveness of Supply-Side Pricing 148
   Demand Contraction: The IMF Package 150
   Need for Financial Reform 152
   Some Problems with Trade Liberalization 153
   Policies for the Future 153
   Alternatives for the United States 157

8. **Central America and the Caribbean:**
   Adjustment in Small, Open Economies
   DeLisle Worrell 159

   The Seventies (1970-79) 162
   The Second Oil Shock and Aftermath (1979-82) 163
   Governmental Responses to the Crisis 165
   Challenges and Responses: An Evaluation 167
   Recommendations 174

About the Overseas Development Council
   and the Contributors 182

Preface:
U.S.-Third World Policy Perspectives

With this first volume, the Overseas Development Council initiates a new policy book series, *U.S.-Third World Policy Perspectives*. This major new innovation in the Council's program is designed to provide those who determine U.S. foreign policy and those who shape international development strategies—in both the public and private sectors—with policy-relevant, timely, and accessible analyses of important issues in U.S.-Third World relations.

ODC's *Policy Perspectives* focus on priority issues on which decisions are yet to be made and seek to identify new policy options or new insights on the implications of proposals already being debated. In its selection of issues and the identification of analysts with expertise to address them, ODC benefits from the views of members of its Program Advisory Committee, listed at the end of this volume. All chapters are commissioned by the Council as part of its policy analysis program.

Like *Adjustment Crisis in the Third World*, each book in the series will offer several perspectives on different aspects of a single policy theme. All of the analyses included will contain specific policy recommendations. While each volume of *Policy Perspectives* will air differing opinions on the central theme, most of the contributing authors are likely to share ODC's basic persuasion that increased interdependence between the United States and developing countries is a *positive* historical development whose continuity requires vigorous, affirmative action by all parties, public and private.

Other institutions and their publications now analyze issues and provide recommendations for policy on various aspects of international economic relations or Third World economic and social development. But none do so with a specific focus on the *U.S.-Third World dimension* of international economic issues. This continues to be the unique trademark of ODC. We believe that a wealth of important and potentially useful research and analysis of immediate significance for policy making is generated in American universities, research organizations, and private commercial institutions. Only a small fraction of this valuable work, however, is available to those who need it *when* they need it. ODC's programs, including the new policy series, strive to help fill this gap.

Policy Perspectives will increase the frequency with which the Council calls attention to U.S.-Third World policy issues and highlights proposals for their resolution. It will incorporate ODC's familiar *Agenda* series of U.S. policy assessments, *U.S. Foreign Policy and the Third World*, on a biennial basis. The next four volumes in the series scheduled for 1984-85 are: *Uncertain Future: Commercial Banks in the Third World; U.S. Foreign Policy and the Third World: Agenda 1985; U.S. Trade Policy and Developing Countries;* and *Development Strategies: A New Synthesis* (see detailed announcement at end of this volume).

We invite readers to send us their comments, criticisms, and suggestions on this and future *Policy Perspectives* as well as their views on issues that need further clarification that might be strengthened by coverage in this new series.

John W. Sewell, *President*
Overseas Development Council

Adjustment Crisis in the Third World:

Overview and Summaries of Recommendations

The Adjustment Imperative and U.S. Policy

Richard E. Feinberg

If development was the dominant theme and aspiration of the Third World in the 1950s and 1960s, adjustment is the painful necessity of the 1980s. In retrospect, the 1970s appear to have been a decade of transition between a golden era of optimism and relatively steady growth and a new period of lowered expectations and austerity. Some developing countries have managed to adjust to a tougher global environment and are beginning to benefit from the incipient recovery in some industrial countries and the resulting modest increase in commodity prices. But most developing nations have yet to accommodate fully to the international realities of the 1980s or to regain positive per capita growth (see Table 1). Some Asian nations are expanding, but most Latin American economies remain deeply depressed. Many countries in Sub-Saharan Africa are unlikely to achieve higher living standards in this century.

Over the past decade, the developing countries have had to adjust simultaneously to four cataclysmic shifts. First, they have had to accept lower living standards to offset the higher costs of oil and capital, the global recession, and, most recently, the retrenchment in international financial markets. Second, they have had to alter investment priorities and relative prices to adjust to the changing costs of energy, food, and other internationally traded goods. Third, their productive structures have been battered by the accelerating pace of technological innovation and by the changing international division of labor as comparative advantage in many

Table 1. Real Growth Rates of Output
(per cent)

	1970-79[a]	1980	1981	1982	1983
Industrial Countries[b]	3.5	1.3	1.6	−0.1	2.3
United States	3.4	−0.3	2.6	−1.9	3.3
Oil Exporters	6.7	−2.0	−4.0	−4.3	−1.1
Non-Oil Exporting Countries	5.0	4.8	2.8	1.5	1.6
Africa[c]	3.7	3.0	1.8	1.2	0.1
Asia[c]	4.8	5.4	5.1	4.5	6.5
Western Hemisphere[c]	6.2	6.1	0.2	−1.6	−2.3

[a] Annual average.
[b] OECD countries, excluding Greece, Portugal, and Turkey.
[c] Excludes oil-exporters in area. Asia includes China.
Sources: IMF, *World Economic Outlook, 1984* (Washington, D.C.: 1984) and IMF, *International Financial Statistics Yearbook* (Washington, D.C.: 1983).

industries has shifted dynamically from one country to another. Fourth, countries are under increasing pressure to expose themselves more fully to these international phenomena—that is, to liberalize their economies. These pressures have come from the Bretton Woods institutions, which are advising policies of austerity and liberalization; from the commercial banks, which refuse to fund programs that merely postpone adjustment; and from the market itself, the most relentless foe of illusions.

The dual task of stabilization (bringing expenditures into line with available resources) and liberalization (freeing prices to reflect international cost structures) makes for a formidable agenda. This combination of income stabilization and price alteration is commonly referred to as "adjustment."

Although the world economy took a turn for the better in 1983, the adjustment process is not going smoothly. As Albert Fishlow points out in Chapter 1, the world economy is plagued by a continuing crisis of debt. Initially, the crisis was defined by whether the international financial system and the developing countries could reschedule enough debt and provide enough new loans to keep debtor countries "liquid." As the Argentine scare of March 1984 signaled, we may now be entering a more conflictive phase of the debt crisis. The question is not just whether governments can squeeze enough liquidity out of their economies to service their debt, but whether they will be willing to pay the political costs of continuing to do so. The prospect of remaining net exporters of capital to the international financial system—as interest payments exceed net new loans—is raising questions regarding the value of playing by the current rules. Politicians are asking whether their nations can service their debt and simultaneously resume development.

The United States has major economic, political, and strategic stakes in the global adjustment process. The incipient economic recovery of the North is weakened by the faltering South. Recession in Third World markets has cost U.S. firms and workers their income and jobs. Now the solvency of the international banking system is threatened. Politically, the repercussions of the adjustment process are everywhere undermining the legitimacy of governments. As a result, financial issues have moved to the top of the diplomatic agenda. The leadership role of the United States—and its competitive position with the Soviet Union in the Third World—will be affected by our capacity to bring the adjustment process to a successful close.

The contributors to this volume share the belief that constructive alternatives exist to the current "wait and see" policies—occasionally interrupted by sporadic actions forced by emergencies—prevalent in many industrial-country capitals. Concrete proposals are presented for new policies at all levels: for the International Monetary Fund and the World Bank, for the United States and other industrial-country governments, and for economic management in developing countries. If some of the innovative proposals involve expenditures and risks, the costs of current policies are every day more evident, and the dangers of systemic rupture persist.

Chronic Crisis

The near panic that gripped the international financial community in 1982 when Mexico and Brazil approached the precipice of default dissipated during 1983. The financial system demonstrated impressive flexibility in pulling together emergency credit packages and in restructuring payments falling due. The international financial institutions and policy makers in key industrial states responded with creativity under pressure. Meanwhile, growth resumed in the United States, West Germany, and Japan. For their part, the developing countries sharply cut their current-account deficits.

In a masterful display of coordination, energy, and innovation, the commercial banking system has rescheduled over $100 billion in debt. Having traditionally reserved rescheduling for exceptional emergencies, banks now accept the frequent, even regular, restructuring of loans. Indeed, banks have agreed to make available new loans as part of rescheduling exercises. The large money-center banks have successfully managed reschedulings involving hundreds of smaller banks, and some regional banks—despite their plans to withdraw gradually from international lending—have been persuaded not to declare slow-paying debtors in default. Although the banks initially justified high interest-rate spreads and rescheduling fees as fair compensation for high risk, more recently they have recognized that such charges were heaping further burdens on already depressed economies, and both spreads and fees have been narrowing.

The international policy community has acted with vigor to prevent banks from suffering catastrophic losses and to keep debt-ridden developing countries afloat. In particular, when the private markets suddenly halted lending—in a freeze-up that might have left key developing countries without liquidity and the means to maintain interest payments—the International Monetary Fund stepped in to fill a dangerous policy void. Moving decisively, the IMF rescued key developing countries by "bailing in" the commercial banks and the central banks of key industrial states. The IMF conditioned its own lending on the willingness of commercial banks to extend fresh loans to financially starved Mexico and Brazil, while the Federal Reserve Board and other central banks provided short-term "bridge" lines of credit. At the same time, the IMF successfully sought a substantial increase in its own resources from member countries.

Facing severe shortages of foreign exchange and needing to gain access to IMF and IMF-coordinated finance, some developing countries have transformed trade deficits into surpluses with astounding speed. The combined current-account deficits of non-oil developing countries dropped from $108 billion in 1981 to an estimated $56 billion in 1983. Inevitably, this precipitous adjustment required a violent contraction of imports and income. With world trade stagnant, exporters in most developing countries lacked the markets, resources, or time to contribute significantly.

Just as the origins of the crisis lie substantially in the global economy, so does improvement in the world economy offer the best and only real hope for recovery. In the 1970s, the sharp increases in

the price of oil created a demand for credit in oil-importing countries that the commercial banks, flush with deposits from oil-sur-
plus nations, were able and willing to fulfill. Some borrowers took
measures to adjust gradually to the real loss of income implied by
the higher price of energy, while others simply kept on borrowing. If
the heavy borrowers acted irresponsibly, they could not be blamed
for failing to foresee the second oil shock of 1979-80 and the subsequent tight monetary policies of the industrial states. Practically
overnight, loans that appeared cheap because their interest rates
were lower than the rate of inflation suddenly became dear, as
interest rates skyrocketed while inflation fell. Since most commercial credits now carry floating interest rates, the real debt burden
facing developing countries quickly reflected these onerous conditions. The heavy borrowers also could not be blamed for failing to
predict the depth and length of the 1980-82 global recession, and
the accompanying declines in world trade and commodity prices.
Nor did many financial experts foresee the panicky closing of the
international capital markets to most developing-country borrowers in 1982. As a result of these unanticipated shocks, the ratios
of debt service to exports and to GNP rose sharply at a time when
the commercial banks were no longer willing to provide much
credit to facilitate gradual adjustment.

Various projections by major institutions and influential private forecasters indicate that developing countries can recover, provided that the industrial world sustains growth rates of around 3
per cent and eschews protectionism, that developing-country terms
of trade improve, that heavily indebted countries restrict consumption and boost exports, that interest rates gradually fall, and that
adequate financing is available.[1] These are clearly very optimistic
assumptions. The industrial countries of the Organisation of Economic Co-operation and Development (OECD) have barely managed a 2-per cent annual growth rate in the past ten years. The
anticipated strong performance of the U.S. economy in 1984 should
drive the OECD as a whole to grow some 3.5 per cent—but its twin
fiscal and trade deficits could presage renewed recession in the
United States in 1985 or 1986. Alarmingly, in recent months interest rates have once again begun to rise.

Albert Fishlow in this volume questions common assumptions
regarding the links between the economies of North and South and
argues that even a sustained 3-per cent growth rate in the industrial countries may not be enough to permit a healthy recovery in
the developing world. He warns that some widely cited forecasts
have overstated the responsiveness of the value of developing-country exports to income growth in the industrial nations. Fishlow

suggests that rising protectionism may result in less trade-intensive world growth. He also points out that typically about one quarter of developing-country exports are destined for other developing countries—many of whose markets have been contracting. For example, Brazil's exports to other developing-country markets fell from $9 billion in 1981 to $6.8 billion in 1982. In 1983, Brazil's estimated exports to Latin America further declined by nearly $800 million.

Furthermore, some developing countries may lack the productive structure to respond quickly to new export opportunities. The recession in some developing countries has been so deep and prolonged that factories are too run-down or outmoded to export competitively. Moreover, foreign-exchange shortages may prevent firms from obtaining the necessary intermediate inputs to production, as well as from importing modern capital equipment. Thus unexpected problems may arise for Third World exports on both the supply and the demand sides.

So far, many developing countries have experienced more stabilization ("expenditure reduction") than genuine adjustment ("expenditure switching"). Many countries have realigned exchange rates, but producers have yet to adjust to the greater profitability of exports. In Chapter 2, Tony Killick and associates argue for an adjustment process that minimizes lost production by designing agricultural and industrial policies to stimulate supply (exports and import-substituting goods) rather than solely suppress demand. By this yardstick, world leaders have managed the adjustment process miserably.

Many developing countries are even failing to manage stabilization, at least as defined by the targets agreed upon with the International Monetary Fund. In several Asian countries—notably Taiwan, South Korea, and Singapore—governments opted for rapid adjustment and have been able to capitalize on earlier reforms to continue an impressive export expansion. The growing economies of India and China—relatively closed and therefore less exposed to the vicissitudes of the global economy—add luster to the Asian picture. But progress in Latin America and Africa has been much more painful and halting. Indeed, the persistent breakdown of IMF stabilization programs is placing the IMF's credibility in jeopardy just when the Fund has taken center-stage in the global adjustment process.

Several authors in this volume explain why so many national stabilization programs, and IMF agreements, are falling apart:

• **Inadequate financing**. Despite the expansion in IMF resources and the IMF's pressures on the banks to extend involuntary loans to major debtors, the availability of external finance has sharply contracted. Industrial-country members are stringently capping the amounts that the IMF can lend to individual countries. Levels of concessional aid are stagnant, equity investment by multinational firms is sharply down, and the commercial banks are dramatically retrenching. At the same time, while nominal interest rates have fallen, real rates remain very high. In 1983, non-oil developing countries were obliged to pay an estimated $52 billion in interest to private creditors, while receiving only some $20 billion in net new loans. The resulting net outflow of approximately $32 billion greatly exceeded the less than $15 billion in net resource transfers by the World Bank and the IMF combined.[2] Inadequate financing has reinforced the contractionary forces in the world economy.

• **Global imbalances**. The IMF was designed to promote open markets and global growth and to assist nations in overcoming balance-of-payments problems "without resorting to measures destructive of national and international prosperity." Finding itself in a prolonged global recession and with very limited resources, the IMF has felt compelled to recommend austerity programs that further reduce world trade and economic activity. At the same time, although the IMF has maintained a rhetoric of free trade and price liberalization, it has been supporting programs in countries where financial crises have forced the introduction of higher tariffs and tighter exchange controls. The IMF has signed a record number of stand-by agreements in a world increasingly characterized by government intervention in markets. Trapped in an environment not anticipated by its founders, and without adequate financial means, the IMF has been unable to accomplish its original objectives.

• **Political sustainability**. Afraid of tarnishing their image of political neutrality, IMF teams have sometimes failed to design programs sufficiently responsive to domestic political realities. Yet, as Joan Nelson argues in Chapter 4, a political strategy is as necessary as a sound economic model to make a stabilization program work. Moreover, whereas "shock treatment" may occasionally be advisable, a rapid economic turnaround is neither politically nor economically feasible in many countries. Riordan Roett warns in Chapter 6 that accumulating political pressures in Brazil threaten not only economic stabilization but also the cohesiveness of the social system and the process of political liberalization. As Lance Taylor notes in Chapter 7, Mexico has sharply cut back income and imports, but social pressures to rebuild and redistribute income endanger the harsh stabilization program.

• **Sense of injustice**. The commitment of many developing-country leaders to implement politically costly austerity programs has been weakened by their belief that the global recession was caused by forces beyond their control—whether OPEC price increases or OECD tight monetary policies—and that they are now being forced to shoulder an unfair portion of the costs of adjustment. As Nelson notes, austerity measures are less politically acceptable when the ultimate beneficiaries appear to be international banks. Moreover, developing countries are well aware that while the United States preaches fiscal austerity abroad, its own budget deficit is approaching 6 per cent of GNP and is partially being financed by borrowing abroad. This borrowing not only permits the United States to grow more rapidly than many developing countries, but, as Colin Bradford argues in Chapter 5, also contributes to higher international interest rates. Moreover, the United States is absorbing capital that might otherwise be available to other nations. In a reversal of history and logic, it has become a net borrower just when many developing countries have become net exporters of capital. True, the large U.S. trade deficit has facilitated developing-country exports; the U.S. trade balance with non-OPEC developing countries has shifted from a small surplus in 1981 to a deficit of $22 billion in 1983. However, the potentially advantageous political impact has been diluted by headline-grabbing decisions that limit the access of particular Third World products. The sense of injustice at the distribution of the costs of global adjustment has continued to ferment.

• **Ideological dichotomies**. The IMF tends to couple austerity measures with reforms that increase the role of the market and of private enterprise. More recently, the World Bank has closely tied its advocacy of export-led growth to internal price liberalization. As Killick points out, this resurgence of orthodoxy reflects political winds in the United States, the pressures of the global recession and inadequate financing, and the shortage of feasible alternatives. While recognizing the importance of "getting prices right," Bradford denies that the current orthodoxy correctly describes reality. He finds that some countries that have been successful exporters have indulged in illiberal pricing practices: "There is a great deal of heterogeneity and complexity in the real world, and the stylized version of the dichotomy between inward- and outward-oriented strategies should be drawn more cautiously." Similarly, Nelson points out that many Third World officials are skeptical of IMF orthodoxy and are therefore less committed to IMF stabilization programs. Expressing the views of a Central Bank official from Barbados, DeLisle Worrell's criticisms of IMF orthodoxy support this contention, as does Lance Taylor's description of the probable course of Mexico's development strategy.

• **National sovereignty**. Perceptions often lag behind changes in the material world. Growing economic interdependence has not been fully matched by a willingness to accept the accompanying reduction in national control over domestic economies. This volume presents contrasting views on how intrusive IMF programs ought to be. Killick argues for a widening of IMF jurisdiction (similar to the expanded role that Stanley Please describes for the World Bank's structural adjustment lending), while Worrell proposes that the IMF focus more narrowly on foreign-exchange targets, leaving the mix of other monetary and fiscal measures to national authorities. Developing countries are not alone, however, in wanting to retain a slipping sovereignty. Bradford interprets recent U.S. fiscal policy and refusal to coordinate macro-economic policies with other industrial states as an attempt to reassert national autonomy.

These political, financial, and ideological strains—together with uncertainties regarding future global growth and developing-country export performance—suggest that despite some signs of progress, severe problems remain. Nevertheless, some industrial governments seem to believe—or at least to hope—that the worst is over and that the crisis has been contained. The danger is that the North may conclude that no concerted action is required. The private sector may concur, as it loses interest in a stagnant Third World that is less able to purchase OECD exports or to play on international capital markets. Governments, banks, and firms will seek to minimize losses, while energies are turned toward the more secure, large, and dynamic intra-OECD markets and the markets of the limited number of newly industrializing country "success cases." The mass of developing countries could become increasingly marginal to the global system.

U.S. Interests

The United States has important stakes in the adjustment process. Economically, U.S. firms and banks have become increasingly dependent upon a healthy and growing developing world. Politically, the fallout from the adjustment process will affect U.S. diplomatic and perhaps even strategic interests around the globe. And America's humanitarian objectives are thwarted by the declining levels of nutrition and the resurgence of disease that are accompanying austerity in many countries.

Economic Interests

Successful adjustment in the developing countries would benefit U.S. firms, banks, and consumers. Expanding and more open Third World markets would serve U.S. exporters and investors, while Americans would enjoy relatively cheap imports from developing countries. U.S. banks would find existing exposure more secure, while markets would gradually expand for additional loans. But these advantages remain largely in the future. So far, the adjustment process has mostly accumulated costs for the United States. Between 1980 and 1983, U.S. exports to developing countries declined by $18.2 billion, eliminating approximately 578,000 jobs.[3] Had developing-country economies maintained their traditional rates of growth, a half million more Americans would have been employed in the U.S. export sector. Moreover, during 1981-83, real U.S. direct investment income from developing countries declined from 1980 levels by an estimated total of $10.4 billion (1980 dollars). An additional $3.6 billion would have been earned had traditional growth rates prevailed. This decline in U.S. exports and in receipts on assets abroad contributed to the alarmingly large U.S. current-account deficit.

Meanwhile, stabilization programs undertaken by developing countries have for the time being facilitated the servicing of interest payments due on accumulated debt. U.S. banks have continued to earn profitable returns from both branch operations and direct lending. However, the developing countries may not be able to continue servicing their debts and attaining adequate import levels at the same time. Thus the compression of developing-country economies threatens the most dynamic U.S. export markets—without ensuring the continued payment of debt service.

Political Interests

It is difficult to demonstrate a clear link between economic trends and politics. Economic growth does not guarantee political stability—indeed it can undermine *status quo* regimes—but prolonged economic decline often makes instability more likely. In any event, as the Kissinger Commission Report on Central America repeatedly asserted, political change, even violent revolution, does not necessarily pose a security threat to the United States.[4] Radical political change may, however, increase the opportunity for the Soviet Union to expand its influence, particularly if a new regime feels insecure and becomes dependent upon Soviet-bloc security assistance.

A smoothly functioning international economy provides the United States with a tremendous edge in its competition with the

Soviet Union for influence in the Third World. The Soviet Union's timid entry into the world economy has left it without much to offer to the Third World's major concern of economic development. Global prosperity provides a continuing inducement for already friendly or nonaligned regimes to remain so. Moreover, it makes regimes that are momentarily dependent on the Soviet Union but active in the world economy more likely to tread the well-worn path to nonalignment or realignment. Prolonged global recession devalues the major asset of the United States in the continuing competition between East and West.

Based on experiences in Europe in the 1930s, economic decline is still frequently associated with the emergence of political authoritarianism. More contemporary experience in Latin America, however, suggests that the relationship between economic pressures and politics may be more complex and less predictable. In several countries, including Argentina, Bolivia, Brazil, Chile, Peru, and Uruguay, economic problems have *increased* pressures for political liberalization. Whereas in the 1930s some democratic regimes were held responsible by their populations for economic decline, more recently authoritarian regimes had the bad luck to be in power when economies collapsed. Contemporary experiences have linked economic contraction and political liberalization, turning conventional wisdom on its head.

In the longer run, however, democracy certainly has a better chance of survival amidst sustained economic growth. Roett warns that continued austerity in Brazil could lead to a resurgence of nationalist authoritarianism. Pressure groups will compromise more readily when each can claim a slice of a growing pie, while conflict can mount when groups are struggling to preserve existing living standards against austerity measures. For those interested in the democratization of Latin America, the global recession has provided unexpected opportunities. Once democracy has been restored, however, renewed global growth will be of great importance.

The combined pressures for stabilization with liberalization threaten to place the United States on the wrong side of Third World nationalism. If the causes of austerity appear to be the erratic, self-interested behavior of banks and the adverse terms of trade (or worse still, protectionism), then developing-country politicians will be tempted to blame their troubles on industrial nations. The IMF often serves as a lightning rod to take the heat off Third World governments, but a persistently visible IMF can focus attention on the international system and its dominant members as the causes of the crisis. Some will argue that an IMF that is simultaneously pressuring for austerity and liberalization is taking advantage of a nation's weakness to tear down those structures that protect whatever autonomy developing nations enjoy. Such reactions inevitably accompany difficult economic times, but they may be greatly amplified if the adjustment process stumbles.

In short, U.S. security interests in the Third World will fare much better if the adjustment process succeeds. Societies are then more likely to be stable and capable of sustaining existing democratic institutions, and less likely to fall under the influence of the Soviet Union or an inward-looking nationalism. Chronic recession also lessens the benefits associated with abiding by the rules governing international exchange. Increased protectionism or financial default become less irrational acts. And demogogues may find a populace more susceptible to the allure of "de-linking" from an inhospitable global system. Already, many nations that have become net capital exporters are shrinking from default less because of the perceived benefits of participating in the international financial system than out of fear of retaliation. A system that depends more upon negative sanctions than upon positive inducements is less secure.

Humanitarian Interests

Finally, humanitarian interests have suffered greatly because of the global recession. The costs of adjustment have been especially severe for the poor in the Third World, where financial safety nets are lacking. Unemployment has reached depression levels in many countries and those fortunate enough to be employed are accepting deflated wages. In a process of de-modernization, factories are closing, workers are returning to rural areas, and farmers are turning away from producing for the market to planting for subsistence.

UNICEF has tracked the consequences of recent economic setbacks on children.[5] For example, available fragmentary data suggest that there has been a decline in height-for-age among youngsters in Zambia's poorer northern regions; infant mortality rates have increased in Bihar, India; the number of children treated for severe malnutrition in Costa Rica doubled between 1981-82; and in São Paulo, Brazil, there are more low-birth-weight babies as well as a significant increase in the number of children given up by their parents because of poverty. Most alarmingly, there is considerable evidence that time lags exist between the shock of economic decline and its impact on child services and child health. The worst social effects of the recession therefore may not yet be fully recorded or felt.

Future Action

The major conclusions and policy suggestions of each chapter in this volume are presented in the Summaries of Recommendations following this overview and will not be repeated here. The Overseas Development Council's *U.S.-Third World Policy Perspectives* series—which this volume initiates—seeks not consensus but diversity of views and debate among authors. Nevertheless, it is pleasing when authors addressing somewhat separate issues from different perspectives reach similar conclusions. Several common themes emerge from their contributions:

• **Since adjustment is unavoidable, it is better to begin early and in an orderly fashion than to wait until financial pressures force a severe and perhaps chaotic contraction.** The adjustment imperative is ideologically neutral and reigns whether regimes are conservative or radical, authoritarian or democratic.

• **Some aspects of the orthodox approach to adjustment are important components of adjustment policy, although they may be insufficient if used in isolation.** "Getting prices right" is often an essential precondition for efficient investment and production patterns (although more may be required). In particular, since the adjustment process generally demands an increase in exports, disincentives such as an overvalued exchange rate should be removed. The liberalization of interest rates and the deepening of financial markets can stimulate greater domestic savings—an important objective, given the poor outlook for the availability of external financing. Nevertheless, price liberalization by itself is no sure cure when other structural adjustments are needed.

• **The IMF and the World Bank should adhere more closely to their commitments to pay more attention to "structural" reforms.** As distinct from monetary and macro-economic matters, "structural" elements encompass the organization of governmental agencies, the price incentives offered to producers, the efficiency of industry, and the investment patterns in agriculture and energy. Please endorses the World Bank's structural adjustment loans that seek to elicit long-term policy reforms in such areas. Killick urges the IMF to take seriously the analysis that led to the establishment in the late 1970s of the Extended Fund Facility: that IMF stand-by arrangements should address structural issues of investment and supply. Such a "real-economy" program would "shift the distribution of productive resources in favor of tradable goods and services plus supporting demand management measures." Nations cannot simply spend their way out of crises (as France and Brazil learned the hard way), yet adjustment should involve the creation of new industries and jobs. According to several of the authors contributing to this volume, although the price mechanism is often an efficient allocator of resources, positive government action in the selective allocation of credit, price incentives, and targeted export-promotion stimuli may be necessary to render firms dynamic and competitive.

 • **The extended "policy dialogues" between the Bretton Woods institutions and member governments should be strengthened.** Traditionally, the IMF has designed one-year programs and the World Bank has concentrated on discrete projects. As Please and Killick emphasize, the severe economic dislocations of recent years have refocused attention on adjustments at the national and sectoral levels that require a longer period to realize. The IMF and the World Bank have been forced to deepen their involvement in national policy decisions. Nelson urges that the resulting dialogues be genuine interchanges and recommends joint studies characterized by open-mindedness and give-and-take. (Offering an alternative view, Worrell is skeptical that IMF staff can match the knowledge of national economists with regard to domestic matters, and so would focus the dialogue more narrowly on foreign-exchange matters.)

 • **The IMF and World Bank should closely coordinate when implementing overlapping programs.** Killick and his colleagues recommend that the IMF give more emphasis to supply-side investments (traditionally the World Bank's purview), while Please extolls the virtues of the World Bank's structural adjustment loans that come tied to broad policy advice (traditionally extended by the IMF). Indeed, Killick asserts that "in contemporary circumstances it is impossible to draw any sharp distinction between balance-of-payments management and the design of development strategies." Yet this programmatic approximation is occurring when IMF-certified stabilization programs are so sapping countries of credit that World Bank projects are being abandoned for lack of funds. Noting this tension, Please suggests that the World Bank's structural adjustment lending programs should not passively allow the implementation of IMF programs to subvert development momentum. He argues that the Bank should more actively encourage the funding of low-cost and replicable investment programs—particularly in sectors such as education, health, housing, and water development.

• **Governments must be firmly committed to adjustment programs if the demanding measures are to be successfully implemented and sustained.** Too many governments are signing agreements that they disagree with in principle and that they believe to be unworkable—simply to receive the first installment or two before straying from the targets. Adjustment packages must build in processes and programs that enhance the commitment of governments. A genuine policy dialogue can build intellectual trust, while an emphasis on new investment can enhance political will by offering positive inducements and hope. Most important, the design and timing of programs should be sensitive to what is politically sustainable. Furthermore, as Nelson suggests, the IMF and other external donors should be willing to alter programs when external shocks unexpectedly knock them off course—so that national authorities feel that they will be held responsible for variables they can control but will not be unduly penalized for exogenously generated mishaps.

• **External financing should be increased to permit countries to meet interest payments on their debt while raising investment and exports.** A world in which developing countries are at once suffering declining living standards and net capital outflows is inherently unstable. Developing countries have been willing to play by the rules because they have believed that their economies would soon rebound. If they begin to foresee prolonged stagnation, the mood will change—as already appears to be the case in some Latin American countries. If interest payments continue to exceed new loans by wide margins, pressures for debt relief will surely mount. To avoid a rupture in the international financial system, the contributors propose numerous ideas to increase net capital flows, including increases in IMF and World Bank resources, guarantee mechanisms aimed at stimulating bank lending and equity investment, and capitalization of some interest payments.

• **The United States should narrow its fiscal deficit, seek lower interest rates, and resist protectionism.** The industrial countries have shifted much of the burden of adjustment onto the developing nations, while the United States has refused the fiscal discipline imposed on other nations. Moreover, tight monetary policies and high interest rates in the United States continue to depress investment and incomes worldwide. Furthermore, if the U.S. recovery is aborted, if protectionist pressures are not resisted, or if global growth is otherwise impaired, the developing countries—especially the newly industrializing countries that are more integrated into the global economy—will be forced to adopt more inward-looking development strategies.

The authors do not, of course, agree on all matters. Opinions differ on the appropriateness of "shock" versus "gradual" adjustment; on how many as well as which variables the IMF should target and how broad its mandate should be; and on the wisdom of liberalization in certain markets. Lance Taylor, for example, is more disposed to selective capital controls and trade barriers. Perhaps more experience and debate will generate a wider consensus on these issues in the future.

The authors do, however, share a strong bias for pragmatism. Their search is not for the justification of preconceived ideologies, but for policies that work. Several authors stress the dangers of overdrawn dichotomies—whether export promotion versus import substitution, politics versus economics, or "free" markets versus government intervention. All the authors accept that market mechanisms are efficient in many circumstances but share a belief that corrective action by national and international authorities is sometimes necessary. The intention of this volume is to improve, however modestly, the quality of those official interventions.

Notes

[1] For example, see William R. Cline, *International Debt and the Stability of the World Economy* (Washington, D.C.: Institute for International Economics, 1983); Thomas O. Enders and Richard P. Mattione, *Latin America: The Crisis of Debt and Growth* (Washington, D.C.: Brookings Institution, 1984); Morgan Guaranty Trust Company, *World Financial Markets*, June 1983; World Bank, *World Debt Tables, 1983-84* (Washington, D.C.: 1983).

[2] IMF, *World Economic Outlook* (Washington, D.C.: 1984), pp. 192, 197, 200, and 209-10; World Bank, *Annual Report, 1983* (Washington, D.C.: 1983), p. 13; and World Bank, *World Debt Tables, 1983-84* (Washington, D.C.: 1983), pp. 3 and 19.

[3] Gabriel G. Manrique and Stuart K. Tucker, "The Costs to the United States of the Recession in Developing Countries," Overseas Development Council, forthcoming.

[4] *Report of the National Bipartisan Commission on Central America* (Washington, D.C.: U.S. Government Printing Office, 1984), pp. 4, 12, 15, 84, 107.

[5] UNICEF, *The Impact of World Recession on Children* (New York: 1983).

Summaries of Recommendations

1. The Debt Crisis: Round Two Ahead?
(Albert Fishlow)

Although debt-service ratios remain very high, fears of the effects of a generalized default have receded in the last year. The financial system has demonstrated its capacity to engineer a sequence of rescues, of which the Argentinian case is the most recent. Moreover, the expectation exists that global economic recovery will improve export performance of the debtor countries.

But optimism may be premature. A careful analysis of the assumptions underlying the hopeful view shows that even small changes in projected trends could dramatically change outcomes. The responsiveness of developing-country trade to recovery in industrialized countries—relative to the adverse consequences of high and rising interest rates—has been exaggerated. Moreover, in the next decade, global growth may be less trade-intensive than in the past. It is highly uncertain that developing countries will enjoy continuously improving balances of payments. Developing countries remain vulnerable to shortfalls in export earnings and must reduce their growth to accommodate. For them, the question is increasingly not only the economic capacity to pay, but also the political cost of doing so.

Present policies are deficient. The success thus far achieved depends upon a fragile convergence of interests between debtor countries and banks. Yet both groups of participants are becoming increasingly unhappy. The last-minute attempts to avert Argentina's default are evidence of the inherent instability of the present arrangements rather than of their adequacy. The outcome was typically short-term, with little indication that the finance needed for effective adjustment and resumption of growth will be forthcoming.

The situation can still be remedied. The large banks can establish a more satisfactory framework for dealing with the problems of debtors. They can (1) forgo commissions and reduce interest charges to the cost of funds on rescheduled debt; (2) extend maturities on rescheduled debt to at least ten years in order to reduce and smooth annual amortization payments; (3) consider countries' capital needs in a longer time frame; and (4) make available new loans to cover interest costs beyond an agreed maximum level (analogous to caps on mortgage rates), which is even now implicitly possible, although regulatory rules would have to be changed to permit explicit capitalization of interest. The banks should introduce these changes in close cooperation with the IMF and the World Bank, establishing more formal and durable institutional linkages.

These measures stop short of other, more comprehensive reforms to restructure global debt that have been proposed. But they have the advantage of greater potential acceptability and they would help create much greater confidence in the management of short-term financial problems. In combination with an expanded role for the World Bank and the regional development banks in supplying public loans—as well as developing-country policies to facilitate exports, stimulate domestic saving, and substitute equity investment—these measures would amount to a significant start toward the continuing transfer of resources needed for economic development.

It is unlikely that even these steps will be implemented unless the industrialized-country governments add their voices to the pleas of the developing countries. By encouraging the banks to treat debt as a long-term development problem and by further underwriting the role of the multilateral institutions, the industrialized countries could move the debt problem toward resolution. If they fail to seize this opportunity, the present lull may prove to be a mere interval in a succession of debt crises.

2. The IMF: Case for a Change in Emphasis (Tony Killick, Graham Bird, Jennifer Sharpley, and Mary Sutton)

Successive U.S. administrations, including the Reagan administration, have regarded the International Monetary Fund as a valuable instrument for the maintenance of the international financial and trading systems. The authors argue that the Fund's effectiveness has been impaired by its failure to adopt adequately to a rapidly changing international economic environment. Many Fund programs are not being completed or are having only modest impact. Arguing on both equity and efficiency grounds, the authors urge the Fund to adopt a new "real-economy" approach to adjustment that seeks to minimize lost production by stimulating supply rather than merely suppressing demand.

Specifically, the authors propose that Fund stabilization programs place greater emphasis on growth and investment in tradable goods—in exports and in import substitution industries. For governments to have adequate time to address structural problems in production, adjustment programs must have a longer time horizon and be more carefully adopted to the specific circumstances of each country. While programs must still pay attention to demand management and to the restraint of consumption, a "real-economy" approach would sometimes permit a more relaxed credit policy—including credit targeting to specific industries or sectors—to increase production.

Developing countries will still have to undertake difficult adjustment programs. The authors urge governments to begin their adaptations to a changing international environment sooner rather than later, controlling demand, "getting the prices right," and following an active policy of exchange-rate adjustment. The challenge is for governments to learn to adopt flexible policies that respond to changing circumstances and that integrate short-term adjustment and longer-term development objectives.

The authors argue that their "real-economy" approach is consistent with the production orientation of the Fund's Articles of Agreement (its constitution) and its Extended Fund Facility. They recognize, however, that more resources would often be required to facilitate adjustment with growth, and they argue for a further increase in IMF quotas, for the use of some of the Fund's holdings of gold, and for the utilization of allocations of SDRs (Special Drawing Rights) for this purpose.

3. The World Bank: Lending for Structural Adjustment (Stanley Please)

In 1980, when financial and development crises of very large proportions loomed before most developing countries, the World Bank instituted its new "structural adjustment lending" (SAL)—nonproject loans designed to elicit policy reforms on the part of recipient countries. As one of the architects of the innovation, now at Oxford, Stanley Please offers an insider's assessment.

The author sees SALs as complementary to the IMF's conditioned credits—focused on supply restructuring (because of the SALs' longer time frame and the Bank's sectoral expertise), but with the sister institutions working on the same country cases in tandem. The author concludes that SALs have enabled the Bank to focus the attention of government leaders on important macro and sectoral policy issues. The "failed" cases (where SALs have been canceled as countries have fallen short of one or another of their monitored undertakings) are interpreted as testimony to the integrity and seriousness of the SAL effort. However, the author suggests that the Bank could probably be a more active advocate of growth and of poverty eradication priorities even within expenditure-cutting stabilization programs. A too passive attitude by the Bank in accepting whatever emerges from the implementation of IMF agreements could subvert the objectives of the SALs. The Bank should be assisting governments to design expenditure programs that preserve development objectives within the parameters of a tight budget.

Please sees the SALs as possibly a major watershed for the institution, not just in the current emergency but in the longer-term future. This arises from his view that the policy framework is critical for successful development and that the Bank is uniquely established to handle development policy issues, but that project operations—the Bank's main line of business—are too weak to handle these policy issues. Certain questions follow from this key recommendation:

- Will the Bank's 10-per cent limit on non-project lending need to be addressed? Probably yes, but only if the answer to the second question is positive.
- Will enough developing countries have sufficient political and technical capabilities to take up serious, structural adjustment programs? On the basis of the record since 1980, the answer is uncertain.
- But if governments are unable or unwilling to undertake the types of adjustments supported by the SALs, then should not donors, including the Bank, reduce the availability of funds that are now supplied to governments not prepared to bite SAL-type "bullets"?

4. The Politics of Stabilization
(Joan M. Nelson)

Both the political commitment of government leaders and public political reactions crucially influence whether stabilization programs are undertaken at all, and, if so, whether they are carried through, diluted, or abandoned. Five case studies and some clues from other countries point toward the following conclusions:

- Where a country's economic structure and institutions permit rapid response to drastic stabilization measures, so-called "shock treatment" is often advisable politically, since leadership commitment and public tolerance are both short-lived.

- A rapid economic turnaround is not feasible in many countries. Where gradualism is the sole constructive option, program design and donor support must both allow for inevitable public pressure and provide credible evidence of progress well before completion of medium-term programs. It may sometimes be desirable to "overshoot" on some measures initially, to provide leeway to ease pressure when public patience dwindles.

- For donors, the need for gradualism should point the way to more adequate assistance in appropriate forms, including program aid in some cases. Consideration should also be given to more flexible and explicit understandings that in effect "insure" programs in progress against adverse shifts in factors beyond the country's control.

- Programs that combine structural adjustment with more conventional demand-constraint and demand-shifting measures can win stronger commitment from political leaders and better acceptance from the public. But they may also entail administrative and political costs not associated with a "pure" stabilization approach.

- Skillful governmental tactics can extend public tolerance of stabilization efforts. Economists usually focus on partial compensation for vulnerable (and/or politically volatile) groups. Evidence suggests that vigorous and frank explanation and persuasion can often be equally or more important, particularly in initial stages. Foreign debt is often a bitter internal political issue. Therefore orderly and more generous rescheduling on a medium-term basis can not only serve economic functions but also help defuse internal political opposition.

5. The NICs: Confronting U.S. "Autonomy"
(Colin I. Bradford, Jr.)

The United States must adjust to the new circumstances of its recently restored hegemonic role in the world economy. The U.S. quest for autonomy in its economic policymaking—whether in the Reagan version of hegemony, wherein the administration's policy priority of disinflation is imposed on the rest of the world, or in the advocacy by some Democrats of a defensive industrial policy for the United States—threatens the world economy with recession and/or protectionism. Today, excessively high U.S. interest rates and the greatly overvalued dollar have wrenched global capital and trade flows, reversing earlier patterns. The current U.S. recovery does not facilitate global adjustment; it is built on the back of world recession and has ushered in an era of sluggish closed-economy growth for the Third World.

U.S. macro-economic policy is no longer a domestic policy for the American economy alone but a fundamental determinant of global economic conditions. If the United States is to fully realize its world leadership role, its macro-economic policy needs to be shaped by international as well as domestic imperatives. For outward-oriented economies that have integrated themselves into the world economy through trade and debt, such as the newly industrializing countries (NICs), the most important "foreign" economic policy of the United States is in fact U.S. *domestic* macro policy.

To achieve positive global adjustment, the United States should alter its fiscal and monetary policy mix, improve the coordination of economic management with other OECD countries, and encourage more investment-oriented IMF programs. The current U.S. policy priority for disinflation at home and abroad is in direct conflict with the survival needs of the NICs. Sluggishness in world trade also weakens the administration's argument that more developing countries should follow the export-led development strategy of the already successful NICs.

Bradford also criticizes the tendency in the United States to identify the export success of some NICs in the 1970s with free-market policies. In fact, the successful NICs applied considerable doses of government intervention. Differing with the findings of some well-known studies, the author denies the existence of a systematic link between export growth and the absence of price distortions. He concludes that "getting prices right" is surely not the only business of public policy.

6. Brazil's Debt Crisis and U.S. Policy (Riordan Roett)

The Reagan administration has taken a "business as usual" attitude toward Brazil in the midst of its debt crisis. Yet the United States has a major opportunity—important for foreign-policy as well as economic reasons—to take the lead in quickly exploring policy options to alleviate the social costs of adjustment and provide a cushion for Brazil's fledgling process of political liberalization.

Chronically falling incomes, rising unemployment, and widespread hunger and malnutrition in both rural and urban areas are producing social pressures that endanger Brazil's delicate transition from authoritarianism to democracy. Furthermore, the author warns that beleaguered leaders might seek to confront the IMF and the commercial banks—and set off a chain reaction in Latin America. Continued U.S. indifference therefore not only risks U.S. political and humanitarian interests, but also may expose the commercial banks to becoming political scapegoats.

Roett urges the United States to consider seriously several proposals to increase capital flows in order to ease Brazil's adjustment process. These include: the creation of a U.S. export development fund; credit insurance facilities coordinated by the World Bank and/or the IMF; measures to increase multinational corporate equity investment; and an IMF-administered political-risk guarantee for new lending by private commercial banks, designed to provide an incentive for both the smaller banks and the "money center" banks to be involved in future plans for recovery.

With the largest debt of any Third World country, Brazil is vitally dependent on international financial assistance. To aid Brazil and other heavily indebted countries, the international financial institutions will need additional resources. The United States should lead, not oppose, the appropriation of new funds for the World Bank, the International Monetary Fund, and the Inter-American Development Bank. The leverage of the World Bank should be increased; the suggestions of a new subsidiary of the Bank that would lend to the Third World at rates less burdensome than the Bank's regular rates strikes the author as sensible.

Finally, the United States must resist protectionist pressures being generated by the rapid growth of Brazilian exports to the U.S. market. If Brazil cannot export, it can neither service its debt nor afford to import U.S. products.

7. Mexico's Adjustment in the 1980s: Look Back Before Leaping Ahead (Lance Taylor)

After the financial crisis of 1982, Mexican economic policy followed orthodox lines: contraction of demand, restriction of the growth of wages to rates lower than the rate of price inflation, and attempts to rationalize the price system. The outcome has been an improvement in the balance of payments—accompanied by severe recession and increased income inequality.

Similar policies also characterized the early years in office of President de la Madrid's two predecessors. Later in their terms, however, both earlier presidents shifted the thrust of their efforts toward economic expansion and income redistribution. A change along these lines may also occur under the current administration.

The author recommends a number of specific policy interventions that could help make the next shift in policy direction more productive. These include the creation of an indigenous capital market to replace the Mexdollar system (dollar-denominated deposits issued by Mexican banks); the "carrot" would be a new financial instrument to hold assets within the country, while the "stick" would be controls on the outflow of capital—and the climate would be improved by a buildup of foreign reserves. Wage and exchange-rate policies are also discussed in light of the adjustment of the Mexican economy in the direction of becoming a chronic oil exporter. There are strong pressures toward an overvalued (lower) exchange rate. Consequently, directed incentives to expand non-oil exports and continued import substitution are proposed.

For the United States, the main recommendation is a generally receptive attitude toward such changes. Given the close linkages between the two countries, overt U.S. attempts to dissuade Mexico from pursuing a more inward-oriented policy could easily provoke unproductive counter-reactions. The United States could ease the transition for Mexico by maintaining financial flows and providing security through reinforced linkages with the safety net of swap arrangements now in existence among the central banks of industrialized countries. A lenient policy on migration makes sense as Mexico grapples with its severe internal distributional problems. Rigid opposition to the likely direction of Mexican policy in the period ahead—or aggressive attempts to web Mexico into a grand North American economic system—will only bring grief to both sides.

8. Central America and the Caribbean: Adjustment in Small, Open Economies (DeLisle Worrell)

Small developing countries should lend their weight to proposals for *international* reform, but they must always stand ready to adopt *domestic* economic policies to cope with the world as they find it. The circumstances of each country must dictate policies. Only some guidelines for good management can be offered on the basis of the experience of the four countries examined: Nicaragua, Jamaica, Barbados, and Costa Rica.

The primary objective of domestic *short-term* economic policy in small, open economies should be to avoid sharp discontinuities that undermine confidence, inhibit investment, and curtail the economy's growth prospects. Economic managers should stay within the limits of their administrative capabilites. There is an urgent need to develop local economic intelligence systems, to allow for strategic decision taking. They should take special care with fiscal policy, their most effective weapon. They have very limited control over relative prices and will find it hard to secure their objectives by relative price adjustment; general administrative controls will also be counterproductive.

Long-term domestic strategies should provide for the development of human resources, particularly the qualities of inventiveness, self-confidence, and organizational ability, which depend on wide exposure to other societies and systems. Export-promotion strategies should concentrate on selected new product lines. These efforts should be complemented by strategies to raise productivity, develop new information systems, and promote energy efficiency.

Reforms in the conduct of international institutions, industrial-country governments, and international commercial banks are also essential if we are to improve on the indifferent record of global economic adjustment in recent years.

The International Monetary Fund needs far larger resources to support its pivotal role in the international adjustment process. More of these funds should be allocated to programs that fund long-term structural adjustments to shocks derived from changes in world prices. IMF conditionality could be made more effective by avoiding intervention in the details of macro-economic policy, focusing instead strictly on the borrowers' ability to pay, using an appropriately defined measure of foreign-exchange reserve availability.

The Fund might intensify efforts to improve economic expertise in the centers of decision making in developing countries.

The international commercial banks need to remedy glaring deficiencies in their capacity to evaluate country risk; their lending might be supported by new forms of international credit insurance.

Also needed are more pervasive and more adequately funded schemes for commodity stabilization, which are in the interest of all countries; developing nations should continue to pursue them even if the advanced industrialized countries remain less enthusiastic.

Adjustment Crisis in the Third World

Chapter 1

The Debt Crisis: Round Two Ahead?

Albert Fishlow

At the end of 1983, the debt of all developing countries, short- and long-term, amounted to more than $800 billion. For the oil-importing developing countries, which account for some 80 per cent of the total, this means more than a third of gross national product. In recent years, debt-service payments alone have equaled half the export earnings of these countries. Small wonder, then, that in the past year some thirty countries have been forced to reschedule more than $100 billion in principal as it came due. Table 1 outlines the evolution of the debt of the major borrowers over the past decade.[1] Its focus on these countries should not, however, obscure the difficult position of many smaller, and in many cases low-income, borrowers; while the debt problems of these smaller debtors do not threaten the stability of the financial system, they do seriously affect the standards of living of their populations.

The sudden inability of Mexico to meet its obligations in August 1982 dramatically moved these statistics from the financial pages into bold headlines. Mexico's $80-billion debt made it the second largest developing-country debtor. If Mexico, with its proven oil reserves of seemingly unlimited value, could not service its debt, what could be expected of countries less favored?

Overnight, the precarious exposure of the world financial system became a matter of grave concern. Banks operate on capital bases that represent only about 5 per cent of their total assets. As a consequence, loans to developing countries far exceeded the resources of the major "money center" banks. If these countries proved entirely unable to pay, the banks would be wiped out. Even serious interruption in debt service threatened sharp reductions in reported profits.

More than the banking sector was in trouble. Countries had used their borrowed money to buy imports from the United States and other industrialized countries. Since the oil crisis of 1973, this demand had helped to stabilize the world economy and to limit recession in the North. Clearly interdependence was more than a rhetorical slogan.

It is not surprising, therefore, that the Federal Reserve Bank, the other central banks (working largely through the Bank for International Settlements), and the International Monetary Fund immediately responded to the Mexican crisis. Fortunately, they also did so with imagination. Emergency credits were made available while a package of Mexican adjustment measures was hammered out. The IMF boldly conditioned its own finance on commitments of new money from the commercial banks. Consequently the banks, as well as Mexico, became subject to IMF conditionality.

These unprecedented arrangements soon became the order of the day. Argentina and Brazil followed Mexico's suit as the flow of voluntary commercial lending virtually ceased after August. In a matter of months—though not without elaborate negotiations involving hundreds of banks—more than $50 billion of debt was rescheduled, about half as much short-term debt was rolled over, and more than $20 billion in new loans was squeezed out of the banks for these three countries alone. By far the most difficult problem was posed by Brazil, whose failure to meet the agreed-upon stabilization targets led to negotiations and renegotiations that dragged on until November 1983, when the government finally accepted additional austerity measures.

In the same month, a reluctant U.S. Congress, after long delay, finally approved an $8.4-billion appropriation to fund an enlarged IMF quota and an expansion of the Fund's General Arrangements to Borrow. The decision came with little time to spare, as the Fund was running out of resources to meet the new needs of developing countries. Initially, the Reagan administration was unenthusiastic about increasing the resources of the IMF. It failed to use the August 1982 annual meeting as an occasion to propose immediate steps to strengthen the financial system's defenses. A month or two later, however, as Brazil tottered, Treasury Secretary Donald Regan became a convert to the cause of a more active role for the Fund. The Congress, more in tune with the administration's earlier lack of enthusiasm, proved more difficult to persuade. It required almost a year, and liberal support, to obtain passage of the measure.

Approval of the Fund's quota increase and resolution of the long-pending Brazil renegotiation with the Fund prompted a great sigh of relief in banking circles. The first significant shock to the spontaneous system of international lending that evolved in the 1970s had been weathered—and without the elaborate changes that some had advocated with the onslaught of the crisis. As the economic recovery in the United States continues, and as it extends to other industrialized countries, the hope is that the developing countries' export earnings will again rise and be adequate to meet their obligations.

But the problem is likely to linger on despite the signs of recovery. The developing countries that have been bearing the brunt of the adjustment are not yet "home free." As the *Wall Street Journal* summed up the situation: "Despite the recent rescue efforts, debt-ridden developing countries face some bleak prospects for the years ahead: anemic export earnings, sluggish investment and crushing interest costs. The total foreign debt of developing countries that don't produce oil, now estimated at $644 billion, is expected to double by 1990."[2] Such a future raises questions of medium-term political, as well as economic, viability. Will the debtor countries continue to accept such a burden, particularly if the magic of global economic recovery proves less powerful than it was in the past?

Even the health of the financial system is far from assured. Ironically, the very success of the immediate response to the crisis signals the end of the market system of Euro-currency financial intermediation that had flourished for more than a decade. Private banking arrangements have been salvaged only by vigorous official intervention. More than a new relationship between the IMF and the commercial banks is involved. Within the United States, the Federal Reserve Board has had to persuade reluctant regional banks of the need to continue to lend to developing countries. Even with improved economic circumstances, few anticipate a return to the buoyant capital market that transferred resources so well in the 1970s. What will replace it?

Doubts thus continue to intrude, with two major questions commanding center-stage: Will industrial-country recovery be the complete solution many hope for? And what is the stance of the developing countries? This chapter addresses both questions and concludes with an evaluation of the existing institutional framework for coping with the debt problem and meeting the medium-term financial needs of developing countries.

Table 1. Developing-Country Debt[a] (billions dollars)

	1973	1974	1975	1976	1977	1978	1979	1980	1981	1982	1983
Non-Oil Countries	130.1	160.8	190.8	228.0	280.3	334.3 300.7[c]	354.5[c]	421.4[c]	492.6[c]	551.3[c]	585.6[c]
NICs[b]	51.3	66.2	82.3	101.5	122.7	149.5 115.9[c]	135.0[c]	160.9[c]	184.5[c]	211.9[c]	217.7[c]
Brazil	13.8	18.9	23.3	28.6	35.2	48.4	57.4	66.1	75.7	88.2	97.0
Mexico	8.6	12.8	16.9	21.8	27.1	33.6					
Republic of Korea	4.6	6.0	7.3	8.9	11.2	14.8	20.5	26.4	31.2	35.8	42.0
Southern Cone	10.1	12.4	12.7	13.0	14.9	19.2	27.5	38.3	51.3	55.2	60.0
Argentina	6.4	8.0	7.9	8.3	9.7	12.5	19.0	27.2	35.7	38.0	42.0
Chile	3.7	4.4	4.8	4.7	6.2	6.7	8.5	11.1	15.6	17.2	18.0
Low-Income Countries	26.4	30.9	34.6	40.1	48.6	54.8	62.7	71.4	75.2	81.8	88.0

Selected Oil Exporters										
15.4	17.9	21.2	27.3	35.3	47.1	58.2[c]	65.2[c]	70.5[c]	78.3[c]	90.0[c]
						99.0	119.0	137.5	160.3	173.0
Algeria										
2.9	3.3	4.5	5.8	8.3	12.7	14.9	15.1	15.3	14.8	17.0
Indonesia										
5.7	7.1	8.9	11.0	12.8	14.5	14.9	17.0	18.0	21.0	23.0
Mexico										
						40.8	53.8	67.0	82.0	83.0
Nigeria										
2.2	2.2	2.1	1.8	1.9	3.6	4.7	5.6	7.9	11.2	17.0
Venezuela										
4.6	5.3	5.7	8.7	12.3	16.3	23.7	27.5	29.3	31.3	33.0
Total[d]										
145.5	178.7	212.0	255.3	315.6	381.4	453.5	540.4	630.1	711.6	758.6

Total, All Developing Countries							
329.3	398.2	472.0	559.9	646.5	724.8	767.7

[a] Short- and long-term debt, including private, non-guaranteed debt. Excludes loans from the IMF.

[b] Newly industrializing countries, here equivalent to IMF category of "major exporters of manufactures," less Argentina but including Mexico.

[c] Excludes Mexico.

[d] Sum of Non-Oil Countries and Selected Oil Exporters.

Sources: *1973-76*—Non-Oil Countries, NICs, and Low-Income Countries from IMF, *World Economic Outlook* (Washington, D.C.: 1983); for NICs and Low-Income Countries, estimated short-term debt—excluded in the source—has been added by the author.

1973-82—Brazil, Mexico, Republic of Korea, Argentina, Indonesia, and Venezuela from William R. Cline, *International Debt and the Stability of the World Economy* (Washington, D.C.: Institute for International Economics, 1983). Algeria and Nigeria estimated from Morgan Guaranty Trust Company, *World Financial Markets*, June 1983, and World Bank, *World Debt Tables* (Washington, D.C.: various years). Chile from Morgan Guaranty, *World Financial Markets*, June 1983, and R. Zahler, "Recent Southern Cone Liberalization Reforms and Stabilization Policies: The Chilean Case, 1974-1982," *Journal of Interamerican Studies and World Affairs*, Vol. 25, No. 4 (November 1983), pp. 509-62.

1977-83—Non-Oil Countries, NICs, Low-Income Countries, and Total, All Developing Countries, from IMF, *World Economic Outlook* (Washington, D.C.: 1984).

1983—Brazil, Mexico, Republic of Korea, and Argentina from OECD, *External Debt of Developing Countries, 1983 Survey* (Paris: 1984); Chile and Venezuela from *Euromoney*, March 1984; Algeria from *Quarterly Economic Review* (*The Economist Intelligence Unit*), No. 1, 1984; Nigeria from *Wall Street Journal*, February 21, 1984; and Indonesia estimated by the author from 1983 borrowing data provided in *Quarterly Economic Review* (*The Economist Intelligence Unit*), No. 1, 1984.

Table 2. Sources of Deterioration in the Current Account of Non-Oil Developing Countries, 1979-82 (billions dollars)

	1978	1979	1980	1981	1982	Cumulative 1979-82
Actual Trade Balance	−36.6	−51.3	−74.3	−79.6	−52.2	—
Adjusted Trade Balance[a]		−46.3	−57.3	−47.8	8.8	—
Oil Effect[b]		5.0	17.0	18.6	14.8	55.4
Recession Effect[c]		—	—	13.2	46.2	59.4
Export Volume[d]		—	—	—	23.2	23.2
Terms of Trade[e]		—	—	13.2	21.3	34.5
Interest Payments on Debt Service (gross)	−19.4	−28.0	−40.4	−55.1	−59.2	—
Interest Rate Effect (gross)[f]		−1.1	.5	11.4	23.0	33.8
Interest Rate Effect (net)[f]		−.5	.2	6.5	14.0	20.2
Actual Current Account	−41.3	−61.0	−89.0	−107.7	−86.8	—
Adjusted Current Account[g]	−41.3	−56.5	−71.8	−69.4	−11.8	—

Source: Actual trade balance and actual current account from IMF, *World Economic Outlook* (Washington, D.C.: 1983).

ᵃ Adjusted Trade Balance: Actual trade balance minus sum of oil and recession effects.

ᵇ Oil Effect: Actual cost of net imports of oil (using oil import price of industrialized countries) minus estimated cost using oil price that varies after 1978 with export prices of oil-importing countries.

ᶜ Recession Effect: Composite of terms of trade and volume effects (does not add because of interaction).

ᵈ Export Volume: Non-oil export value times cumulative negative percentage deviation between actual export volume of oil-importing countries and volume predicted by 3.2 per cent industrialized-country growth in 1980-82.

ᵉ Terms of Trade: Cumulative negative percentage deviation between actual non-oil terms of trade (export prices of non-oil, oil-importing countries; import prices of oil-exporting countries in 1973-74, 1979-80, non-oil countries in other years) and terms of trade predicted by 3.2 per cent OECD growth and deceleration of industrialized-country inflation at 1 percentage point per year beginning in 1979.

ᶠ Interest Rate Effect: Based on difference between the 1975-78 average real interest rate and actual real rates. For short-term interest payments, the U.S. prime rate was used. Interest on long-term and medium-term loans was calculated by using the real U.S. prime rate with a weight of 1/3 and the OECD long-term fixed interest rate with a weight of 2/3, corresponding to portfolio weights reported in OECD, *External Debt of Developing Countries*, 1982. Rates were applied to average annual debt, obtained by using average of year-end debts. Net interest effect includes the offsetting earnings from short-term assets. This method approximates well the actual gross and net interest payments reported in IMF, *World Economic Outlook* (Washington, D.C.: 1983).

ᵍ Adjusted Current Account: Actual current account minus sum of oil effect, recession effect, and net interest effect.

A Liquidity Crisis?

The current optimism contrasts with the public mood of early 1983. Shortly after the Mexican financial collapse, *Time* magazine christened the Third World's exposure a "debt bomb." Others more analytically inclined differentiated between a liquidity crisis and a solvency problem—that is, between a short-term interruption of cash flow versus a long-term inability to repay debts. They insisted that there was no structural problem. Thus the World Bank, in its 1983 report on external debt, stated that:

> There is no generalized debt crisis: rather, the mutual difficulties of developing countries in servicing foreign borrowing and of commercial banks in obtaining service payments on foreign lending are an outgrowth of the broader economic problems that grip all of the world's economies. The resolution of these difficulties lies in a restoration of economic health to the global economy and a resumption of strong growth in international trade.[3]

It is of course true that the oil price shock of late 1979 and the subsequent recession and rise in interest rates greatly affected the balances of payments of developing countries. Table 2 depicts the impact on the non-oil countries of a deteriorating international environment. Overall, between 1979 and 1982 the combined consequences of higher oil prices, reduced export earnings caused by recession, and higher interest rates added $135 billion, or almost 40 per cent, to the current-account deficits actually experienced by these countries. By 1982, when all three effects were strong, almost all of the $87-billion current-account deficit could be attributed to adverse external shocks.

Increasingly, recession and interest-rate rises dominated the initial hike in oil prices and made their impact felt on all developing countries—whether oil importers or exporters. The foreign-exchange earnings of developing countries, and hence their capacity to service the debt, were progressively affected. Even prudent managers could not predict effects of this magnitude. It is this generalized experience that makes the debt issue more than a matter of imprudence on the part of a few countries; it also leads to the view that world economic recovery will eliminate the problem.

Looking ahead rather than backward further bolsters the liquidity interpretation. Like the IMF's 1983 medium-term scenarios and Morgan Guaranty's balance-of-payments model, William Cline's recent projections for nineteen of the largest debtors reemphasize that:

If this growth rate [3 per cent annually for industrialized countries] can be achieved, the debt problems of the developing countries should be manageable and should show considerable improvement. . . .The central result of this analysis is that the debt problem can be managed, and that it is essentially a problem of illiquidity, not insolvency.[4]

Although this assessment has merit, it requires qualification in two important respects. First, it is not entirely adequate to speak of countries as if they were firms. For a firm, solvency is defined by an excess of assets over liabilities; otherwise it is bankrupt, and its creditors may be driven to seek its dissolution. Countries, on the other hand, cannot go into bankruptcy in the same sense. Their assets cannot be seized by a court and liquidated. Countries are solvent if they can manage to pay back their debts over some undefined future. They are liquid if they manage to service them now. What is of interest is whether developing countries will be liquid in the future, not whether they will have paid back their debts.

Thus the liquidity-solvency distinction is of limited practical significance. What is more relevant to whether current debt is too large is the relationship between the average interest rate on debt and the rate at which exports are growing. Suppose countries have equal exports and imports. Then they will have to borrow each year to cover their interest payments, and their debt will grow at the same annual rate as the interest rate. If exports grow faster, the debt/export ratio declines, and there is a better prospect both for continuous servicing of the debt and for acquiring more. If the interest rate exceeds the export growth rate, however, the only way to prevent the debt/export ratio from rising is by cutting back on imports. Only by running a merchandise surplus—that is, by transferring real resources to creditor countries—can debtors control the debt/export ratio.

That, of course, is exactly what many countries have been forced to do since 1982, as interest rates have remained high, exports have languished, and capital flow has dried up. The merchandise surplus, acclaimed as a sign of healthy adjustment, therefore is not a good index of solvency. Rather, it is a measure of the current disequilibrium that requires developing countries to pay more in interest than they receive in new loans.

The disequilibrium is substantial. Most of the net flow from South to North came from the Latin American countries, where much of the Third-World debt problem is concentrated. These countries' resource transfer amounted to $20 billion in 1982 and to $30 billion in 1983, representing 19 per cent and 27 per cent respectively of the value of exports of goods and services. As a recent report of the U.N. Economic Commission for Latin America states: "Thus was prolonged a situation that, taking into account the relative degree of development of the region, can only be qualified as perverse."[5] More generally, for the major borrowers, the positive net transfer of $17 billion in 1981 was converted to a net outflow of $7 billion in 1982 and then a still larger net outflow of $21 billion in 1983.[6]

As long as interest rates remain higher than export growth, therefore, it can reasonably be asked whether debtor countries are solvent. The only way they can deal with their debt is to borrow excessively or to become capital exporters. Neither makes sense, and the debtor countries are acutely aware of this anomaly.

The second objection to the prevalent characterization of the debt problem as a simple liquidity crisis is an extension of the first. It is not obvious that it will be as easy for the debtor countries to achieve even larger merchandise surpluses in the next few years, as some of the optimistic balance-of-payments projections suggest. The latter assume that economic recovery in the industrialized countries will give such a large boost to trade that debtor-country imports will not have to continue to bear the full burden of adjustment, permitting growth to resume comparatively soon.

This picture is simply too rosy on two major counts. One is the overstatement of the responsiveness of developing-country exports to income growth in the industrialized countries. The other is the possibility that global development in the future will be less trade-intensive than in the last two decades. The following discussion considers each of these points in turn.

A Closer Look at the Assumptions[7]

The principal determinants of the rate at which the dollar value of developing-country exports will grow are (1) the rate at which their volume grows, (2) the change in their prices relative to inflation, and (3) the value of the dollar vis-à-vis other currencies.

Optimistic estimates of the responsiveness of export volume to economic recovery in the industrialized countries of the Organisation for Economic Co-operation and Development (OECD) generally are based on the past relationship between OECD import volumes and OECD growth. This seems to exaggerate the likely effect of recovery on the major developing-country debtors. Their export volume has already held up better than trade among the industrialized countries because of more effective competition, spurred by the necessity to earn foreign exchange as recession loomed. As Table 2 indicates, not until 1982 was there an adverse effect from slower industrialized-country growth. The flip side is that as the industrial economies recover, developing-country sales to them cannot be expected to spring back as much as their imports as a whole, since developing-country exports did not fall as much in the first place.

Projections of buoyant export performance may also overestimate the effect of recovery on terms-of-trade improvement. Data on individual countries are sparse, but even this limited information, together with available regional aggregates, suggests lower responsiveness to recovery than the optimistic assessments assume. Those assessments also place special weight on the lift that possible dollar depreciation could give developing-country earnings. A falling value of the dollar seemingly can inflate the dollar prices of developing-country exports proportionally and hence provide immediate relief for their predominantly dollar-denominated debt. With the dollar considerably overvalued, it is easy to see how its potential decline by 10 or even 20 per cent in the near future could become a dominant factor in inflating export prices—the more so because, unlike generalized inflation, it would not be compensated by rising interest rates.

The assumption that dollar prices of exports will increase exactly as much as the dollar depreciates is not an obvious one and indeed is not borne out by the past behavior of developing-country terms of trade, which seem to have moved inversely with the value of the dollar. For example, in the last case of significant dollar depreciation in 1978, when industrial-country income was growing at a rate of 4.1 per cent, export prices of primary commodities fell considerably. The unit value of the manufactures exported by developing countries failed to rise as rapidly as the value of the industrial countries' manufactured exports. As a consequence, the aggregate terms of trade of oil-importing developing countries declined at an annual rate of 3.4 per cent.

The implications of alternative patterns of increased export prices are presented in Table 3. Scenarios A and B maintain the same assumptions of a 10-per cent depreciation of the dollar in 1984 and a 5-per cent annual inflation. Scenario B translates these into an equal rise in export prices, to which a terms-of-trade improvement of about 4 per cent is added. Scenario A, in recognition of the mixed statistical evidence relating to past price behavior, is less generous. It assumes that developing-country import prices will rise by almost 13 per cent as a result of dollar depreciation and inflation, as past performance confirms. But it makes no further allowance for improved terms-of-trade in addition to the large increase in prices of traded goods relative to inflation.

Scenario A, unlike Scenario B, also excludes the potential additional effects of individual developing-country devaluations on the aggregate volume of developing-country exports. These account for a further, but small, difference. Part of the reductions that such devaluations may afford in supply prices will be offset by compensating removal of export subsidies under pressure from developed-country governments. Moreover, exporters who are devaluing will tend to jostle one another's market shares; there is a fallacy of composition in simply aggregating individual country responses. Finally, the intent is to measure not how much more developing-country debtors will have to sacrifice to improve their trade balances, but rather the impact of the external environment.

All other components of Table 3 are calculated on a similar basis. The results then reveal how sensitive the improved situation of the principal oil-importer debtor countries is to the estimated rise in export prices. Scenario A's scaling down of the 1984 surge in export value from Scenario B's rate of about 27 per cent to a rate of 19 per cent means that debt will have to grow almost *twice as rapidly* as projected in Scenario B. Debt/export ratios fall, but much more slowly, making obvious the continuing precariousness of the situation if the actual outcome is even marginally less favorable than Scenario B.

Differing forecast methods, as has been suggested here, do not fully agree. Neither do expectations about the likely extent of dollar depreciation, nor even about the continuity of economic recovery over the 1984-86 period. They merely add further misgivings. Scenario A's modest restatement of the rate of potential export growth establishes the vulnerability of the debtor countries to what may be a false optimism. Moreover, a rise of two percentage points in interest rates is sufficient to cut the decline in the debt/export ratio reported in Scenario A by a quarter.

Some of the widely cited projections that show the debt problem to be behind us—such as those of Cline and of Morgan Guaranty—therefore must be viewed with caution. Other forecasts support the more cautious note sounded in this chapter. Both the Data Resources and Wharton projections, for example, indicate far smaller increases in the value of developing-country exports, in aggregate as well as for the largest debtors, than the Scenario B projections in Table 3. The OECD has recently forecasted an increase in export prices of only 4 per cent for developing countries in 1984 to go along with an export volume growth of 7 per cent; this

Table 3. Alternative Balance-of-Payments Projections for the Larger, Oil-Importing Debtors[a] (billions current dollars)

	1983	1984	1985	1986
Scenario A				
Exports[b]	125.2	149.5	166.4	185.2
Imports[c]	135.4	157.2	172.1	192.0
Interest[d]	29.3	30.1	30.7	32.6
Current Account[e]	−30.9	−28.3	−26.7	−28.6
Debt[f]	327.6	354.3	377.6	403.0
Net Debt/Exports	1.88	1.69	1.62	1.54
Scenario B (Cline)				
Exports	125.2	158.8	179.9	199.8
Imports	135.4	159.3	174.6	194.8
Interest	29.3	30.1	29.6	30.2
Current Account	−30.9	−20.2	−12.6	−12.6
Debt	327.6	346.6	355.8	365.5
Net Debt/Exports	1.88	1.55	1.40	1.28

Source: William R. Cline, *International Debt and the Stability of the World Economy* (Washington, D.C.: Institute for International Economics, 1983), Scenario B data, p. 53.

[a] Includes Brazil, Argentina, Republic of Korea, Philippines, Israel, Turkey, Yugoslavia, Chile, Portugal, Thailand, Romania, and Hungary.

[b] Exports, 1984-86: 1983 base year times real growth of 6 per cent times price increase of 12.6 per cent in 1984 and 5 per cent subsequently.

[c] Imports, 1984-86: 1983 base year for non-oil imports times Cline's real growth estimate times price increase of 12.6 per cent in 1984 and 5 per cent subsequently; oil imports from Cline.

[d] Interest, 1984-86: Based on debt at end of previous year, with rate weighted at 2/3 of LIBOR plus premium, 1/3 at fixed rate, less income on reserves.

[e] Current Account, 1984-86: Incorporates estimated services and transfers in addition to trade balance and interest payments.

[f] Change in Debt, 1984-86: Current account deficit less estimated direct investment and reserve acquisition of .2 times change in imports.

11-per cent gain in export value is even less optimistic than the 19-per cent growth assumed in the export series of Scenario A and the 27-per cent growth assumption underlying Scenario B.[8] The increase in interest rates thus far registered in 1984 adds an annualized claim of some $4 billion on those export earnings.

There is also good reason to question whether experience over the last two decades is an accurate guide for predicting the near future. The world has emerged from an exceptional period in which trade growth has been unusually responsive to increased production. Indeed, going back even to the Pax Britannica of the nineteenth century, it is impossible to find a period of comparable trade intensity. Some of the characteristics of the present structure of the global economy argue against simple resumption of recent tendencies:

1. *Protectionist sentiments are stronger, as clearly evidenced by the number of recent petitions for the restriction of trade in the United States.* Within a single week in January 1984, four escape clause actions were filed, not alleging unfair trade, but merely injury; during the preceding three years, only five such cases had been brought. Developing countries competing with our basic industries—and they tend to be the newly industrializing-country debtors—have become a special target. Under the formula proposed for carbon steel imports, for example, the share for Japan and the Common Market would hardly be affected, while that for developing countries would decline from a current market share of about 10 per cent to a mere 3 per cent.

The reasons for this intensification of protectionism are partly cyclical. High rates of unemployment continue to arouse political pressure against competitive imports. The overvalued dollar, making imports cheaper in the United States, is another cause. But more enduring changes are at the same time taking place in the world economy. Comparative advantage in some of the standardized, low-technology goods such as steel, automobile parts, and simple machine tools has shifted to advanced developing countries. The real complaint is about competition, not about subsidies. Moreover, among the industrial countries, the pattern of recovery is not symmetrical. Europe has been lagging, and its governments are increasingly susceptible to appeals for protection. In such circumstances, market opportunities for debtor countries are less bright than they were a decade ago.

2. *The present commitment to restrain inflation reduces the likelihood of replicating the commodity booms of the last decade, and, with them, periods of sharply improved terms of trade.* Demands for stocks are unlikely to expand as rapidly with non-inflationary real recovery. Increases in the prices of primary products will encounter resistance from purchasers who will see them as changes in relative prices rather than as tied to general inflation. High real interest rates will have the same effect of moderating inventory acquisition.

3. *Focus on the magical effects of recovery in the industrialized countries ignores the consequences of debt-imposed depression in the developing countries for Third World trade growth.* Trade among developing countries is responsible for about a fourth of developing-country exports. This market has been growing rapidly for the manufactured exports of the largest debtors, but the restrictions now imposed on imports in some debtor countries are so severe that they adversely affect this export potential.

These concerns are more than theoretical. Despite the initial stage of industrialized-country recovery in 1983—which was more vigorous at a growth of 2.5 per cent than had been predicted—the value of non-oil developing-country exports rose only modestly. Indeed, preliminary results for the most indebted Latin American countries for 1983 show continuing deterioration in the terms of trade, along with absolute declines in export prices.[9]

Faith in recovery therefore may be misplaced, especially if high real interest rates persist. This view differs from the Cline assessment, which stresses the virtues of industrialized-country growth even at the expense of high interest rates. Cline claims that a 1 percentage point increase in growth is worth seven times as much in foreign exchange as a 1 percentage point decrease in the interest rate.[10] Alternative, and equally reasonable, estimates of export responsiveness to recovery more than halve that margin of superiority. Especially debtors with high debt/export ratios will therefore continue to be vulnerable until permanent industrialized-country growth produces cumulative effects. Moreover, the level of interest rates paid is partly a matter of negotiation involving the countries and the banks, and therefore subject to direct policy influence; the rate of growth of exports is less easily manipulated.

An exclusive focus on the balance of payments misses another important effect of high interest rates. The higher the cost, the greater the transfer of income abroad and the lower national income. Interest payments must be made at the expense of other applications of resources. Countries are poorer as a consequence. With debt/GNP ratios of one half and more for some of the debtors, each percentage point rise in the interest rate translates for them into a one-half percentage point reduction in national income.

Even from the vantage of the balance of payments, the effect of continuing high interest rates is to promote perverse resource transfers. The Cline projections of Table 3, favorable as they seem, derive their dramatic decline in debt/export ratios from progressively larger trade surpluses. In the absence of credit, imports (essential for growth) must be restrained to make room for interest payments despite rapid expansion of exports.

Such future restraint, because of the favorable growth in exports, is less severe, however, than that actually experienced in 1983. Although exports stagnated, the balance of payments of the principal debtors did not deteriorate. On the contrary, current accounts improved, especially those of oil exporters like Mexico and Venezuela. These debtor countries had little alternative but to compress their imports dramatically to adapt to the lack of new loans. They did so at the expense of income growth. For the oil exporters, this meant learning the necessity and possibility of import substitution, which had been practiced earlier, and no less painfully, by the oil importers.

In the last analysis, therefore, the debt problem is more than a mere liquidity crisis that will be fully resolved by an improved cash flow. At high interest rates, there is a greater possibility that export growth will be inadequate. The implication is not that the debtor countries will be unable to pay, but that repayment is likely to be a continuing real burden that these countries will bear disproportionately. The IMF says as much:

> The results of Scenario A [recovery and open markets] are less favorable as far as growth is concerned, and imply stronger adjustment efforts, than those presented last year. In part because of a lower flow of bank lending, the new Scenario A envisages . . . a lower deficit . . . despite conditions that would be less favorable for exports. The result is that the aggregate real GDP of non-oil developing countries in 1986 is now expected to be about 5½ per cent less than previously estimated. The volume of their imports is projected to be nearly 13 per cent less.[11]

Optimism about international recovery enjoys the unwarranted luxury of ignoring the consequences for the continuing willingness of developing countries to pay under adverse conditions. Realism requires a closer look.

The Politics of Adjustment and Default

The principal debtors, and they are concentrated in Latin America, have not, as we have seen, fared well in recent years. Rescheduling has been accompanied in almost all cases by programs of stabilization and austerity under IMF auspices. Growth has declined or even become negative, the prime factor assuring a reduction of imports. For Brazil, the fall in income has already exceeded that of the Great Depression in duration and severity.

Retrenchment has not proved popular. The decline in real income necessarily imposes private costs and evokes resistance. It is not difficult to construct a coalition in opposition to policies that guarantee certain losses and only potential benefits. To a beleaguered public, stabilization looks worse than the malady it is intended to cure.

But framing the opposition in terms of private self-interest characterizes it too narrowly. If it were not for past stabilization experiences that proved unsuccessful, and a respectable literature skeptical of orthodox policy, dissent would not run so deep. What has been added this time is the further conviction that the debtor countries are being forced to bear the cost unfairly. In their view, they were not alone in erring by borrowing excessively. Banks also loaned too much, sometimes aggressively. Yet the banks continue to receive their interest payments, at the expense of essential imports that must be foregone. Inappropriate fiscal policy in the United States that contributes to high interest rates may be criticized by the IMF, but it goes unpunished and undebited for the difficulties that it has imposed on the adjustment of others.

A recent letter to *The Economist* from a Brazilian reader made the point simply:

> Citizens of the "first world" refuse to understand that recession, for us, means more starvation, more children abandoned by miserable parents and a sharp increase in infant mortality and illiteracy. . . . If [an] illiterate Brazilian finds out that the loss of his job was caused by a recession provoked by the obligation to pay back the money which first-world bankers enticed us to borrow, plus interest, he will certainly become a sort of Sandinist, or worse.[12]

Under mounting social pressure, and in conjunction with external interest payments that exceed new borrowing, some form of relief is now openly discussed in the major Latin American debtor countries. Whichever euphemism is used—whether unilateral renegotiation or moratorium—the threat of possible default is barely veiled. Clearly the willingness to consider such a drastic solution, despite its potential costs of interrupted trade and impaired access to capital markets, is greater the more extreme the economic decline. Up to a point, austerity can improve the prospects for repayment. But applied too long and too painfully, austerity provokes a hostile rejection of submission to external claims. Rational calculations showing the potential high costs of default lose their force in the face of the clear and present high costs of internal depression.

Nor is the challenge ahead simply a matter of international

recovery stimulating the exports needed to pay. The debt now comes to more than 50 per cent of national income in Argentina, Mexico, Peru, the Republic of Korea, the Philippines, and Chile. As noted earlier, at high interest rates, a large income transfer is required. In Chile, for example, a 7 per cent real rate of interest translates into payment abroad of more than all the income received by the poorest fifth of the population.

These adverse realities are provoking reaction. Political turbulence and social unrest have surfaced in many of the debtor countries, especially in Latin America, but also in the Philippines and elsewhere. Where political participation is most open, governments have been most responsive. It is no accident that the popularly elected president of Argentina, with a degree of legitimacy not seen in at least a decade, has been among the most active in insisting upon debt relief. The neighboring dictatorship in Chile has been more acquiescent, preferring to avoid confrontation with the banks.

Nostalgia for the simpler days of authoritarian governments is, however, misplaced. Those regimes, if not already rejected, are losing credibility as they fail to cope with current economic difficulties. The continuing payment of interest will have to be legitimized by consent rather than repression. Moreover, the new political forces gathering strength have learned from some of the populist errors of the past. The new leaders are critical of their countries' asymmetrical integration into the world economy of the 1970s, which saw larger capital inflows rather than expanding export shares. They recognize the need for continuing export growth as the only medium-term solution to overhanging debt. There is no illusion that foreign resources will again be available in the proportions of the recent past. Instead, internal savings will be required, and consumption will have to be curtailed. There is also an understanding that sheer expansion of the public sector constitutes no more acceptable a development strategy than does sheer dependence on market forces. Finally, there is little faith in massive income redistribution as a short-term panacea.

These are important bridges to a consensual stabilization policy that addresses both internal requirements and debt service obligations. Paradoxically, an effective strategy may well require measures far more drastic than those tailored by the IMF. Both Argentina and Brazil face depression as well as triple-digit inflation. Conventional monetary and fiscal policy is likely to be inappropriate, or, at best, quite costly. Realignment of the internal debt, control over the public sector, reductions in real interest rates, and a halt to the spiral of wages and prices are all simultaneously needed. Design of a correct policy mix is not an easy task. Nor is that of reconciling legitimate popular claims with domestic austerity. But popular governments hold out a hope of succeeding in these matters where their authoritarian predecessors failed.

Their claim for debt relief and guarantees against deterioration of the international environment is essential to that hope. Stabilization has a chance of success only where there is some degree of freedom for domestic policy. If the balance of payments is the only priority, adjustment will be sacrificed to immediate foreign-exchange needs. Even if the rest of the world recovers, internal disequilibrium will remain a constant provocation for unilateral default.

The Present Policy Mold

In mid-1984, the elements in place to deal with the debt problem are formally little changed from what they were in August 1982. What has been added are additional resources from the IMF quota increase and the considerable experience gained through the repetitive tasks of renegotiating debt and hammering out country adjustment packages case by case. These are by no means trivial. Still, the absence of further change derives less from complete satisfaction with the present policy than from a lack of consensus on appropriate, more far-reaching reforms.

Financial circles are far from tranquil. In a June 1983 assessment, *World Financial Markets* criticized the "relatively optimistic, laissez-faire school that assumes the current debt situation is a fairly short-term liquidity issue," to be solved primarily through developing-country adjustment along with some recovery in the industrial countries. "By ignoring long-term structural elements of the international debt problem or overstating the prospects for global recovery, this approach risks forcing excessive deflationary costs on borrowers. It is also overly optimistic about market forces providing ample new borrowing."[13] The events of the intervening year give little reason for a different conclusion.

The present situation derives its stability from the fragile convergence of the immediate interests of creditor banks and debtor countries. Banks are committed to extending additional credits to countries currently in difficulty only because they have to. Lending is involuntary. It is done because the IMF has imposed conditionality and because of the threat of default that would cause bank balance sheets and profits to suffer. To avert defaults that would expose the precariousness of their financial accounts, the banks—with some hope of ultimate repayment under better conditions in the future—are caught in a "lending trap" that is the counterpart of the "debt trap" ensnaring countries. Countries must borrow to meet part of their interest payments, thereby increasing their debt without obtaining resources for adequate imports to underwrite recovery or even export expansion. They continue to make their payments because they fear the immediate losses from trade that might be interrupted as a result of default, and they are not prepared to forgo the net capital flows they need and expect in the future.

Such circumstances serve neither party well. Banks have been led to shortsighted efforts to obtain larger profits to compensate for their perceived greater risk. This has taken the form of increased margins, both one-time fees and ongoing premiums over the deposit rate. For the reschedulings completed in 1983 for Latin America, amounting to some $44 billion for seven countries, banks obtained commissions of between 1 and 1.25 percentage points, as well as revised spreads that have usually added about a full percentage point to previous ones. These markups might have added $70 million to the profits of the nine largest U.S. banks, applying the highest marginal tax rates. These additional profits translated into an increased after-tax return of about 25 per cent on the old loans to those countries—quite independently of higher spreads being charged on new loans.[14]

Ironically, the absolute effect on total bank profits is relatively small, as is the effect on the borrowers. The cost of the higher premium over LIBOR (London Interbank Offered Rate) to Mexico is about 1 per cent of foreign-exchange earnings, for example, since what is relevant to the country is the total interest rate, not the margin. But the ill will is considerable about imposing, arbitrarily, increased costs of servicing an already burdensome debt. Such charges are not market-determined, since the lending is involuntary; pressed by Mexico, Argentina, and Brazil, the banks in fact subsequently agreed to some reduction of their spreads. Indeed, the countries were joined in their protests by Federal Reserve Board Chairman Paul Volcker—motivated, no doubt, by concern for system stability. In the last-minute rescue of Argentina, the much reduced 1/8 per cent spread on the $100-million bank loan was a central issue.

At the same time, of course, the large money-market banks, especially in the United States, are themselves not pleased by the continuing and opposing demands on them by countries and regulators. The banks are being forced to set aside larger loan-loss reserves to satisfy bank examiners and a Congress concerned about excessive bank exposure. Tax treatment of such reserves is less favorable than in Europe. They must also cope with second-tier banks that have much less to gain from a continued lending relationship with developing countries and do not want to renew outstanding loans, even at higher spreads. Michigan National Bank has even taken Citicorp to court over the involuntary extension of a $5-million participation in a Pemex loan. For new money, the money-market banks can no longer count on tapping their regional colleagues.

The debtor countries, for their part, have fared badly. Despite Keynes's oft-quoted dictum about the advantage of large rather than small debts in dealing with creditors, the countries have been able to extract only modest additional resources from financial markets—and those only for the price of austerity programs. They have been forced to give priority to achieving trade surpluses and, in deferring to this single policy objective, have failed to design more adequate and longer-term adjustments.

The Fund has performed three essential functions in making this delicate arrangement work. First, it has offset individual bank prudence that would call for a reduced commitment and even shorter maturity of loans by enforcing lending targets based upon initial exposure. This new conditionality imposed on the bank overcomes the free-rider problem inherent in a pure market relationship, whereby each bank would hope the others would contribute, enabling it to get its money out; such behavior, since it would have had all of them backing away, would make them all worse off. Second, the Fund has devised adjustment programs that assure lenders of developing-country efforts to meet their obligations and thereby avoid the moral hazard of countries simply borrowing more without intention to repay. Finally, the IMF, in conjunction with the Bank for International Settlements, central banks, and industrial-country governments, has made available public resources to satisfy immediate liquidity requirements and to supplement the private market.

Central authority thus has been indispensable to a continuing bank-country relationship. The principal virtue of this tripartite debt regime has been its cushioning of the impact of debt problems on the financial system. But strains have been evident. Countries have reacted against the discipline imposed by the Fund; Venezuela, for example, still has not reached agreement on a stabilization program. In the case of Brazil, the banks have found their loans in danger of being declared non-accruing because the Fund took so long to certify a mutually acceptable stabilization package. Most recently, Argentina extended negotiation of an interim-loan and stabilization agreement with the IMF until the last possible instant. The financial participation of other Latin American countries in the final arrangement carries a dual message: a willingness to cooperate, but also an implicit threat of more organized resistance to higher debt-service costs.

As successful as this ad hoc arrangement has been in responding to the crisis so far, it has two serious deficiencies. The first is that it has contributed to a continuing short-term mentality. The banks still see advantage in minimizing the amount of additional lending or renegotiation they are induced to undertake. Even when they accept modifications, as in reducing interest rates, the very absence of rules creates additional uncertainty and further postpones the restoration of normal capital flows. They, and even the Fund, prefer to keep a country on a short leash and constantly accountable. Although this may limit the moral hazard problem of countries borrowing without intent to pay, it does so at the risk of miscalculating the provocation to default. Yet precisely that possibility reinforces the preference for dealing not only with one country at a time, but also with only one year at a time. The structure is thus potentially unstable.

The second deficiency is that current policies fail to address the adequacy of the long-term supply of capital. Quasi-socialization of the international banking system by the Fund in an emergency is one thing; continuing imposition of broader systemic goals is quite another. There is no reason to believe that the maximization of private profit will produce the right amount of capital for the right developing countries in the future. One of the causes of the present crisis is precisely such market failure.

According to all present signs and past historical reaction to external debt problems, voluntary lending will not recuperate quickly. Current U.S. economic policy makes the prospects even bleaker. The last quarterly report of the Bank for International Settlements called attention to the evolution of a segmented financial market:

> On the one hand, Western banks have now virtually stopped all voluntary lending to the third world and Eastern Europe, because of concern about repayment. But business transactions among the industrial nations appear to be picking up briskly as American banks accelerate their borrowing from other Western countries to finance America's payments deficit.[15]

Trying exclusively to avert the worst is not necessarily equivalent to a good, let alone the best, solution to the current financial dilemma. The present policy context is fraught with dangers. A last-minute rescue may fail. Recovery may not continue at its current pace, which will only impose more demands upon a potentially unstable bank-country relationship. Social costs in some of the developing countries may lead to failure to live up to stabilization targets. The continuing pattern of adjustment through trade surpluses may evoke even more pronounced tendencies toward protectionism, with significant consequences for the overall structure of the trading system. Reaction against rapidly rising imports from the newly industrializing countries can spill over to imports from industrial-country competitors. These possibilities, and with them slowed industrial-country growth, are very real. That reality contributes to a pervasive uncertainty, which is itself a constraint on the recovery of the global economy in the 1980s.

Radical Proposals for Restructuring Debt

In the aftermath of the Mexican shock, when the prospects for muddling through seemed much dimmer and the perils more immediate, a variety of more radical reforms were suggested.[16] Despite their differences, the proposed reforms shared common features. One was the reduction, in a decisive fashion, of the current debt service being demanded of developing countries—to alleviate the present foreign-exchange drag on their economic growth. Another was the reduction of the future developing-country debt burden through a transfer of resources from creditor banks and/or industrial countries—in the form of "writing down" the debt or rescheduling it on favorable terms. Thus the burden of past mistakes would be allocated more explicitly and equitably. A third theme was an enhanced role for a public presence in financial markets to monitor and influence lending and borrowing as well as country adjustment.

The form most typically advocated for achieving these multiple objectives was purchase of the banks' developing-country loans by an existing, or a new, international agency. Banks would sell their loans at a discount in exchange for the securities of the agency, thus substituting a known, but limited, loss for their present uncertain exposure. The agency, in turn, would recontract the debt of the countries at longer maturities and lower prices, passing along the bank write-down and possibly additional concessions from special governmental appropriations. The new arrangements would thus improve the quality of bank portfolios, shift the debt to an international development institution whose concerns would be broader, and distribute the costs of excessive debt accumulation more equitably among banks, industrial countries (through foregone taxes on potential bank profits and capital contributions to the agency), and developing countries.

All of these plans have, however, been criticized for their short-comings.[17] The most salient problem has been the failure to provide explicitly for flows of new capital once previous debts have been reorganized. Another is the volume of public resources required to fund purchase of the bank loans, even if capital is only fractionally paid in. Although the agency would issue its own securities, like the World Bank, and no actual expenditure need occur, an appropriation for capital would be necessary and subject to the resistance recently encountered in the expansion of IMF quotas. A third short-coming of these approaches is the proposed generality of their application, which would encourage even sound debtor countries to relax their adjustment efforts in favor of unneeded debt relief.

These observations have merit, but they exaggerate the deficiencies inherent in the plans. One of the increasingly accepted indictments of the present situation is, after all, the failure to assure new lending in the needed amounts. In this respect, even these radical proposals share the optimism of those who believe that, in the long term, capital markets can be trusted to provide the necessary resources. It would not be difficult to impose continuing involuntary lending by banks, since they need not eliminate their entire portfolios, and since the demand for new loans would not be as great with reduced debt service and better economic perform-ance. Moreover, other proposals that emphasize future guarantees to elicit larger capital flows have fared no better.

Such a reservation is therefore not the fundamental reason that nothing is being done. Nor is it the amount of public money required. If all the countries supplying fresh capital to the Fund had appropriated equal amounts of paid-in capital to an entity in the business of refinancing developing-country debt, and if that entity, in turn, had augmented its resources threefold (by using its paid-in capital to go into the market), this could have effected a transfer of about $90 billion in loans—close to a third of banks' gross exposure in non-oil developing countries. Nor is it impossible to devise criteria that would exclude unworthy debtors.

The real issue is not the technical adequacy of the proposals. Designs can be perfected, and additional features added. The precise distribution of costs among banks, industrialized countries, and developing countries can be negotiated. The problem is that nothing is being done—not even an increase in the capital of the World Bank in order to permit more official lending—because the present system responds only under duress. Banks are unwilling to opt for modifications even if both they and the system would be better off. To admit the need for change is to confirm the inadequacy of current arrangements and to risk testing them. All along the banks have been saying that the problem is minimal—even while agreeing to reschedule some $100 billion in debt. To call for help that did not come would be counterproductive; at best, therefore, banks are reactive and limited to short-term palliatives under their control.

The situation of the developing countries is even worse. The leading debtors must proclaim their commitment to the current arrangements and the unfailing integrity of their obligations if they are to have access to the financial assistance they continue to need. For all the talk of a "debtor's OPEC," incentives for individual compliance are much stronger than group repudiation. Different individual-country circumstances and the prospective lack of a united front make any other policy risky. Foreign ministers may advocate general resolutions, but central bankers continue to pay periodic visits to New York and Washington to deal concretely with the debt problem. The Argentine experience graphically illustrates these tendencies.

The multilateral agencies, for their part, are without independent power; they have limited resources and must rely on the private banks for the lion's share of lending, even when it is involuntary. And they have little scope for committing the industrialized countries, as the continuing struggle to achieve larger capital bases reveals.

A More Feasible Alternative

The reason for today's inaction is not the absence of a potentially better framework for dealing with the debt problem, but lack of leadership by the industrialized countries, and especially by the United States. As the crisis atmosphere of 1982 recedes, case-by-case emergency care rather than systemic reform looks more alluring. Insistence upon the adequacy of the market limits adaptation to its failures. Making the debt issue a narrow liquidity problem conforms to such a mindset. Absent a financial collapse, the costs remain implicit rather than budgetary. Taxpayers pay economically through slower growth, foregone trade and investment, and ultimately jobs; they also pay politically, through increasing alienation of the developing world. Such costs are considerably greater than direct appropriations.

This political reality, and the new threat posed by higher interest rates, call for identifying a more feasible set of measures.

Much of the initiative rests with the large banks, in the United States and elsewhere. They can guarantee against resurgence of higher debt-service payments as a consequence of higher interest rates, while the effects of economic recovery are still uncertain. Walter Wriston, chairman of Citicorp, entitled his recent article in the *Wall Street Journal*: "LDCs Just Need a Little Help From Their Friends."[18] The banks could prove such friends by introducing elements of additional stability in the present policy framework.

First, in rescheduling debt, they can cancel commission fees and reduce interest charges to their cost of funds. This would afford some material relief for the countries with the most severe debt problems, and at the same time recognize bank responsibility for a share of the difficulty.

Second, banks can extend maturities on rescheduled debt to at least ten years, thereby reducing and smoothing annual amortization payments. There is also an advantage in consolidating debt into medium- and long-term maturity. Short-term credits have proved exceedingly difficult to renegotiate and are the most difficult to monitor. Yet the effect of diminished finance upon the level of trade is immediate and negative.

Third, banks can agree to capitalize interest payments when these exceed a specifically agreed ceiling. Such a practice is commonplace in domestic mortage lending, where there is a cap to inflation indexing. Although present regulatory provisions would have to be altered to permit automatic and explicit postponement of interest payments, the same effect could be realized through informal arrangements. The practical effect of such additional lending would be to assure the use of foreign-exchange receipts for needed imports rather than interest payments.

Fourth, a longer time-frame for determining external capital requirements can be substituted for the present annual, and sometimes shorter, perspective. In such a framework, debt falling due over several years could be restructured in a single, timely agreement. Banks can participate more actively, in conjunction with the IMF and World Bank, in negotiations with debtor countries. More durable institutional linkages are necessary to reflect the new realities.

These steps would be to the banks' own advantage. They would be a constructive move toward a much more positive, workable, and predictable framework for bank-country interaction rather than the present potentially non-cooperative game. Passiveness is a formula for developing-country discontent and continuing uncertainty in financial markets. The banks' stake need not be left to others to defend.

Developing countries can contribute to this design as well. Their capacity to formulate and implement effective adjustment strategies is clearly central. Vague talk of moratoria is no substitute for domestic economic policy. Mutual confidence can be restored by evidence of stabilization within the context of a more full-blown, medium-term development strategy. Such a strategy will inevitably require larger domestic saving and larger exports. It is necessary to show what can be done with the debt relief that is asked.

The industrialized countries, in their turn, have perhaps a last decisive opportunity, at small expense, to promote these repairs to the present system of managing the debt problem. They can do so not merely by encouraging others but by confronting the other dimension of the debt problem: the adequacy of long-term transfers of resources to the developing countries. As *World Financial Markets* recently commented:

> It is time for the United States to reassert leadership in the field of development economics and finance. The industrial countries can no longer neglect the need for adequate long-term capital flows to developing countries, which commercial banks are ill-equipped to provide. This will entail continued support for official institutions such as the IMF and World Bank, and also reforms to enhance their overall effectiveness.[19]

In the final analysis, the debt problem is a development problem, involving not only finance but also trade. As such, it does not affect the performance of the developing countries alone, but has increasing, if still unequal, ramifications for the prosperity of developed nations as well. Nor is the issue a technocratic one, devoid of political content. Our long-term relationships with Third World countries and their choices of development strategies are at stake. Until these realities are acknowledged, the debt problem will continue to defy resolution and the present recovery may prove a mere interval in a succession of crises.

Notes

[1] See Table 1 and sources indicated there for different debt estimates at the end of 1982. The estimate of more than $800 billion is from World Bank, *World Debt Tables, 1983-84* (Washington, D.C.: 1984), p. xii. Such a total incorporates the broad developing-country definition of Table 1, and includes IMF-loans as well.

[2] *Wall Street Journal*, November 25, 1983, p. 1.

[3] World Bank, *World Debt Tables, 1982-83* (Washington, D.C.: 1983), p. vii.
[4] William R. Cline, *International Debt and the Stability of the World Economy* (Washington, D.C.: Institute for International Economics, 1983), p. 71.
[5] Economic Commission for Latin America, *Balance preliminar de la economia latinoamericana durante 1983* (Santiago, Chile: December 1983), p. 29.
[6] World Bank estimates from *Debt Tables, 1983-84*, op. cit., p. x.
[7] For a fuller treatment, including statistical evidence, see Albert Fishlow, "Coping with the Crisis of Creeping Debt," Working Paper No. 18, Department of Economics, University of California, Berkeley, February 1984.
[8] See the Wharton *World Economic Outlook*, October 1983, and the DRI results for the Latin American principal debtors in Thomas O. Enders and Richard P. Mattione, *Latin America: The Crisis of Debt and Growth* (Washington, D.C.: Brookings Institution, 1984); OECD, *External Debt of Developing Countries, 1983 Survey* (Paris: 1984) p. 10.
[9] Economic Commission for Latin America, *Balance preliminar*, op. cit., Table 11.
[10] Cline, *International Debt*, op. cit., p. 65.
[11] International Monetary Fund, *World Economic Outlook, 1983* (Washington, D.C.: 1983), p. 20.
[12] *The Economist*, October 15-21, 1983, p. 4.
[13] Morgan Guaranty Trust Company, *World Financial Markets*, June 1983, pp. 11, 12.
[14] These estimates start from the terms and sums rescheduled reported in *Latin American Weekly Report*, May 20, 1983, plus subsequent news accounts. On average, spreads were 1 per cent higher than during the period when the loans were initially contracted in the late 1970s, allowing for intervening grace periods. Commissions for rescheduling ranged between 1.25 and 1.5 per cent, of which 1 per cent was regarded as profit (taking into account the World Bank typical commission payment of 0.25 per cent).
Commissions are presumed to be paid initially, even if not accounted in bank earnings in that fashion, and to yield a return of 10 per cent a year. The average annual value, spread over the life of the loan, is therefore greater than the simple average (approximately twice as large).
Equivalently, one can approximate the increased returns on old loans, excluding the effect of commissions, by noting that the spread on rescheduled loans has doubled. Since such rescheduled loans are about one quarter of the total extended by banks to these countries, the effect is about a 25 per cent rise in after-tax earnings. The calculations are reported in *Wall Street Journal*, December 5, 1983.
[15] Quoted in *New York Times*, January 26, 1984.
[16] Among the authors of various swap proposals are Peter Kenen, Felix Rohatyn, and Richard Weinert. I myself advanced a similar proposal, much earlier, that the World Bank absorb some of the commercial bank portfolio of developing-country loans in exchange for World Bank bonds. See Albert Fishlow et al., *Rich and Poor Nations in the World Economy* (New York: McGraw-Hill, 1978), pp. 67-68. Many of these plans, and others, are cited in Cline, *International Debt*, op. cit., pp. 114-15.
[17] These criticisms and others are summarized in Cline, *International Debt*, op. cit., pp. 117-19.
[18] *Wall Street Journal*, March 14, 1984, p. 30.
[19] *World Financial Markets*, February 1984, p. 13.

Chapter 2

The IMF:
Case for a Change
in Emphasis

Tony Killick, Graham Bird, Jennifer Sharpley,
and Mary Sutton

A large proportion of oil-importing developing countries have been experiencing persistent, nonviable balance-of-payments deficits in the 1980s. Much of the deterioration in their payments situation in recent years has stemmed from largely irreversible adverse movements in their commodity terms of trade. This implies that a deteriorating current account is no longer *prima facie* evidence of the pursuit of excessively expansionary domestic demand policies and that restoration of a healthy balance of payments requires longer-term changes in the structures of production and demand.

Although many of the problems now confronting developing countries emanate from a more hostile worldwide economic environment, economic adjustments to strengthen the balance of payments are nevertheless inevitable, for it cannot be assumed that enough funds will become available at sub-market terms for longer-term financing to be a sustainable alternative to corrective measures. Adjustment is thus unavoidable in most developing countries that are in deficit, and it is the *costs of adjustment* that turn a payments deficit into a "problem." A variety of domestic and global factors severely limit the ability of these countries to achieve adjustment without heavy social costs.

This implies that the key task is to minimize the adjustment costs associated with the required strengthening of the balance of payments. Conceptually, the approach presented in this chapter is set in a cost-minimizing framework—although admittedly the language of quantification is used loosely and the "costs" cannot be reduced to some simple measure of welfare foregone. The most important single determinant of adjustment costs, viewed from this perspective, is the extent to which adjustment is achieved by suppressing demand rather than by stimulating supply. Closely related to this is the availability of financing and, therefore, the required speed of adjustment. In the face of a balance-of-payments crisis, a government must look for quick-acting measures, which almost certainly means opting for cuts in demand.

Unfortunately, the IMF has not set its programs within a cost-minimizing framework. It has treated the balance-of-payments objective as overriding, and has been reluctant to give weight to other government purposes when designing stabilization programs. From the point of view of a developing country, the Fund approach is *potentially* a high-cost one: The IMF can offer limited amounts of financial support, it stresses demand management, its programs are largely short-term, and it is preoccupied with a small number of quantified performance criteria. The emphasis is on "potentially," however, since the evidence suggests that the actual impact of Fund programs has been limited. Although it seems clear that the deflationary effects of Fund programs are seldom as bad as they are reputed to be, on the other hand the Fund typically falls short of its own objectives in the area of global balance-of-payments management.

It must be admitted, however, that most of the Fund's past critics have not progressed far in setting out constructive alternatives. Clearly a policy of neglect by developing-country governments offers the worst outcome of all: an involuntary "adjustment" brought about by an inability to borrow abroad and by interruptions in import supplies that result in greatly reduced capacity utilization, large reductions in investment, shortages of key consumer goods, and much hardship. It is also clear that a policy of "de-linking" does not offer a cost-efficient alternative; even in the unfavorable climate of the early 1980s, developing countries were still deriving major benefits from international trade. The onus is thus upon those interested in reformist solutions to suggest alternatives that promise to be more cost-efficient.

In this paper we set out such an alternative approach, based on the findings of our recent detailed examination of economic stabilization policies in developing countries and of the role of the IMF in these programs.[1] Urging changes in policy both by individual developing countries and by the IMF, we set out a package of measures—a "real-economy" strategy—to address the *structural* aspects of balance-of-payments problems.

The Case for Change in IMF Conditionality

Lest it be thought that we seek to convert the IMF from its traditional role into a purveyor of long-term development aid, we begin by setting out our initial premise. Specifically, we start from the statement of objectives set out in the Fund's Articles of Agreement. Those who created the Fund at Bretton Woods, and those who have joined it since, presumably have believed that all members stand to benefit from having an effective organization that would facilitate international monetary cooperation and the growth of international trade and exchange stability and that would provide material assistance to members seeking to correct payments imbalances. We share that belief. But the results of our analysis indicate that in some respects existing Fund policies may be an obstacle to the effective execution of the Fund's responsibilities, at least in relation to some of its developing-country members.

The case for change can be stated as follows. The influence of deteriorating terms of trade and other exogenous factors has worsened the balance-of-payments situation of most oil-importing developing countries. Yet the control of domestic demand remains the thrust of Fund programs—even though attempts at structural adaptation chiefly by means of demand restraint are likely to be high-cost solutions. It is, moreover, universally accepted (not least by the Fund) that structural adaptation is necessarily a lengthy process. Conventional stand-by arrangements of one year's duration are not well designed to assist with this task, even if they are set within some kind of medium-term framework.

The changing geography of the Fund's clients must also be considered. The great majority of stand-by credits, as well as those made available under the Extended Fund Facility (EFF), have in recent years been lent to the *poorer* developing countries (although Argentina, Brazil, and Mexico were major exceptions in early 1983), but it is precisely for the circumstances of the *low-income* countries that the Fund's traditional policies are least suitable. It is worth recalling here one of the conclusions of our Kenya case study: In terms of its attitudes toward economic policies, its appreciation of the potential gains of maintaining an open-economy stance, and its avoidance of the grosser forms of economic mismanagement, Kenya appears to be exactly the type of developing country that could most easily do business with the Fund. Yet the relationship has been a troubled one and all programs (except the most recent) have broken down. If Kenya and the IMF cannot work out an effective relationship, what African government can? The Kenya situation is a specific illustration of the general difficulty of applying the Fund's stabilization approach to the circumstances of *low-income* developing countries.

The IMF Articles of Agreement refer to the maintenance of high levels of employment, income, and economic development as "the primary objectives of economic policy" that the Fund can assist through balance-of-payment assistance. But in practice the Fund has sometimes appeared to treat these objectives as secondary to the restoration of payments equilibrium and has tended to neglect the potentially negative impact of its programs on the "primary objectives" set out in its Articles. As already indicated, however, our study found that Fund programs often have only a modest impact, for good or ill. For reasons that are far from exclusively attributable to the Fund, a high percentage of programs become inoperative during their intended time frame, which is generally only one year. Even in cases where a credit is fully drawn, it seems that only limited improvement can be claimed in the balance of payments and in other macro-economic variables. Finally, while the Fund sought hard to adapt its resources, facilities, and conditionality to changing circumstances following the first oil shock, some of that adaptation was undone by a return since 1981, partly at the instigation of the Reagan administration, to policies more like those of the late 1960s than of the late 1970s. As others have pointed out, one of the effects of the tightening up in conditionality since 1981 has been to give a further contractionary twist to a world economy already in recession.

For all these reasons, there is an overwhelming case for a major change in the content of conditionality—at a minimum, a reversion to the late-1970s attempts to adapt and to accommodate developing-country members. The case flows simply from the Articles of Agreement: Given the changing nature of its clientele and their problems, the Fund's current approach to the design of stabilization programs reduces its ability to carry out certain of the purposes written into its Articles.

It should in all honesty be added that our recommendations for change spring not only from our concern about the Fund's faithfulness to its Articles, but also from our persuasion that it is desirable to redress the present tendency of international monetary arrangements to increase income disparities between nations. In the past few years, the powerful members of the Organization of Petroleum Exporting Countries (OPEC) and the industrial nations of the Organisation for Economic Co-operation and Development (OECD) have been able to shift much of the burden of adjustment onto developing-nation oil importers, which is why this group of countries is plagued with such intractable deficits. "Adjustment," it seems, is a prescription largely reserved for low-income deficit countries (but not the USA!), even though simple accounting logic dictates that aggregate deficits cannot be reduced unless there is a matching reduction in surpluses. It is also difficult to dismiss the accusation (by President Nyerere of Tanzania, among others) that the IMF has been employed as an instrument of control by the rich and powerful nations over the poorer—as an active agent in an asymmetrical adjustment process that places the greatest burdens upon those least able to bear them. At a minimum, it is surely desirable that the Fund's policies be designed to minimize this burden and its adverse welfare effects on those already living in poverty. Thus the equity case is immensely strong, even if it is not broadly shared. But whether that case is accepted or not, there is an equally strong *efficiency* case for change.

Perhaps at the heart of some of the Fund's difficulties is the view that there should be a fairly standard stabilization program— some well-defined "conventional" approach. It is not our intention here to suggest that the Fund switch from a standard demand-management approach to a standard real-economy approach. In fact, we place importance on the role of demand management and would be the last to deny that governments often worsen their external problems by domestic mismanagement or inertia. What we do urge is that the Fund use a richer *mix* of policies, recognizing the mutual interdependence of demand- and supply-oriented policies and adapting stabilization programs to country circumstances within a less confining intellectual frontier. Fundamental to our approach is the premise that the design of such programs must be directly related to the causes of the problems they address.

Two polar cases may help to clarify the need for a sufficient differentiation of approaches. At one extreme there is what might be called the "classical IMF problem" of a persistent payments deficit attributable largely to excessively expansionary fiscal policies. With the terms of trade assumed to be roughly steady, the chief task is to bring aggregate demand (and therefore the budget) under control, increase the incentive to export, reduce the incentive to import, and create domestic conditions conducive to an inflow of supporting finance.

At the other extreme, there is the "structural" case of a country that is pursuing responsible fiscal and monetary policies at home but that is confronted with an enormous increase in the unit cost of imports, a depressed foreign demand for its traditional exports, and a persistent, serious deterioration in its terms of trade. These external factors may be aggravated by structural weaknesses of a more domestic origin, or such weaknesses may themselves be the principal source of difficulty: lagging agriculture, high-cost industry, or an inefficient marketing system.

Obviously, most countries experiencing payments difficulties fall somewhere between these polar cases and therefore require a blend of policies designed to tackle both demand and supply weaknesses. It is equally obvious, however, that in the last decade or so, particularly since the second oil shock and the general recession of the early 1980s, the "structural" sources of deficit have become more important relative to excess-demand sources.

The "real-economy" approach we urge is particularly relevant for the circumstances of countries confronting essentially *structural* problems.

A "Real-Economy" Strategy: Adjustment With Growth

Often the best approach to economic management involves a program primarily aimed at re-orienting the productive system. Such a "real-economy" strategy places greater weight on supply-side measures, in contrast to approaches that emphasize the control of aggregate demand. There are strong *a priori* reasons for expecting the real-economy approach to be most cost-efficient if it can be successfully implemented. *Such a strategy of adjustment with growth would permit equilibrium to be restored at a higher overall level of economic activity and it would minimize the conflicts between the policy objectives of stabilization, growth, and social welfare.* A wide variety of problems are more amenable to solution in the context of economic growth than they are in a recession:

- Sectoral shifts and industrial restructuring are easier to secure, since what is chiefly in question is differential rates of expansion rather than the absolute decline of the disfavored lines of activity.
- The level of saving and thus investment can be sustained.
- The absorption problem is easier to solve by raising income than by cutting spending.
- Financing the government's budget becomes easier.
- The politics of adjustment becomes less sensitive.

The approach advocated here emphasizes the importance of designing balance-of-payments programs that stimulate output and productivity. It tackles key bottlenecks and constraints within the productive system and goes beyond conventional macro aggregates to a wide variety of specific micro-economic measures.

The objective of a strategy of adjustment with growth is to create a viable balance of payments in a manner that also promotes, or at least minimizes conflicts with, that group of government objectives called "economic development." The key target variable will generally be the *current account* of the balance of payments; it is only by reducing the current deficit that a country can safeguard against the danger of generating a financing gap that cannot be filled or against building up an unsustainably large volume of external debt-servicing obligations. The emphasis will thus be on increasing the volume and value of exports, reducing *net* dependence on imports through efficient import substitution, and maximizing net inflows (and minimizing net outflows) on the "invisibles and transfers" account, through measures such as stimulation of the tourist industry, encouragement of the repatriation of earnings from nationals working abroad, and more efficient domestic provision of insurance and shipping services.

The growth of output envisaged in this strategy can be thought of as coming from two sources: from the improved utilization of existing productive capacity and from increases in that capacity. Greater capacity utilization may be particularly important both because it is common for countries experiencing a payments crisis to be operating well below the trend level of output, and because greater output from existing capacity should not, in principle, be subject to long gestation lags in a situation in which time is of the essence.

When it comes to expanding productive capacity, a strategy of adjustment with growth calls for a relative increase in the output of tradables—all goods and services that enter significantly into world trade—vis-à-vis non-tradables. From the viewpoint of a specific country, tradables are items that are or potentially could be exported, together with items that are imported or are home-produced substitutes for imports. Almost all goods are traded or potentially tradable, but some goods, and a larger proportion of services—for example, domestic water supplies, health services, and construction—do not normally lend themselves to international commerce. Although a wide range of policy instruments can be deployed to assist the relative expansion in the output of tradables, measures to change the structure of commodity and factor price incentives are of crucial importance (as will be shown below). On the export side, of course, the feasibility of the real-economy approach will be affected by the rate of recovery of the markets of the OECD countries at present, by their buoyancy in the future, and by trends in protectionism. To the extent that the payments crisis has been largely caused by rapidly rising import prices, however, this

trend will itself create new, profitable, import-substituting investment opportunities and possibly also improved ability to compete in
non-traditional export markets.

The strategy so far described may produce quick results, but
only when there is much excess capacity in the traded goods sector
that can be rapidly mobilized. In many circumstances it would be
unwise to base plans on major improvements in utilization, for
although most countries operate well within their production frontier, the obstacles to remedying this situation are often deep-
seated—otherwise the problem would be less widespread. The alternative of expanding the production frontier, although in a sense
a more fundamental solution, is bound to be slower-acting because
of gestation lags. In the meantime, balance-of-payments deficits
must be expected to persist, even if on a diminishing scale, and
these will have to be financed somehow.

Although there are no grounds for being dogmatic even on this
point, there must also be a general presumption in favor of gradual
programs rather than shock treatment approaches. In large part
this follows from what already has been said about the need for
actions that will stimulate output but will involve gestation lags. It
also seems likely that the loss to "psychic welfare" is less when
people have time to adjust their lives to altered circumstances and
policies than if traumatic changes are suddenly thrust upon them.
Gradual programs are also likely to be easier to monitor and control; the risks of major policy mistakes are thus probably lessened.
The Chilean experience suggests the high costs of the shock approach, now apparently abandoned.[2] What we particularly fear is
the danger of overkill through a combination of devaluation, interest-rate reform, budgetary stringency, and credit restrictions.

It must be noted, however, that a general preference for gradual programs further emphasizes the need for longer-term financing. The strategy advocated here envisages a more adequate flow of
financing than is often available, including concessional flows to
those countries that cannot (or should not) meet their needs from
commercial sources. The role of supporting finance is particularly
important, since a country's ability to meet its import needs will
have a great influence on the utilization of productive capacity and
the volume of new capital formation. One of the criticisms of programs emphasizing the limitation of imports is that they may deny
essential intermediate and capital goods to precisely those sectors
that need to expand if the structural problem is to be overcome.

But if increases in the production of tradables are at the heart
of the real-economy strategy, this does not mean that demand
management can be abandoned. To go back to essentials, payments

adjustment entails a reduction in absorption (consumption plus investment) relative to income. One of the attractions of the real-economy strategy is that its *primary emphasis is on the expansion of income, thus obviating or lessening the need for an absolute reduction in consumption and investment.* But in the absence of demand management and incomes policies, there is every likelihood that consumption and investment would expand quite as fast as income, thus subverting the entire program. With this approach it would be essential to protect the investment component of absorption; it is chiefly consumption that would have to be restrained. The same destination is reached by another route when it is recalled that the objective is to reduce the *current-account* deficit. According to the basic model of income determination in an open economy, if exports are to rise relative to imports, then savings must rise relative to investment. Since we have already determined that investment should not be cut, it follows that savings must be raised, again entailing that the chief burden must fall upon consumption. This is an unwelcome fact, since the countries on whose predicament we here focus generally have low average incomes and many people living in absolute poverty. But without much-enlarged, near-permanent international flows of concessional finance, there seems to be no alternative to austerity. This is the sharp end of the truth that the adverse movement in the terms of trade suffered by most oil-importing developing countries represents a transfer of real income from them to their suppliers. All that can be said in mitigation is that the real-economy strategy offers less draconian consumption curbs than an approach based more heavily upon demand restraint.

But is not the restraint of consumption likely to require conventional fiscal and monetary policies of the type associated with IMF programs? If so, are we really offering an alternative? There are, in fact, major differences between the two approaches—the most important being the level of output (and consumption) at which a viable balance of payments may be restored. Furthermore, supply-oriented measures, if successful, will increase the demand for real money balances, which is primarily a function of real income. Other things being equal, this will mean that a given payments outcome will be consistent with a larger real volume of domestic credit, which, in turn, may assist a further round of increased capacity utilization and capital formation. In addition, as discussed below, safeguards can be introduced against the danger that fiscal and monetary restraints may undermine the pattern of structural change that we advocate. On the other hand, we do not wish to exaggerate the extent to which our suggestions differ from IMF policies. In the present context, we consider the changes we advocate to be an important difference of emphasis—of viewing demand management as an essential supporting measure to a supply-oriented strategy, rather than treating it as the centerpiece, with or without supplementary supply measures.

One other basic principle of the real-economy strategy is that, like the Fund, we consider balance-of-payments adjustment to require a *package* of measures. The danger inherent in any such comprehensive approach, however, is that the effective implementation of a large number of mutually reinforcing and carefully phased policy measures is likely to test the most powerful government and the most efficient public administration—and countries vary greatly in this respect. It is therefore essential to tailor the program to the practical capabilities of each country.

The complexity and diversity of real-economy approaches to balance-of-payments adjustment can be illustrated further by considering the range of policy instruments available to governments for achieving the objectives set out earlier. Table 1 gives a partial inventory of this range of instruments—partial both because it is largely confined to measures affecting the agricultural and industrial sectors and because, even within these two areas, it would be quite easy to add to the list. Each country has its own peculiarities of, for example, institutional framework, policy traditions, and sectoral needs; and comparisons of specific country policies reveal an exceedingly rich variety of instruments in use.

No attempt is made in Table 1 to rank the relative importance of various instruments. What it does make clear, however, is the wide range of available and relevant policy instruments. The distinction between macro-economic and micro-economic policies (which has been used to limit the coverage of IMF program conditionality) tends to break down in the context of adjustment with growth. Apparently macro-economic instruments (such as the exchange rate) affect the productive sectors in differential ways, just as micro-economic measures aimed at a particular activity (for example, tourist promotion) can make an important contribution to the macro-economic objective of payments adjustment.

Implications for IMF Practices and Policies

How might the principles of a real-economy strategy be incorporated into the policies and practices of the Fund? Would it not be a radical change? We think not, because the reasons for moving toward this type of program are almost identical to the rationale presented by the Fund itself for introducing its Extended Fund Facility and subsequently for its policy adaptations of 1979-80. The

Table 1. Partial Inventory of Policy Instruments Affecting the Production of Tradables

Tax Measures

Import tariffs (and the associated pattern of industrial protection)
Export taxation
Taxation of land values
Taxation of gasoline and other fuels
Investment incentives (such as tax holidays)
Reform (strengthening of tax administration, for example)

Government Expenditure Measures

Agricultural research and development; extension training
Rural infrastructure (roads, storage facilities, cattle digs, etc.)
Land conservation/reclamation
Food and other buffer stocks
Subsidies on food and other essentials
Agricultural input subsidies (for fertilizers, for example)
Geological surveying and exploration
Export subsidies and insurance
Industrial infrastructure (for example, power, water, and communication)
Industrial estates
Research and development of more appropriate industrial technologies
Investments in local resource-based energy projects (such as hydro-electricity)
Port facilities

Legal and Regulatory Measures

Export quality and health controls
Land reform; land registration
Import and export controls
Price controls

Other Institutional Measures

Strengthening relevant state-managed bodies
Improved distribution of agricultural inputs
Co-operative development
Export advice and technical assistance
Promotion of tourism
Strengthening public-sector project selection and execution procedures
Improved negotiating stance vis-à-vis multinational corporations (for example, on oil exploration or mineral exploitation)

Financial, Pricing, and Related Measures

Interest-rate and other financial reforms
Sectoral credit allocations (including rural credit, and allocations as between public and private sectors)
Pricing policies (for example, for agriculture, some state-managed enterprises)
Exchange-rate adjustments
Incomes policies

analysis presented in an internal Fund document in mid-1980 is scarcely less relevant today:

> The problems of adjustment in present circumstances are particularly complex. It is clear that the correction of the large payments imbalances cannot be achieved within a short period. . . .Moreover, important structural changes in the oil importing countries will be necessary, if these countries are to achieve a gradual correction without seriously endangering growth prospects. The task of bringing about the necessary adjustment is made more difficult in the present circumstances by the fact that inflationary expectations have become deeply entrenched in most countries. Sustained anti-inflationary corrective actions, taken simultaneously, tend to dampen the growth of world trade and this makes it more difficult for each country to shift more resources into the export sector. In order to maintain a reasonable and durable rate of economic growth, adjustment has to be set within a relatively long time frame and it has to be concerned with structural improvements in the pattern of output and demand.

Publications by IMF staff members have similarly urged the importance of measures to change the structures of demand and supply.[3]

To a large extent, then, what we are proposing for the Fund is not new. We are essentially calling upon the Fund to have the courage of its own analyses and to continue the process of adaptation begun in the late 1970s but seemingly aborted in 1981. Although only a shift of emphasis, the change from demand management as the primary means of payments adjustment to a supporting role nevertheless would be a significant one for the Fund. In the context of a strategy of adjustment with growth, it would be most important to design demand-control measures so that they protect savings and investment to the fullest possible extent, leaving the chief burden of reducing absorption (consumption plus investment) relative to income to be borne by consumption. Similarly, to the extent that the programs continue to incorporate relative or absolute reductions in government spending, it would be essential to include safeguards to prevent the cuts from falling on those public expenditures that could promote needed changes in the economic structure. This is a more subtle task than simply trying to protect the capital budget vis-à-vis the recurrent budget. The capital budget includes military equipment, office buildings, and a wide variety of other items unlikely to make much of a contribution to payments adjustment, while the recurrent budget contains items such as agricultural research and extension, which can be essential to program success.

Adaptations would similarly be needed in the Fund's traditional approach to credit control. The role of domestic credit in a real-economy approach is far more ambiguous than under a monetary approach. Monetarists stress the negative effects of increased credit on the overall balance of payments, which are likely to occur partly because of the use of credit to finance imports. However, domestic credit is also likely to have a positive effect on investment and therefore on the potential pace of structural adjustment. Drawing attention to the positive effects of credit on the productive system, a recent Fund study suggests that "at least in the longer run, increased levels of profitable credit will strengthen the current account performance rather than place a burden on the balance of payments."[4] Excessively tight credit restrictions could deter supply-side adjustment by reducing industrial capacity utilization and by making it more difficult or costly to finance adequate inventories of inputs and work in progress.

The upshot of these considerations is that more credit is likely to be justified in a structural program than in a demand-oriented one and that greater attention will have to be given to credit allocation across the economy, perhaps through the use of selective controls. This is not, however, an invitation to print money; increased credit to finance consumption (broadly defined to include housing and other durables) is particularly to be discouraged.

For reasons given earlier, going beyond these rather general prescriptions should be attempted only in the context of a specific country situation—to assure that programs are "tailor-made" to fit the specifics of particular cases. To give some concrete idea of what a real-economy program incorporating these various suggestions would be like, however, our larger study (see footnote 1) sets out a specific illustration of what shifting to a real-economy approach would mean in the case of Kenya.

The chief features of this approach are that:

(1) The program would be set in a cost-minimizing, growth-oriented framework and designed to be consonant with the government objective of poverty alleviation.

(2) It would be a medium-term program, to be executed over five years.

(3) The emphasis would be upon a program arrived at by consensus, reflecting a genuine government commitment. In this connection, as well as in monitoring the program, we place

some importance on the role of an IMF resident represen-
tative.

(4) A substantial number of measures to stimulate the production of exportable and import-substituting goods and services
relative to non-tradables would be included, with at least the
same status as other provisions of the program.

(5) Quantified performance criteria would be replaced by a
broader set of "review indicators." Performance under these
indicators would not govern eligibility for continued access to
the credit, as in the case of existing performance criteria; like
those criteria, however, they would trigger a review mission,
whose job it would be to form a rounded judgment of overall
progress with the program and to make recommendations
about continued access on that basis. A review mission could
be dispatched at the initiative of either the government or the
IMF.

(6) There would be an agreed timetable of execution for all or
a large proportion of the program elements, and there would
be explicit provision for the ways in which progress would be
monitored.

(7) In addition to lending its own resources, the Fund would
initiate actions to attract additional supporting finance from
other multilateral, bilateral, and perhaps commercial sources.

There is no doubt a good deal to argue about in the specifics of these
proposals, as well as gaps to be filled in. But one point should be
unquestionably clear: This approach does not offer a deficit country
the soft option of obtaining a lot more money without taking tough
policy measures.

It might be objected at this stage that the IMF has already
conducted—in the form of its Extended Fund Facility—an experiment that went some way in the direction of our suggestions, but
that the experiment did not work well, and consequently the EFF is
now used much less than it was a few years ago. Our own analysis of
the effectiveness of the EFF leads us to conclude: (1) that in
1978-81, EFFs were more likely to break down than were stand-by
arrangements; (2) that EFF programs produced weaker results for
the balance of payments when compared with prior outcomes, but
that the comparative performance was ambiguous in relation to
program targets; (3) that EFF programs were notably more successful in protecting real economic growth; (4) that neither type of
program made much impression on the inflation rate, although the
EFF result was clearly the better with respect to program targets;

and (5) that the unpopularity of the EFF within the Fund had a great deal to do with the special presentational and accounting difficulties that resulted from program breakdowns.

Thus, in comparison with stand-by programs, no clear EFF inferiority (or superiority) emerges. However, the conditionality freeze of the second half of 1981 resulted in a far greater reluctance by the Fund's Executive Board to agree to new EFF credits. The Reagan administration and certain European governments were not happy with the Fund's move toward medium-term programs and a more active role in global recycling. There were internal Fund reasons for not resisting very strongly the political pressures against continued extensive use of the EFF. In all fairness, it must also be said that the program's supporters were not able to point to a strong performance record.

In any case, the EFF does not represent a definitive test of a real-economy strategy. The "structural" elements in this facility have a somewhat uncertain status, given that they are essentially superimposed upon conventional demand-management measures, with the key performance criteria remaining the conventional ones of quarterly credit ceilings and the like. Any effective supply-side conditionality contained in EFF agreements was *additional* to the Fund's conventional conditions. It was, in other words, an uneasy compromise, and it did not satisfactorily bridge the gap between the Fund's intellectual recognition of the need for a changed approach to adjustment and its traditional practices. In fact, credit ceilings were *more* stringent in EFFs than in stand-by arrangements.

Possible Sources of Additional Financing

If much IMF lending were to take the form advocated here, it would require more funds because these are longer-term programs necessitating the provision of supporting finance for a number of years. From what sources might such money come? We identify the following five possibilities.

1. In many ways *further quota increases* are the most straightforward alternative. The ratio of quotas to world imports has fallen dramatically since the 1960s, just when the size of payments disequilibria has been rising, and the 1983 quota increase has gone only a small way toward a restoration of this ratio. Furthermore, using increased quotas to raise resources would permit the Fund to expand the loans it extends at sub-market interest rates. On the other hand, a portion of the value of increased quotas would be expected to be used for the low-conditionality facilities, so that the

proportion of low-conditionality finance will rise. However, it should also be expected that higher quotas would not only raise the Fund's resources but also increase demand for them.

2. Although it offers a useful and often expedient way of meeting potential crises of liquidity, *ad hoc borrowing* does not seem to offer a satisfactory long-term solution to the shortage of resources, since it does not provide a reliable source of finance. For example, the scope for future borrowing from Saudi Arabia hinges crucially on the price of oil and the size of the Saudi balance-of-payments surplus, which, however, is highly sensitive to conditions on the world oil market and to OPEC politics. Moreover, this is a rather expensive source of finance.

3. *Direct borrowing by the Fund from private capital markets* raises a number of questions. Would the IMF "on-lend" these funds at commercial terms similar to those under which it borrowed, or would it attempt to transform the maturity and terms of loans? If it were to on-lend at softer terms than those at which it was borrowing, where would the finance for such subsidization come from? Would all developing countries benefit from such arrangements, or would there be distributional variations, particularly between the more and less creditworthy developing countries?

Any incentive for private banks to lend to the Fund would have to arise from the rate of return offered and their own assessment of the risks involved, which could be influenced by the uses to which the extra resources were put. Since the banks would presumably assess the risks as less than those involved with lending directly to developing countries, they would probably be prepared to accept a lower rate of return. Lending to the Fund could be attractive to commercial banks as a means of widening their asset portfolios, since it would enable them to combine high-return, high-risk lending directly to developing countries with lower-return, low-risk lending to the IMF. However, it might also induce them to pull even further out of direct balance-of-payments financing, an area in which the Fund has the greater expertise. Furthermore, IMF lending financed by commercial borrowing might be concentrated particularly on the higher-income developing countries—unless an interest-rate subsidy could be devised. It might thus be unpopular with low-income countries. It might also be unpopular with middle-income countries, which might regard IMF borrowing as crowding out their own direct borrowing, compelling them to turn to the Fund and its conditionality.

4. Resort to *gold sales* is, of course, not a new idea, since the Fund already has used sales of its gold to finance operations of its Trust Fund. The IMF has thus accepted that this constitutes an

appropriate use of its gold. The pros and cons of using gold in this way have been thoroughly investigated elsewhere.[5] What emerges is that there is a strong case for such sales on equity grounds, and no legitimate argument against them on efficiency grounds.

The main problems relating to gold sales relate to: (1) variations in the market price of gold, causing fluctuations in receipts from any given volume of sales; (2) the fact that the major beneficiaries might turn out to be the purchasers of gold—mostly industrial rather than developing countries; and (3) the unanswered question of what happens when all the gold has been sold.

The first problem simply makes the exercise of maximizing receipts that much more complex, but this has not prevented the auctioning of gold in the past. The second problem could, in principle, be dealt with by introducing some form of international gold capital gains tax, although it seems highly unlikely that this would be acceptable. The only practical solution would then be to use IMF gold as collateral for raising private loans, rather than selling it— but in this case the finance made available would not be concessional. The third problem might be resolved by using only the interest from the investment of receipts from gold sales rather than the full capital value; while this would imply a continuing flow of finance, it would of course also mean that initially less finance would be available.

5. Most proposals for *an SDR link* keep the creation of Special Drawing Rights separate from the activities of the General Account. In principle, however, the link could be organized to provide extra resources for the General Account, and schemes of this nature have been discussed within the Fund. In effect, SDRs would be used to augment other Fund resources. Although the mechanics of this type of link vary, one important implication is that the SDRs thus created would be allocated to borrowing countries on a conditional and quite possibly repayable basis, and would thus lose many of their previously distinctive features. Under this form of link, the appropriateness of IMF conditionality would again be a crucial issue.

These various methods of increasing IMF resources are not, of course, mutually exclusive. Although each deserves consideration—and each may well present some technical as well as political difficulties—our own preference is for a package including further quota increases, gold sales, and an SDR link. A major reason for preferring this combination is that it would leave the IMF in a position to provide special financial relief (through interest subsidies and the SDR link, for example) to low-income developing countries whose poverty and balance-of-payments situations make application of the standard borrowing terms inappropriate.

It should by now be amply clear that the view we take of the role of the IMF is not only positive but also cast within the Fund's historical terms of reference to assist member governments in overcoming payments imbalances. To the extent that we are critical of IMF practices, it is because we do not think that they are currently framed in a manner likely to achieve the Fund's stated objectives— and because we believe that in the past the Fund has not placed enough weight on other economic (not to mention political) objectives of policy as constraints upon the design of stabilization programs. The real-economy strategy is not an attempt to convert the IMF into another development agency; it is an assertion that in contemporary circumstances it is impossible to draw any sharp distinction between balance-of-payments management and the design of development strategies.

The Case for Change in Developing-Country Policies

If our emphasis so far has been on changes in IMF policies, this is not because we see these as exclusively responsible for the adjustment problems that currently confront most developing nations. Our country studies point to numerous weaknesses in developing-country government policies as well. The case for change within many developing nations is as strong as the case for change at the IMF.

In our own analysis of developing-country policies, we found that policy deficiencies were often linked to a reluctance to come to terms with the harsh realities of the two oil shocks and the recession in the industrial world, as well as a reluctance to place sufficient weight upon economic stabilization as a policy objective. That many of these countries' problems have been "wished upon them" by convolutions in the world economy over which they had no control is obviously true. But this does not remove the need for adjustment. And while the worsened external environment has been a major cause of their payments deficits during the past decade, domestic policy weaknesses have often compounded the difficulties. Undoubtedly the best policy advice for developing countries is to avoid situations in which it becomes necessary to seek IMF assistance!

The events of the early-1980s have left many developing-country governments in little doubt that shortages of foreign exchange today constitute a massive obstacle to the fulfillment of the material aspirations of their peoples. Once such shortages are recognized as the binding constraint upon development, it follows as a matter of logic that policies designed to deal with this problem *are part of the development effort.* Quite apart from loosening the hold of the foreign-exchange constraints, successful stabilization will also reduce uncertainties and risks, which is a key task of planning and is itself likely to have a beneficial effect on economic performance. The task then becomes one of building adjustment into the country's development strategy and planning. Clearly the real-economy strategy has much to say about the desirable content of developing-country development strategies.

One source of difficulty in this context is that planning in these countries has conventionally been regarded as a once-every-five-years effort to write a medium-term development plan. Quite apart from the numerous other difficulties and disappointments to which it has led, this approach to planning has the great defect of inflexibility. It does not lend itself to accommodating the types of exogenous shocks to which the developing world has been subjected in recent years. If stabilization policy is to be effectively coordinated with other aspects of the development effort—and plans are commonly weak in this area—planning will have to be much more flexible than has typically been the case in the past. In particular, it will need to facilitate the coordination of short-term fiscal and monetary measures with long-term policies.

More concretely, we urge developing-country governments to accept a number of propositions about their domestic policies to which some have demonstrated resistance in the past. First, demand management *is* crucially important if adjustment and therefore development are to be achieved. This does not mean "fine tuning," which is impracticable, but rather the achievement of *general* control over the level of absorption (particularly consumption) relative to income, including the avoidance of large-scale deficit financing. Second, relative prices *do* matter crucially in the allocation of resources and, therefore, in achieving structural adjustment. Over the years a considerable volume of empirical research has accumulated that gives the lie to any generalized "elasticity pessimism," except in the very short term. Although "getting prices right" can only be part of the answer to the adjustment problem, programs that swim against the tide of perverse price signals are unlikely to be successful.

This view is of course addressed particularly to "left-wing" governments—for it is they who are most likely to be skeptical of the market mechanism. That there is no intrinsic incompatibility between socialism and the use of market signals as an allocative mechanism is suggested by the existence of a large literature of venerable pedigree giving a positive role to prices in a socialist economy, as well as by the *practices* of various socialist governments:

> In Hungary and Yugoslavia, state-owned firms operate in a market system and respond to price signals, with domestic prices being linked to world market prices through the exchange rate, import tariffs, and export subsidies. Of greater relevance to economies of lower levels of development, China also attempts to decentralise the process of decision-making, with increased use made of the market mechanism.[6]

Since the distinctive feature of socialism is its concern to reduce inequalities, left-wing governments tend to cling to price controls and subsidies as means of achieving this objective. But price controls often have perverse effects, and the major beneficiaries of subsidies are by no means invariably the poorest of the poor. This is particularly true of subsidies to a wide range of state-owned enterprises. In a high proportion of cases, it is the relatively affluent urban population that gains the most; the persistence of subsidies is more a tribute to the political clout of town dwellers than it is to the idealism of the government.

Left-wing governments also are most likely to reject calls for demand and wage restraints and to neglect the balance-of-payments. But it is our view that a disregard for the basic tenets of demand management is bound to undermine attempts to build a socialist society. Socialists should seriously ponder the advice of one sympathetic writer:

> The great importance of correct financial policies during attempts at transition to socialism and the fact that it is precisely socialist governments. . .which need most to follow deliberate and often strict financial policies is very rarely recognised by economists and politicians on the Left. . . . [Such policies are needed] so as to avoid too large an expansion of total demand, as this will inevitably lead to scarcities, high inflation, and foreign exchange crisis. Very high levels of inflation will not only disrupt market links with the remaining private sector, but even more importantly will make an effective system of planning and control of the rapidly growing State sector very difficult, if not meaningless.[7]

The author goes on to stress the importance of proper balance-of-payments management and incomes policies, arguing that otherwise economic disruptions will undermine the political foundations of social reforms. Active policies of economic management thus should be seen as a necessary feature of any transition to socialism. The approach to adjustment discussed here envisages a large and active role for the state; in no sense does it advocate a laissez-faire solution.

An active exchange rate policy is a particularly important application of our general recommendation that governments make positive use of the price mechanism. On this matter we are in general agreement with the IMF. But here the "structural" case is predominant, since it is the exchange rate that determines the relative prices of tradable and non-tradable goods. Moreover, generalized "elasticity pessimism" is particularly inappropiate when it comes to trade—although there are, of course, particular circumstances in which elasticities are small. There is, no doubt, much force in the argument that what ultimately determines the export prospects of developing countries is the income elasticity of demand for their goods (mainly in industrial countries), but this is not an argument against the use of exchange rates. It is precisely non-traditional exports, which in general are likely to have the larger income elasticities of demand, that are most responsive to exchange rate depreciations. Moreover, we consider use of the exchange rate to be generally preferable to wholesale exchange controls, which are actually liable to weaken the underlying balance-of-payments situation by discriminating against exports—although there are crises in which controls are inevitable.

Active use of the exchange rate also is a more positive (and perhaps a more distributionally progressive) alternative to severe demand repression. Far more weight is thrust upon the control of aggregate demand in a country facing a payments crisis if it insists on an unchanged exchange rate. Currency depreciations reduce the need for additional measures of demand restraint both because of their own demand-absorbing effects and because they do more to stimulate appropriate supply (production of exports and import substitutes), thus limiting any requirement for absolute reductions in absorption.

A final concern we wish to raise about policies pursued in developing countries relates to the widespread practice of holding interest rates well below the inflation rate—what is known as "financial repression." In principle, interest-rate reforms that create positive (or less negative) real interest rates are likely to have a number of advantages: They will tend to encourage domestic saving and inflows (or reduced outflows) of capital from the rest of the world; they will tend to channel available investment resources into higher productivity employments; they may, by increasing the demand for money and money-substitutes, reduce the necessary degree of credit restraint and employment; and they are likely to enhance the effectiveness of the conventional instruments of demand management, particularly by increasing central bank control over the money base.[8] It must be cautioned, however, that developing-country experiences with financial reforms that have raised interest rates have been far from uniform. South Korea, Taiwan, and Indonesia are commonly cited as success stories in this respect; but such policies also have had negative results, as exemplified by the experiences of Chile.

Especially in many of the poorer developing countries, a key determinant of success in applying an interest-rate reform is the degree of efficiency of the financial system as a means of mobilizing savings and channeling them into productive investment. It should not, however, be taken for granted that a sufficient array of investment opportunities promising high rates of return will always exist, or be perceived to exist. If they do not, raising interest rates can result in a seriously reduced investment rate. Finally, if interest-rate policy is not carefully coordinated with exchange-rate policy, unwanted results can arise via the foreign asset component of the money base.[9] The greater the degree of exchange-rate flexibility, the greater the danger of "overkill" through higher interest rates, which invite an unwanted inflow of short-term capital that tends to push up the exchange rate and/or swell the money base. The general case against financial repression nonetheless holds, as long as due caution is exercised in the design of policies to eliminate it.

Conclusion

We thus envisage a range of actions that can be undertaken, both by the IMF and by developing-country governments, to ease the balance-of-payments constraint. Especially in the latter case, but also to some extent within the Fund, the changes could be adopted with little further ado. The major thrust of our proposals regarding the conditionality of the Fund is controversial, however, and would require policy decisions by those who govern its actions. Thus any major changes in such policies will perforce be an outcome of international diplomacy, which places the issue of IMF policies toward developing countries firmly within the context of the North-South "dialogue."

At present, several of the key industrial-country governments do not regard it as in their interests to agree to the types of changes advocated here. The task of international diplomacy thus is to change these perceptions of national interest, for it is in no one's interest to continue with policies that are manifestly not working well. Confrontationalist tactics are unlikely to be helpful in this task. Whatever the difficulties and frustrations, and however unpromising the present state of North-South relations, there is in the end no alternative to reform by consensus.

Notes

[1] This article is drawn from the concluding chapter of the first volume of a major two-volume study organized under the auspices of the Overseas Development Institute in London. See Tony Killick, Graham Bird, Jennifer Sharpley, and Mary Sutton, *The Quest for Economic Stabilisation: The IMF and the Third World* (vol. 1) and *The IMF and Stabilisation: Developing Country Experiences* (vol. 2) (London and New York: Heinemann Educational Books and St. Martins Press, in association with Overseas Development Institute, 1984). The comprehensive ODI Study examines in detail the cases of Indonesia, Kenya, and Jamaica.

[2] See Ricardo French-Davies, "The Monetarist Experiment in Chile: A Critical Survey," *World Development*, Vol. 11, No. 11 (November 1983), pp. 905-26.

[3] See, for example, Karim Nashashibi, "A Supply Framework for Exchange Reform in Developing Countries: The Experience of Sudan," *IMF Staff Papers*, Vol. 27, No. 1 (March 1980), and Andrew D. Crockett, "Stabilization Policies in Developing Countries: Some Policy Considerations," *IMF Staff Papers*, Vol. 28, No. 1 (March 1981).

[4] Peter M. Keller, "Implications of Credit Policies for Output and the Balance of Payments," *IMF Staff Papers*, Vol. 27, No. 3 (September 1980), p. 464. See also Paul Krugman and Lance Taylor, "Contractionary Effects of Devaluation," *Journal of International Economics*, Vol. 8, No. 3 (August 1978), pp. 445-56.

[5] David A. Brodsky and Garry P. Sampson, "Gold, SDRs and Developing Countries," *Trade and Development*, No. 2 (Autumn 1980); and David A. Brodsky and Garry P. Sampson, "Implications of the Effective Revaluation of Reserve Account Gold: The Case for a Gold Account for Development," *World Development*, Vol. 9, No. 7 (July 1981), pp. 589-608.

[6] Bela Balassa, "Structural Adjustment Policies in Developing Economies," *World Development*, Vol. 10, No. 1 (January 1982), pp. 35-36.

[7] Stephany Griffiths-Jones, "The Role of Financial Policies in the Transition to Socialism," *IFDA Dossier*, No. 28 (March-April 1982), p. 71; see also Stephany Griffiths-Jones, *The Role of Finance in the Transition to Socialism* (London: Frances Pinter, 1981).

[8] See Anthony Lanyi and Rusdu Saracoglu, *Interest Rate Policies in Developing Countries*, IMF Occasional Paper No. 22, Washington, D.C., November 1983.

[9] See Donald J. Mathieson, "Financial Reform and Capital Flows in a Developing Economy," *IMF Staff Papers*, Vol. 26, No. 3 (September 1979).

Chapter 3

The World Bank: Lending for Structural Adjustment

Stanley Please

At the start of the 1980s, the developing world faced the prospect of a marked deterioration in its external economic circumstances, including recession in developed countries, related declines in primary-product prices as well as in market access for other exports, high oil prices, and a rising burden of debt aggravated by high real interest rates. These unpropitious external circumstances were intensified further by a widespread failure of developing countries to take effective steps to assure their ability to meet the debt-service obligations on the large flows of funds obtained from commercial banks during the second half of the 1970s. It was clear that unless both these external and internal factors were recognized and addressed, the consequent deterioration in the balances of payments of developing countries would develop into financial crises that only the most draconian of demand-restricting measures would be able to handle. Such measures would inevitably fall heavily on investment programs and on other efforts essential in the developing world for stimulating growth, providing basic needs, and alleviating poverty.

It was with these concerns in mind that the World Bank[1] introduced its program of structural adjustment lending (SAL) in 1980. Despite some improvement in the global economic situation since then—revival in industrial countries, lower oil prices, and some increases in primary-product prices—these concerns remain as valid now as they were in 1980. Moreover, what was merely feared in 1980 has become reality in many countries as governments have found expenditure-cutting programs to be the only option available for dealing with an immediate external financial crisis.

Successful adjustment to the external shock of a deteriorated world economic environment requires programs that combine national financial discipline with measures that speed the reduction of the import dependency of countries in deficit and increase their export-earning effectiveness compared with countries in surplus. Programs supported by the International Monetary Fund have been directed at these twin objectives. It has been pointed out, for instance, that while "demand management measures and financial stability may have been *proximate* instruments and objectives of Fund policies, the full attainment of supply potential has always been the *ultimate* aim"; most policy measures—whether interest rates, measures to achieve greater financial viability of public enterprises, taxes and subsidies, or exchange rates—have impact both on aggregate demand and on the pattern of supply.[2]

But the process of speeding and deepening structural adjustment so that balance-of-payments viability can be achieved *at a higher level of real income and with greater attention to the needs of developmental policy* requires programs reaching beyond the measures included in IMF programs. Among these additional sectoral and sub-sectoral concerns that are important to the structural adjustment and development processes are:

- the relative roles of the public and private sectors in economic activity;
- the way markets are permitted to develop or are organized by governments;
- the process and criteria by which the level and structure of agricultural prices are determined;
- the industrial policy framework within which industry operates and expands, as determined by tariffs, import licensing systems, and investment promotion schemes;
- the appropriate structure of energy pricing and taxation that will both induce an efficient supply of energy to reflect projected comparative costs of imported and domestic sources and at the same time bring about whatever level of energy conservation is considered desirable; and
- a well-formulated public expenditure program.

IMF conditionality has not attempted to address these complex structural and sectoral issues to any great extent—and probably quite rightly so, given the other important responsibilities of the Fund and the specialties of its staff. In relation to these areas to policy, Fund conditionality has been limited to the most glaring cases of economically inappropriate prices, such as those of food, domestic oil, or exports. The World Bank, on the other hand, has always been deeply concerned with these issues. Its economic work has always given considerable emphasis to sectoral and sub-sectoral pricing issues—involving not only prices of the factors of production and selling prices, but also tariffs, subsidies, and industrial incentives. Institutional development also has been an important and growing part of the Bank's economic work.

However, despite the importance that the Bank attributes in its economic work to appropriate policies for achieving development and structural adjustment objectives, its Articles of Agreement legally preclude its engagement in anything other than project lending except in special circumstances. The Bank has interpreted this obligation fairly rigorously. Since the late 1960s, there has been an agreed ceiling of 10 per cent of World Bank commitments for non-project lending. Yet these operations have until recently represented no more than 6 per cent of annual commitments. In fact, prior to 1980, non-project operations were undertaken only in response to a few cases of immediate and urgent need stemming from natural disasters or "man-made" ones (such as postwar reconstruction in Nigeria or Uganda); from serious declines in the terms of trade due to export price declines (such as Zambia's past experience with copper or Colombia's with coffee); from import price increases (most obviously in the price of oil in 1973-74, and again in 1979); or from other acute needs such as India's need for help in financing imports of intermediate goods and spare parts for more fully utilizing its existing industrial capacity rather than for financing new projects.

Until 1980, these non-project operations all emphasized the need for quick disbursement of World Bank funds and focused on policy issues only incidentally, if at all. Even sectoral and sub-sectoral lending that has gone beyond narrowly conceived project lending has been limited and has rarely made policy issues central in the design of operations. For instance, sectoral lending has been virtually restricted to a few highway authorities with which agreement has been reached on a program of projects to be prepared, appraised, and supervised by the national agency.

The Bank has thus always been confronted with the problem of how to make an effective link between its commitment and disbursement of project funds and its concern with broader issues of policy and institutional development. In this respect, the contrast with the

IMF could not be starker. In making its more conditioned distribution of funds, the IMF commits and makes available its resources purely and simply against the willingness of a government to formulate and agree on a program of policy changes and subsequently to implement the agreed program. The Fund, therefore, is an operational institution that is mainly concerned with providing financial support for packages of policy reform. The Bank, however, is an operational institution that is close to being exclusively concerned with providing financial support for individual *projects*, notwithstanding its recognition of the fact that its mandate as an international development institution can only be implemented if policy packages that address issues of structural adjustment and development are being formulated and implemented by governments.

It was in the context of an increased need both for deeper, more sustained adjustment programs and for additional external financial support for such programs that the Bank launched its structural adjustment lending program in 1980. The SAL program represented the Bank's first attempt to introduce on a systematic basis a form of lending that focused expressly on policy and institutional reform. It was also an effort to provide more structure and discipline both within the Bank and in the Bank's relationship with its member countries regarding policy and institutional reform than had been possible previously.

Structural adjustment lending has been limited both in the number of countries participating—sixteen to date—and in the volume of World Bank funds allocated to SAL operations, which has risen from approximately $700 million in 1981 to about $1,250 million in 1983 (fiscal years). Despite this limited scale and extent, SAL operations already have had the obvious effect of forcing the Bank's operational management to take policy reform more seriously. It is, of course, another question whether SAL programs have had an impact on the willingness, or ability, of governments to adopt more far-reaching and sustained policy reforms than would have been adopted in the absence of SAL operations. An even more important question is whether SAL programs have encouraged governments undertaking policy reforms to provide also for *sustaining* these reforms by simultaneously improving the political as well as technical institutional setting in which policy is formulated and implemented.

However difficult and tentative such a comprehensive evaluation of the SAL program would at this stage necessarily be (and it is not attempted here), it is a central issue for those interested in and responsible for determining the future role of the World Bank. The

Bank's mandate is to engage in the financing of projects in support of the achievement of the long-term development objectives of its developing-country members. The SAL program has moved the institution into non-project lending on a systematic basis and has placed policy issues rather than project issues at center-stage. The context of its introduction is the financial crisis that most developing countries have been experiencing since 1980. But should the SAL program simply disappear when the immediate intensity of the crisis eases? Or does experience with the program to date suggest that the Bank should rethink its role and the design of its operations more generally? Is there a possibility that SAL lending will be seen in retrospect not so much as a diversion to meet an immediate crisis but as a watershed in the role of the Bank and in the way it executes this role?

Structural Adjustment Lending

In each case structural adjustment lending consists of some three or four discrete lending operations over approximately five or six years. Its purpose is to provide quick-disbursing, balance-of-payments support to a country that is prepared both to formulate a structural adjustment program and to reach agreement with the Bank on such a program.[3] SAL programs have three components:

- a statement of structural objectives to be achieved in five to ten years;
- a statement of the measures that will be taken over approximately five years to achieve the objectives; and
- a monitorable set of actions to be taken by a government either before the Bank's Board approves the SAL operation or during the approximately year-long disbursement period.

The disbursement of funds under each SAL operation is typically tranched, or phased, to ensure both that the adjustment program in general is on track and that specific measures included in the monitorable program of action actually are implemented.

Quick disbursement of Bank funds to provide immediate support to a country's balance of payments has not been the primary focus of Bank attention under SAL, although it has been a necessary part of the concept. In any case, the aggregate amounts involved have been relatively small. Moreover, SAL funds are not additional; they do not increase the total agreed level of World Bank lending, which is determined by IDA replenishment decisions and by a slowly rising ceiling on IBRD lending related to the IBRD's capital base. In practice, SAL funds are disbursed more quickly than those committed under regular Bank operations and are not tied to particular commodities or particular country procurement, unlike many other sources of finance. For some countries, the financial "bridging" that is in effect provided by the SAL program (while policy measures take effect) may not be unimportant—even though the program's central purpose is to give greater urgency and robustness to the Bank's concerns and involvement in policy issues relating to structural adjustment.

Three features of SAL operations help achieve this central objective. First, the program's comprehensiveness of coverage applies to both economy-wide and sectoral issues of policy and of institutional reform. In terms of macro-economic policy, for instance, SAL operations typically cover agreements on the size and composition of the public investment program and sometimes on important components of recurrent expenditures. As regards sectoral coverage, the loans cover the directly productive sectors of agriculture and industry as well as the energy sector.

Second, SAL operations have a single-minded concern with policy reform. Bank project operations have never been weak on conditionality; on the contrary, it could be argued that they have attached too many conditions—conditions ranging from detailed technical, administrative, and financial issues relating to a project, through sub-sectoral policy and institutional concerns, to larger questions of sectoral and macro-economic policy. The problem with such a broad spectrum of conditionality is that it becomes diffused and weakened, with an understandable (and appropriate) priority given to the narrower project conditions and, to a lesser extent, sub-sectoral conditions. The broader agreements on sectoral and macro-economic issues tend always, because of their indirectness, to lose their strength and therefore their credibility. SAL conditionality, in contrast, is concerned entirely with macro-economic and sectoral policies. This focus has given the preparation, formulation, negotiation, monitoring, and disciplining of programs of policy reform far greater importance than these processes receive in project lending. The commitment of funds for a limited period of twelve months or so, with an intermediate tranching provision after, say, half the commitment has been disbursed, has made the monitoring of policy implementation a continuous process.

The third notable feature of SAL operations is that they involve agreement on a monitorable program of action. This program embodies precise and detailed actions of both policy and institutional changes that a government obligates itself to undertake. Some of these precise action programs emerge from studies that are, in their terms of reference and schedules of work, an integral part of the monitorable program. Actions based on these recommendations provide the basis for subsequent SAL policy agreements.

One of the Bank's major concerns at the macro-economic level has been with the public sector's use of resources—and particularly with the public investment program. SAL agreements have covered: specific changes in the institutional arrangements by which public investment programs are determined and monitored; changes in the sectoral and sub-sectoral balance of the investment program; agreement on project selection criteria; determination of a core program of highest priority projects that will be protected from budgetary cutbacks if financial resources are more limited than envisaged; and annual presentation of rolling, two- or three-year public investment programs.

This emphasis that SAL operations give to institutional reform is a feature of SAL operations that extends beyond public investment programs. For instance, in the case of agricultural pricing, which involves agreement on precise changes in output or input prices or in tax and subsidy arrangements, considerable emphasis also has been given to agreement on institutional measures to improve the criteria used to determine the level and structure of agricultural prices, as well as the timeliness of announcements of price policy in relation to the cultivation cycle, etc. Moreover, SAL agreements have reflected the importance of improved marketing efficiency if pricing policy is to have the full intended impact on production. Thus SAL agreements have included measures both to limit the public sector's role in agricultural marketing (where this has exceeded the capacity of the public sector to provide marketing services efficiently) and to improve the efficiency of public-sector marketing agencies and their policies.

Constraints on the Program

The introduction of the SAL program has resulted in the Bank's reaching its 10-per cent ceiling on non-project lending in the past two years. An important issue, therefore, is whether this ceiling is constraining the development of SAL operations and their effectiveness. The Bank's Board, while reaffirming the ceiling in 1982, indicated its willingness to review this decision if the ceiling is considered too constraining. Three separate questions shape this issue: Does the ceiling limit the number of countries with which the Bank could develop a SAL program? Does it limit the effectiveness of SAL operations? Does it encourage the development of alternative operational options that do not count as non-project operations and, therefore, fall outside the 10-per cent ceiling?

It is unlikely that the number of participating countries has been kept down by the 10-per cent ceiling. Only a few governments are interested in structural adjustment lending; many governments have been unable to formulate and implement structural adjustment programs of a scope and depth acceptable to the Bank, and among those who are prepared to move along these lines, some are unwilling to do so at the behest of the Bank. The first situation is clearly more worrisome than the second. It raises the question of whether these unwilling governments are pursuing structural adjustment policies that can achieve both their developmental objectives and their goal of medium- and long-term viability of their balances of payments—and therefore whether their programs justify existing levels of external assistance, including project lending by the Bank. Although project lending has a very important continuing role to play in the lending program of the Bank, it would clearly be undesirable if it came to be seen by some countries as the "easy option" for those unable to address critical policy issues.

In the future, the number of countries receiving SAL support will be determined not only by how many new countries request it, but also by how many "drop out" of the program. To some extent this will occur "automatically," as a consequence of the decision that a SAL program for any one country should be limited to a maximum of four or five operations over five to six years. (Only Turkey has reached this limit so far.) Countries will also be phased out of the SAL program if they are unable to maintain in full the agreed program of structural adjustment measures (as has happened in the cases of Bolivia, Guyana, and Senegal). Finally, certain countries whose immediate balance-of-payments situation has improved might be phased out of SAL operations despite the fact that the structural adjustment measures required to avoid future balance-of-payments problems need to be sustained. If countries are phased out for this reason, it will be because a decision has been taken that structural adjustment lending is only justified in "special circumstances," and that improvement in the immediate balance-of-payments situation disqualifies a country from such assistance. The alternative view is that SAL should be used more actively to anticipate and avoid future balance-of-payments crises—and their "remedies," which inevitably mean severe reductions in developmental expenditures.

It is difficult, therefore, to estimate how binding a constraint the 10-per cent ceiling will be on the number of countries receiving

SAL support. In a substantive sense it must be hoped that it will prove to be the main binding constraint, as this would imply that more countries are able to formulate and sustain structural adjustment programs and are seeking Bank support for them. Consequently, any reconsideration of the ceiling on non-project lending should start from a recognition that, at a time when domestic policy reforms to achieve structural adjustment are still desperately required, it would be foolish to constrain the Bank from providing support to any government willing to implement such a program. The danger of this happening is not very great in the cases of small countries for which SAL operations can be handled within the 10-per cent ceiling. It is clearly much more of a constraint in relation to the larger and medium-size countries (such as Brazil, Mexico, and Nigeria), at least until some other larger recipients of SAL support (for example, the Republic of Korea, the Philippines, or Thailand) "graduate" from the program.

The number of countries that can be supported by the SAL program under the 10-per cent ceiling obviously depends on the size of the individual country programs that are then in operation. Although the dollar amount of each is flexible and certainly does not correspond to a country's need as reflected in its foreign exchange gap, there is a minimum amount below which the "seriousness" and "credibility" of the Bank's involvement in the monitoring and disciplining of major policy issues becomes suspect. It is difficult to define this lower limit in any precise way, but it has been considered to be best expressed as a percentage—about 30 per cent—of the Bank's lending program to a country. So far, this percentage, in combination with the number of countries seeking SAL support, also has been consistent with the 10-per cent ceiling.

Would a higher level of SAL support to a country have resulted in a broader, more extensive, or more rapidly implemented program of structural adjustment measures? Within the bounds of realistic levels of SAL support, probably no significant increase in the strength of the program would have occurred. There is no continuous supply curve of measures reflecting an increased willingness to improve the structural adjustment program for each $1-million, or $10-million, increase in SAL support. If the matter is thought of in these terms at all, the curve should be seen as very stepped: from zero willingness to discuss and agree to a program with the Bank unless a minimum loan commitment is made, to a step representing a much greater willingness by a government to improve its program provided that the level of support by the Bank is much higher than 30 per cent. This level of Bank support, however, would be inconsistent both with the Bank's total lending program to the developing world—fixed by the availability of IDA funding and the slowly rising ceiling on lending determined by the IBRD's capital structure—and with its other non-SAL responsibilities.

It needs to be reemphasized in this connection that the funding of the SAL program has to be within existing IDA and IBRD levels of lending—that there is no "additionality" for SAL lending operations. Funds for a structural adjustment loan in any country have to be taken either from resources that would otherwise have been allocated to other operations in the country or from a reallocation of funds from other country programs—or, most likely, a little from both. As regards the second of these "sources" of funding, a government's willingness to formulate and agree on a SAL program is evidence of "good performance" and is therefore likely to result in an increase in the country's allocation of IDA and/or IBRD funds. However, the leeway both for country reallocations and for reducing longer-term development project lending to make room for SAL lending is clearly limited. It is this limited scope for SAL additionality *even to each country* that represents the major barrier to a more positive attitude toward SAL operations by many governments. Although the speed of disbursements from IDA and Bank funds is likely to be increased—and this is of course a very attractive feature of SAL—the increase is a once-only gain.

In summary, the absence of additionality for SAL represents the major constraint on SAL lending. But this constraint relates primarily to whether or not a country is willing to agree with the Bank on a SAL program in the first place. Once such a relationship is established, the 30-per cent guideline probably does not have any adverse impact on the strength of the program of measures agreed. To the extent that it has relevance in any one country, the 30-per cent guideline can and has been implemented flexibly.

A third factor to consider in examining the impact of the 10-per cent ceiling that applies to non-project lending is the definition of what is included within the ceiling. Since 1980, only a few non-SAL operations—such as Bangladesh's import credit (virtually a SAL operation in recent years) and the one-time reconstruction operations in Uganda and Zimbabwe—have in fact been counted as part of the ceiling. Of much greater significance is the list of operations that have been excluded from the definition of non-project lending: agricultural rehabilitation projects (Uganda, Sudan, Tanzania); export development projects (Jamaica, Mexico, Costa Rica); public-sector management projects (Peru, Turkey); and technical assistance projects (Mauritius, Mauritania, Bhutan, Tunisia). There clearly is a spectrum of operational lending concepts between "pure" project lending and the "pure" non-project lending of the SAL program. The line drawn for defining the 10-per cent ceiling on non-project lending is somewhat arbitrary, but the line itself has gained considerable significance in the design of Bank operations in support of structural adjustment programs. For the Bank has been able to use sectoral and sub-sectoral operations having an overwhelming focus on policy and institutional reforms in support of adjustment programs even in countries in which it does not formally have a SAL program. These operations have not been subject to the 10-per cent ceiling. Yet while these operations have been useful in supplementing SAL programs in countries in which such programs exist, they never have had—nor were they conceived as having—the same degrees of comprehensiveness in support of adjustment programs as actual SAL operations. On the contrary, in countries in which for political and/or technical reasons a full SAL program was not initially possible, these sectoral and subsectoral operations have been thought of as first steps toward the development of a SAL-supported program. Thus, although the development of these operations has eased the constraint of the 10-per cent ceiling, the ceiling still has relevance.

A question frequently asked, of course, is whether these operations *should* be excluded from the 10-per cent ceiling; some of the questioners suggest that these operations are designed to avoid the constraint of the ceiling. The feature that most concerns these critics is that the sectoral and sub-sectoral operations in question support policy reform *directly*, rather than *indirectly*, through project lending. This is of course the very feature considered most relevant and attractive by those who desire an active role for the Bank in support of adjustment programs.

Qualitative Evaluation

It is both too early and conceptually enormously difficult to undertake a full-scale evaluation of SAL operations. Clearly the easiest approach would be to list the component parts of the monitorable action programs supported under each SAL operation and then to determine the extent to which they were implemented. Indeed, this exercise is more easily undertaken for Bank SAL operations than it is for IMF operations. While IMF operations comprise a series of macro-economic targets (such as those relating to the balance-of-payments deficit or to public-sector borrowing) that are determined by both policy actions and non-policy variables (such as the weather or export prices), SAL operations relate purely to policy actions taken by the government. Thus a SAL program might, for instance, include agreement to increase agricultural producer prices, to permit more freedom of entry into agricultural output and input marketing, and to take other actions to stimulate agricultural output. What is then monitored is not the target of increased agricultural output but the implementation of the agreed actions. If in fact, contrary to expectations, agricultural output should fall, this will either be due to non-policy factors or to an incorrect diagnosis of why agricultural output was not increasing as rapidly as expected. The government should not be held responsible for either of these situations.

If SAL operations were evaluated in this manner they would undoubtedly show a good track record. The Bank has been very strict in ensuring that governments adhere closely to certain agreed actions. This has not been for purely legalistic reasons. On the contrary, where actions have been taken that were not agreed upon but that were clearly effective substitutes, this has been fully acceptable. In addition, strict compliance with a SAL agreement has not always been interpreted as 100-per cent implementation, particularly where the defaults have involved relatively minor actions, or where it is known that the procedures for taking certain actions are well advanced but are taking somewhat longer to be completed than anticipated.

While the record of compliance under SAL agreements has in general been good, both governments and the Bank have tended to underestimate the time it takes to implement action to reform policies and institutions. In part this delay is simply due to the time it takes to mobilize political support for the agreed actions, often as much a problem in one-party dictatorial systems as in any other country. In large part, however, the delay results from the complex nature of the actions to be taken to reform policies and institutional arrangements once there is movement beyond the generalities of "providing incentive prices," "permitting more managerial autonomy to parastatal managers," and other broad recommendations that typically emanate from the general analysis of a problem.

Any substantive evaluation of SAL operations must, however, proceed beyond the simple test of whether structural adjustment measures have been implemented as agreed, including the timeliness of their implementation. To what extent have SAL operations induced governments to adopt reform measures they would not otherwise have implemented or would have implemented less rapidly? This line of examination would ultimately seek to determine whether SAL operations can be credited with some of the success a country might have had in achieving such structural adjustment objectives as the maintenance or revival of international creditworthiness, the stimulation of export earnings and foreign-exchange savings in economically efficient ways, and action on developmental priorities through the adoption of better targeted and more efficient public expenditure programs. Ambitious evaluation exercises of this hypothetical "with/without" type are notoriously difficult and speculative even at the project level; they are even more problematic at the level of broad policy and institutional reform. No such evaluation is attempted here.

Probably the most relevant question that can be asked at this stage is one that is more internal to the World Bank—although any answer to it is also fraught with some of the problems of comparing actual and hypothetical events. Has the Bank done all it possibly could within its mandate and within the limits of its financial and staff resources to encourage and support countries facing the severe and unexpected deterioration in the global economy in the early 1980s? Specifically, has the SAL program made such encouragement and support by the Bank more effective than would otherwise have been possible? Clearly governments are sovereign within their borders and are responsible for their own policies, whether these are well- or ill-suited to the development and structural adjustment needs of their countries. The relevant test for the Bank is whether it has used its resources in ways that maximized its positive impact on programs to meet these development and structural adjustment needs. If it has done so and the country in question nevertheless "collapses" in some sense (as some middle-income, semi-industrialized developing countries have in terms of their foreign debt crises, and some Sub-Saharan African countries have due to continuing production crises), the Bank can still maintain that it designed its operations as effectively as possible to try to avert such collapses.

Evaluated in this way, structural adjustment lending can claim to have been extremely effective. The Bank has been able to mobilize far greater attention to the reform of critical policy and institutional issues than was previously possible. The mere adoption of a form of lending expressly in support of reform programs has provided a clear signal to governments of the extent to which the Bank is willing to modify its own operational practices in major ways in the light of the crisis that they face—provided that governments show a comparable willingness to face up to the urgency of the need. In addition, as already noted, the SAL process has itself provided ways to make policies and institutional issues central in the Bank's operational relationship with a government. Thus the program forces both the Bank and the government to seek acceptable solutions to these issues at whatever level of decision making is appropriate. In fact, one of the program's major achievements is that in many cases it has helped to establish forums within governments for the handling of important policy issues that otherwise were likely to remain unresolved because they fell between the responsibilities of different ministries and agencies.

It is likewise very difficult to believe that any operational concept with a less direct focus on and support for programs of structural adjustment could have given this same degree of assistance. The frequently mentioned alternative to SAL—that the Bank's project lending program to a country, or part of this program, be based on agreement on a structural adjustment program—can in no way match the sharpness of focus and support provided under SAL operations.

Public Expenditures

A major criticism of IMF-supported programs has always been that in concentrating on the total level of government expenditures, they countenance undesirable reductions in economic and social expenditures. One of the objectives of SAL was, in effect, to provide an external "lobby" for expenditures designed to achieve developmental objectives. To some significant extent, this has been achieved. In particular, some programs have been agreed upon to reduce or eliminate, in a phased manner, expenditures that no longer serve priority economic or social objectives. Most important in this connection is the phasing out of subsidy programs. Whatever their original objectives—and often, these were well conceived, as in the case of encouraging fertilizer use during the early years of its introduction as part of a new agricultural package—many of these subsidies have become "counter-developmental" in terms of both efficiency and poverty-alleviation objectives. Furthermore, under SAL operations, considerable attention has been given to public investment programs, to their sectoral allocations, choices of projects, and other aspects. In particular, the Bank has attempted to ensure that the cutting back of public investment is done in an efficient manner. Instead of cutbacks across the whole range of projects (with the consequence that all projects take longer to complete), a more selective exercise is undertaken, with some projects being excluded from funding completely while others proceed on a priority basis.

The Bank has probably been insufficiently active, however, in stressing that if a structural adjustment program is to be supported under SAL, aggregate social and economic expenditures should not be the residual recipient of government resources in order that IMF targets can be met. There has been a tendency for the Bank to accept this aggregate as a "given" arising out of the IMF-supported program and simply to address the question of how the expenditure can be more efficiently allocated. Of course, in a situation of falling domestic real incomes and balance-of-payments problems, government real expenditures are bound to fall. It is unlikely that economic and social expenditures will escape these reductions. Yet a too passive attitude by the Bank in accepting whatever emerges from IMF agreements could subvert the objective of structural adjustment lending, which is to ensure that development momentum is maintained while macro-economic balance is achieved. In a very few instances, SAL programs have included agreements to maintain or increase real expenditures on priority social and economic services, but these have been exceptions.

The Bank also has not gone very far in assisting governments to design expenditure programs that help achieve developmental objectives within a tight budgetary situation. Expenditures on education, health, or housing can be more effectively targeted toward poverty groups and can be designed in ways that reduce unit costs very considerably. The Bank and other external donors have been working with developing-country governments for many years to develop low-cost, replicable programs to provide basic infrastructure or services, such as housing, sewage, water supply, and health and education delivery systems. Most of these activities have been at the level of *projects*. The present and prospective economic situation facing developing countries now makes it even more urgent to help intensify the implementation of efficient but low-cost and replicable socio-economic *programs*. Structural adjustment lending provides an operational channel through which these policy issues can be handled more effectively than typically has been the case under project operations. By strengthening emphasis on this area, SAL would be contributing not only to the adjustment process, but to the longer-term needs of development.

Discussion of these issues provides a fuller context for attempting to answer, at least in part, the questions raised at the beginning of this chapter: Is structural adjustment lending to be regarded as a diversion to help deal with a global crisis or as a watershed in the Bank's mandate and operational design? If an appropriate framework of policies is as important as investment for achieving growth and poverty alleviation objectives, should not the Bank put policy issues at the center of its operations as a matter of long-term strategy? If so, is this consistent with a mandate that makes the Bank overwhelmingly a *project* lender in the absence of exceptional circumstances?

The SAL program has for the first time disciplined Bank staff and management to treat policy issues as central to its operations and not simply as add-ons to project operations. The view expressed in this chapter is that the attempt to make *policy* conditionality the "tail" of *project* lending—especially with too wide a span of conditionality—almost inevitably means inadequate discipline toward policy issues. The absence of priority attention for policy considerations does not arise from lack of concern about or commitment toward policy reform on the part of staff and management. If this view is accepted, and if it is also accepted that the Bank, acting alongside the IMF, has a comparative advantage over other financial agencies in pursuing policy issues with governments, then SAL should be regarded as a watershed in the evolution of the Bank. The SAL program has provided an experience upon which governments and the Bank's management should build when looking to the institution's future role in the international effort to eradicate poverty.

Notes

[1] The term World Bank includes the International Bank for Reconstruction and Development (IBRD) and the International Development Association (IDA). IBRD lends to governments or against a government guarantee on non-concessional terms (17-20 years at 10.08 per cent, May 1984). IDA lends on concessional terms (50 years at a 0.75 per cent service charge).

[2] Manuel Guitián, "Fund Conditionality and the International Adjustment Process: The Early Period, 1950-70," *Finance and Development*, Vol. 17, No. 4 (December 1980), pp. 23-27.

[3] For earlier descriptions of structural adjustment lending and the considerations that led to its introduction, see especially Pierre M. Landell-Mills, "Structural Adjustment Lending: Early Experience," *Finance and Development*, Vol. 18, No. 4 (December 1981), pp. 17-21, and Ernest Stern, "World Bank Financing of Structural Adjustment," in John Williamson, ed., *IMF Conditionality* (Washington, D.C.: Institute for International Economics, 1983), pp. 87-107.

Chapter 4

The Politics of Stabilization

Joan M. Nelson

In Mexico in the autumn of 1983, one in every three manufacturing workers was unemployed. In Brazil at the same time, a bitterly contested wage control bill was passed to hold salary increases below inflation, in effect mandating a 13-per cent average cut. In Senegal in 1982, the government raised the controlled price of imported rice—the urban staple food—by 30 per cent, which more than wiped out the earlier sizable subsidy on rice; in August 1983, it increased the price by another 25 per cent. These were but three instances of a broader pattern of worsening standards of living in countries that have introduced serious stabilization programs. The crucial question for the success of these programs is at least as political as it is economic: How long will people tolerate austerity?

Stabilization[1] is inherently painful, but there is no avoiding the pain. The alternative to planned and guided adjustment is chaotic adjustment, entailing even higher costs in terms of controls, scarcities, inflation, unemployment, and atrophied output and growth. Yet the batting average of planned stabilization programs, especially in the poorer countries, has not been good. A high proportion of such programs are abandoned in midstream. Others are technically completed, in that performance targets are met and all installments of the loan drawn, but serious difficulties often begin again within a matter of months.

The frustration of such attempts has many explanations: completely uncontrollable events, such as adverse weather or shifts in

99

the terms of trade; unmet expectations of supplementary external finance, whether private capital inflows, rescheduling, or aid from bilateral sources; and perhaps shortcomings inherent in the approach to stabilization itself. The past few years have brought intense debate about the design of stabilization programs, especially in poorer countries, and some changes in practice. Aspects of this debate are reviewed in other chapters in this volume (especially Chapter 2); here the focus is on the often mentioned but little analyzed political dimensions of stabilization efforts.

In country after country, internal political pressures—and politicians' fears of such pressure—have led governments to postpone corrective action until the economic crisis is acute or to dilute or abandon programs before the necessary economic adjustments are accomplished. Theorists and practitioners involved in stabilization programs are well aware of the importance of politics for the success or failure of those efforts, yet explicit and systematic attempts to examine political constraints remain controversial, for several reasons.

It is often argued that international organizations and bilateral aid agencies should not become involved in the political dimensions of the programs they assist. This argument is both illogical and impractical. There are, of course, sound moral and practical reasons why neither international organizations nor other nations should deliberately intervene in internal politics—even if governments do regularly give it a try. In the case of stabilization programs, however, serious outside attempts to anticipate political and administrative obstacles and to design programs to cope with them are more likely to be constructive and practical than interventionist. Failure to identify and lessen such obstacles is in fact both irresponsible toward the governments and peoples concerned and wasteful of the external agency's resources.

Political issues are also sometimes conveniently and simplistically dismissed as only a matter of sufficient political "will" on the part of the government concerned. Either the government has sufficient will or it does not. If it does, political analysis is unnecessary; if it does not, there is not much to be done about it. Although commitment to stabilization on the part of the top political leaders of a country is indeed crucial, that commitment is itself a factor that outside agencies may be able to influence. Commitment is also a matter of degree, and different degrees of it may call for differently designed programs. Still more important, even a strong commitment to stabilization may not be sufficient to overcome political obstacles unless programs are also designed to address those obstacles.

The costliness of failed programs—in terms of resources expended and sacrifices suffered for little or no lasting gain—also argues persuasively for greater attention to political sustainability; so do the dangers of a legacy of counterproductive cynicism and bitterness. Recent debate and experimentation with program design, both by developing countries and by multilateral and bilateral agencies, have moved policy and practice toward programs that are longer in duration, less reliant on monetary instruments, and more explicitly attentive to structural adjustment on the supply side. Stabilization and structural adjustment can usefully be viewed as a continuum, with "stabilization" programs focused on demand management and potential short-run gains in foreign-exchange earnings or savings, while "structural adjustment" programs emphasize supply-side changes that usually take several years to bear fruit. The boundary between the two is not well defined, and actual programs usually include elements of both (indeed, the same reforms may promote both). But some programs clearly approximate "pure" stabilization while others have a much stronger adjustment element.

Increased emphasis on structural adjustment makes it all the more urgent to take steps to assure political sustainability. Over a period of several years, opposition can coalesce. The costs and risks of relying on coercive suppression of opposition are correspondingly heightened. But the new emphasis on a longer time horizon also provides more opportunity for phasing, for gradual application of measures, for manipulation of the sequence in which measures are introduced, and for midcourse adjustments to respond to both technical and political signals. Thus the mixed record of past efforts, the pressing nature of current problems, and the evolving nature of stabilization and adjustment programs all point toward the need for more systematic political analysis.

Determinants of Political Sustainability

The odds that a stabilization effort will be abandoned or seriously diluted in midcourse because of leaders' political concerns or popular political pressure are directly affected by:

- the strength of commitment to the program on the part of the country's leadership;
- the government's ability to implement the program and manage political responses; and

- the political response that the program evokes from influential groups.

These factors are not independent of each other; indeed, they interact dynamically. Each is also of course strongly influenced by the anticipated and actual economic impact of the program. And each reflects a series of more basic attitudes, institutions, and relationships, some of which are discussed in this chapter.

Both the overall approach and many of the more specific observations in this chapter are based on a comparative study of five countries that the author completed for the U.S. Agency for International Development in mid-1983. The cases examined included:

Ghana—from the overthrow of Nkrumah in 1966, through the military and the civilian regimes that followed, to the coup of January 1972.

Zambia—from the adoption of a two-year stand-by agreement with the International Monetary Fund in April 1978 to January 1983.

Kenya—from Kenyatta's death in 1978 and Moi's succession to the presidency through 1982.

Sri Lanka—from the mid-1977 landslide election of a United National Party government committed to a more market-oriented economy through the re-election of President Jayawardene in autumn 1982.

Jamaica—from the several unsuccessful stabilization efforts of 1977-78 by the Manley government to the 1980 electoral victory of the Seaga government and its initial reforms.

With the exception of Jamaica, these are all quite poor nations. In 1980, their gross national product per capita ranged from $270 in Sri Lanka up to $560 in Zambia (where distribution, however, leaves the bulk of the population extremely poor); the corresponding figure for Jamaica was $1,040. Kenya, with just under 16 million people in 1980, is the largest of the five; Jamaica, with 2.2 million, the smallest.

The reason for focusing the case studies on small, poor, highly trade-dependent countries is that these are the nations whose experience has evoked the most acute disagreement and uncertainty about the effectiveness of conventional approaches to stabilization. All case studies covered at least five years; they were not confined to a single "stabilization episode" (usually defined as the duration of an IMF stand-by agreement). One of the most interesting patterns noted is the way in which the experience of earlier periods affected later decisions and political reponses.

Leadership Commitment

The country cases examined certainly confirm the importance of committed leadership to an effective stabilization program. "Will" alone is not sufficient, but it is clearly necessary. Reluctance to adopt firm stabilization measures is generally prompted either by fear of political repercussions or by lack of confidence that stabilization measures will in fact improve the situation—or both. "Commitment" is usually born of duress—of painful recognition that the economic and political costs of failure to act are probably greater than the costs of action.

The record suggests that politicians are "damned if they do and damned if they don't" when it comes to the political consequences of their stabilization decisions. A firm stabilization program predictably provokes protest; but so does continued economic deterioration. Leaders' decisions may be influenced by a less obvious consideration: the public will evaluate government policies on the basis of a "before and after" rather than a "with and without" comparison. Once a government adopts stabilization measures, the public is likely to blame it for any subsequent economic hardship, even if the hardship might have been greater in the absence of such measures. Therefore politicians are likely to see the adoption of stabilization measures as speeding up and strengthening public reaction to hardship, and as inviting reaction against the government itself, instead of attributing at least some of the suffering to external forces such as changed international prices or rapacious foreign creditors. Moreover, to the extent that stabilization measures shift the burdens of economic hardship to the groups capable of effective protest (for instance, civil servants), the adoption of a program may intensify the political risks inherent in an already tight economic situation. Finally, in some cases the announcement of a stabilization program may ignite political opposition because elements of the public or opposition parties can point to IMF involvement as government "capitulation." In other cases, IMF involvement may be politically convenient to the government, which may be able to blame austerity on the IMF or to use the Fund's presence to reassure some elements of the public—or both.

Political leaders must balance their fear of intensified protest, more sharply focused on the government itself, against the possible political benefits of increased foreign exchange available through a stand-by agreement—and perhaps from other public and private sources whose support is influenced by the IMF "seal of approval." Clearly the volume, timing, and conditions attached to foreign financial support will affect its political value. For example, assistance that can be used only to reduce overdue foreign debt is considerably less attractive than assistance that can be used to increase imports.

Many political leaders are not only concerned about political repercussions, but also very skeptical that stabilization will produce economic benefits at all (other than the temporary relief of stabilization assistance). Case studies indicate that such skepticism is not a marginal issue but a major obstacle to commitment, often as important as fear of political risk. In many countries only a very small number of economic officials have the training to grasp complex and abstract economic relationships and the implications of alternative macro-economic policies. Furthermore, aspects of conventional stabilization and adjustment programs are counter-intuitive. The public and even most officials find it hard to understand why a shortage of foreign exchange (expressed as a balance-of-payments deficit and import restrictions) will be relieved by *lowering* the value of their currency in relation to those of others. Since the connections between poor economic performance and distorted prices are not understood, the conviction is widespread among politicians and officials as well as the public that devaluation and other price changes are formulas forced on developing nations by the IMF either for obscure theoretical reasons that have little application to their own circumstances or, worse yet, to protect the interests of rich international financiers.

Even when the economic rationale of stabilization is well understood, political leaders often lack confidence in it. Skepticism flows in part from the linkage of stabilization with economic liberalization. Many IMF-supported programs and all World Bank structural adjustment loans stress reduced direct government intervention in the economy and greater reliance on market incentives in the state-managed sector. These prescriptions run counter to deep-rooted biases against free markets and in favor of centralized decision making and controls. Throughout the developing world—as was true historically in Western Europe—most officials and intellectuals and much of the public tend to doubt that the profit motive can be socially constructive, view middlemen as unproductive and exploitative, and place considerable confidence in the effectiveness of state economic controls to pursue national goals.

More fundamentally, disappointing experiences with past stabilization efforts also contribute to skepticism. The objective causes of such disappointments are an important and controversial set of issues, going beyond the scope of this chapter. For the purposes of political analysis, perceptions of and reactions to past situations are more important than their accurate economic interpretations. India's experience with devaluation in 1966 has colored public attitudes ever since; similarly, the drastic and apparently ineffective devaluation in Jamaica in 1978-79 led the Seaga regime that followed to shun open devaluation and to resort instead to an indirect equivalent until late 1983.

Another prevalent negative perception is that a country's economic difficulties are mainly due to forces beyond its control and that corrective policies therefore are not merely painful but also fruitless. For instance, national economic problems in Ghana in the late 1960s were generally traced to the "Nkrumah debts," for which the assumed solution was rescheduling or repudiation. And in Zambia in the late 1970s, the obvious role of low world copper prices and the Zimbabwe war masked the contribution of internal policies and actions to the serious economic decline.

These sources of skepticism about stabilization clearly apply with varying force in different situations, but they are widespread and together add up to a formidable list.

Ability to Carry Out a Program

Even leaders who are committed to stabilization face a formidable array of constraints, including divisions and challenges within their own elite circles, inadequate central financial control mechanisms, and other problems of bureaucratic management and efficiency, as well as the risks of resistance from specific interest groups or the public at large. This brief discussion focuses on only a few important issues within this range of concerns that tend to be overlooked or underestimated.

Budgetary discipline is a major component in almost all stabilization programs. Yet containing budgets has proved to be an extremely difficult target for governments to meet. A survey of 70 IMF stand-by arrangements during the period 1963-72, and a second review covering 105 stand-bys between 1969 and 1978, found that most unsuccessful financial programs failed because of fiscal problems. By 1977 and 1978, fewer than a fifth of the programs were able to limit expenditures as planned.[2] The political difficulty of further cuts, especially in those countries where budgets already have been constrained for several years, is well recognized. Less obvious are the reasons for slow progress and, in many cases, for the apparent lack of interest in improving financial and budgeting control mechanisms—an elementary step that would seem to strengthen the hand of political leaders.

It is likely that in many countries political leaders prefer keeping most budgeting authority in their own hands to establishing powerful, institutionalized procedures and staffs for advance coordination and on-going vetting of expenditures. When top political leaders rely on their own control over allocation of resources to maintain the loyalty of faction-ridden or personally ambitious lieutenants (as in Kenya and Zambia in the early 1980s), they cannot lightly relinquish such control to an anonymous group of technical bureaucrats. Thus even when the benefits in terms of greater budgetary discipline are evident, political leaders may not be willing or able to move toward such a system.

The prevalence of patron-client patterns of politics affects the capacity of many governments to enforce not only austerity but also adjustment measures that move away from direct controls and toward greater reliance on market mechanisms, including more realistic pricing within the public and state-managed sectors. In at least four and perhaps all five of the background cases discussed in this chapter, politicians relied extensively on doling out material favors as a key to staying in power. If ability to direct jobs, contracts, licenses, foreign exchange, subsidized goods and services, and other benefits to political friends and away from political enemies is the main means that politicians have to build and maintain political support, they cannot easily give up such control to price mechanisms that do not distinguish supporter from opponent.

Public Responses

Reactions to stabilization by specific groups and the public at large are determined by the actual impact of the policies, by interpretations of those policies, and by the varying political capabilities of different groups. Austerity measures such as wage freezes and budget cuts harm many groups and benefit few immediately. Measures that alter relative prices, including devaluation, have a more mixed impact. Who loses and who gains—and their relative importance—may differ in poorer countries and semi-developed or advanced ones. In poor countries, much of the urban middle and working classes are employed in the public sector or work for industries that depend on imported fuel, materials, and intermediate inputs. As consumers, the same groups also rely heavily on imported goods, often even for staple foods. They are therefore particularly vulnerable to budget cuts and devaluation, both as producers and as consumers. Conversely, interests that elsewhere generally benefit from and therefore support devaluation in particular are often weaker in poorer countries, where there is little export-oriented industry and where producers of import-substituting foods are usually poorly organized politically.

Political responses are shaped not only by the actual effects of policies but also by how people perceive and interpret those effects.

Subjective interpretations that are crucial for political reactions include:

- the attribution of responsibility for losses or gains;
- the expected duration of losses;
- confidence that policies will help solve problems; and
- the perceived equity of impact—among classes and, in many countries, among ethnic groups and/or regions.

Because these interpretations are so important, the government's presentation and explanation of stabilization measures can have an important influence on sustainability.

Actual effects and interpretations of them determine how people feel about stabilization. What they *do* about how they feel of course depends on their political clout. In semi-industrialized nations, the reactions of organized labor and business associations are often crucial. In many of the poorer developing nations, few private-sector groups are organized or influential enough to exert much pressure. In contrast, civil servants, officials in the many public corporations and semi-autonomous agencies, and the military are all potentially important political interest groups, partly because of their organization, awareness, and control over important assets and partly because of the absence of powerful private groups.

Political responses to stabilization are not only the reactions of specific interest groups and of organized opposition parties in countries where these operate. There is also a more elusive yet important element: the public mood with respect to economic policies. There are times when a broad section of the public is convinced that basic changes are unavoidable. Such conviction often grows out of years of economic stagnation or decline, perhaps punctuated by repeated but limited and ineffective stabilization efforts. Among the clearer examples are Peru in the late 1970s and Turkey in the years just before and after 1980. The public's sense that a change of direction was imperative was demonstrated at the polls in Sri Lanka in 1977 and in Jamaica in 1980. A public mood in favor of economic reform clearly improves the prospects for temporary tolerance of austerity—a "grace period" during which the government has a contingent grant of confidence. Such a mood is also likely to inhibit protests by specific groups that otherwise might create serious problems.

But the grace period will expire in a matter of months, or surely within a year. By that time, continued acquiescence depends on evidence visible and acceptable to the relevant political groups that the medicine is working, even if it must be taken for a longer time. At this point, the issue of what people will accept as evidence of progress becomes critical.

Economic indicators that are significant to one group are not necessarily important to others. Central Bank and Ministry of Finance officials focus on cuts in public sector and trade deficits, reduced overdue debt payments, and/or increased international reserves. Large and medium-size businesses and the private financial community probably watch the same indicators, and in some countries sophisticated trade union leaders also may accept such evidence of progress. Small firms are likely to focus on more immediately *tangible* concerns, such as availability of credit and foreign exchange for imported inputs. Workers and consumers are also likely to gauge progress by improvements that affect their daily lives: increased availability of preferred staples and near-staples, slowed inflation, reduced unemployment, more adequate or less frequently interrupted basic national and municipal services. Even modest improvements of a horrendous situation can generate hope and sustain tolerance, while the lack of credible evidence of progress can produce a psychological tailspin. The dynamic of public mood suggests that, where feasible, it may sometimes be desirable to "overshoot" on some measures initially, to provide some leeway for easing pressure after early acquiescence wears thin.

Political Sustainability: What Governments Can Do

The actual design of a stabilization program—the mix of measures applied, their phasing, the choice of a more rapid or more gradual approach—all contribute, positively or negatively, to the program's political sustainability. So do the tactics used to defend the program.

The Speed of Adjustment: Shock Treatment or Gradualism?

One frequent issue that relates to the political as well as the economic implications of program design is the attempted speed of adjustment. Advocates of "shock treatment" are convinced that public tolerance for sacrifice is brief and that the courage of politicians is likewise limited. If the adjustment process is too gradual, opposition will gather and the process will be derailed. Those who urge gradualism counter that the greatest political risks are associated with sudden cuts in consumption, employment, and sometimes output. Gradualism permits phasing aspects of the program to avoid pressuring too many important groups at once, and may even avoid goading any major groups into action. The government can then deal separately with whichever groups do protest, using appropriate tactics of persuasion, partial compensation, or restraint.

Although these contrasting assumptions cannot be proved right or wrong in general, the conditions under which each is likely to apply are worth careful consideration. The political logic of the shock approach depends on the ability of the economy to respond rapidly to drastically altered signals and resource availabilities (that is, reduced consumption). A rapid economic turnaround permits some loosening of austerity while generating hope; once the initial "hump" is surmounted, the program can be expected to generate considerable support. When such a strategy is feasible economically, it may well make sense politically. But it is clearly not appropriate for most of the poorer economies, where institutional and economic rigidities rule out a rapid adjustment. It is also obviously risky for weak governments, which may not survive the "hump."

Poorer and less flexible nations, especially those of Sub-Saharan Africa, confront a cruel double dilemma in their efforts to adjust. In many cases, their economies are not capable of rapid adjustment. Exports are usually concentrated in one or only a few products, and much of the investment essential for growth includes crucial imported components. The changes necessary to diversify and expand production cannot be induced by stabilization alone—by belt-tightening and changes in relative prices—but will require years of investment and institutional and human resource development. In such nations, a shock approach can indeed "balance" the budget and the trade account, but only by reducing consumption, government services, production, and employment far below any level that could facilitate real adjustment—that is, changes in the composition of production and expanded productive capacity. Indeed, in such economies a draconian approach can seriously weaken the capacity for real adjustment.

Yet many of these nations lack the resources—internal and external—to pursue the more gradual yet purposeful course that offers the best promise. Available resources are so badly out of line with needs that there is no avoiding drastic cuts in imports and domestic spending, whatever the costs to progress toward sustainable adjustment and resumed development. For such countries, debates about the optimal speed of adjustment have a bitter theoretical flavor without more adequate inflows of financial assistance.

Even for those poorer countries with some room for choice of strategies, the more gradual approach to stabilization, which is the most promising in economic terms, still poses formidable political problems. The gradual approach is sometimes portrayed as a political "soft option"—or at any rate softer than the shock approach. In principle it can lessen political risks—partly by allowing more flexibility in timing and phasing of measures to minimize political backlash and partly by making time for real economic adjustments to take hold, thereby reducing real costs. When stabilization measures are combined with medium-term, supply-side-oriented, structural adjustment measures, the combination is also much more likely to gain positive commitment from political leaders. Stabilization is mainly a negative set of prescriptions designed to correct certain key imbalances in an economy. Although leaders may sometimes be convinced that the medicine is necessary, it is hard for them to dispense it with enthusiasm. A more fundamental readjustment program, although also painful, enlists more constructive energies and corresponding psychological involvement. It also can be presented to the public in a more positive and persuasive manner than a straight austerity program.

But a program combining short-term stabilization and medium-term structural adjustment measures also has clear political risks. Structural adjustment may threaten some groups and interests more fundamentally than does austerity. The longer timetable permits opponents of adjustment measures to become organized and articulate, and to join forces with each other. Unless international economic conditions and financial assistance improve substantially, for most poor countries a medium-term program means prolonged austerity, with only modest changes and improvements to sustain hope and confidence. Far from being a soft option, successful management of a sustained stabilization and adjustment effort over several years requires political leadership and skill of a high order; it is probably more difficult than the challenge of maintaining transitional order and acceptance during a "shock" program in countries where a rapid economic turnaround is feasible.

Since stabilization and adjustment programs are policy packages, the handling of their major components also raises political issues. Unfortunately, almost no systematic comparative analysis is available on the political implications of various options. For example, overvalued exchange rates are almost always part of a financial crisis. What are the probable political repercussions of a large, one-time devaluation versus several smaller steps? Of various flexible exchange-rate mechanisms, following devaluation, to guard against further erosion of international competitiveness? Conventional wisdom argues that dual exchange rates (two or more different exchange rates for different types of commodities or transactions) are usually inadequate economically and awkward administratively, yet political leaders often prefer dual rates to devaluation. Under what conditions does a split rate have real political advantages? There has been remarkably little effort to address such questions.

Similarly, we know very little about the conditions under which a government can successfully reduce costly, unsustainable food subsidies—another common theme in stabilization and adjustment programs recently and a topic that universally gives politicians nightmares. Some such efforts have produced massive riots (as in Cairo in 1979) and coups (as in Liberia in 1980), yet elsewhere (as in Sri Lanka in 1978 and 1979, and in Senegal in 1982 and 1983) major cuts provoked no serious threat. Common sense argues that government-mandated price increases should not be introduced when domestic food supplies are low. Thus Senegal, on the one hand, resisted outside pressure to cut its subsidies on imported rice in 1981, when drought had shrunk domestic substitutes; and thus Sri Lanka, on the other hand, successfully slashed subsidies and rations during a period when domestic rice supplies and the economy generally were expanding rapidly. Similarly, trade liberalization in poorer countries is politically easier and economically less risky when exports are expanding. Therefore it seems likely that liberalization efforts should focus initially on export promotion. But solid, empirically based support for such general propositions is not available. Nevertheless, more systematic efforts to assess the probable political impacts of alternative policy options for specific countries might well yield more sustainable programs.

Tactics of Sustainability

In presenting and defending programs, governments can use persuasion, partial compensation, containment of opposition—and in some instances also diversion or obfuscation. Economists have tended to think mainly in terms of *compensation*. Wage adjustments in the public and private sectors, as well as concessions and exceptions of various kinds for specific businesses and firms, are widely used to mute opposition to stabilization. Most commonly, wage freezes are lifted for the lowest-paid workers (as in Zambia in 1979-80) to partly counter increased prices resulting from devaluation, reduced consumption subsidies, or higher taxes. Stabilization case histories are also studded with salary hikes for civil servants—often following several years of wage freeze and serious erosion of real incomes, but often also with the consequence of breaching government expenditure ceilings agreed upon with the IMF. Thus in Kenya in 1981, an unbudgeted increase of 23-30 per cent for civil servants contributed to bank borrowing (deficit finance) at more than twice the ceiling stipulated in the stand-by agreement. Although it is hard to "prove" that such concessions have in practice warded off seriously threatening protests, they almost surely have served to defuse spreading unrest.

Sometimes it may be possible to offer the public, or some part of it, partial *compensation of a non-economic nature*. In Peru in the late 1970s, stabilization efforts gradually became linked to a time-table for the restoration of civilian rule. On at least one occasion, anticipated protests were averted partly by a veiled threat that confrontation over economic policy would end the political transition. In Jamaica after 1980, and in Turkey during the same period, new governments cracked down on widespread political violence at the same time that stabilization efforts were launched. For much of the urban population, this meant a welcome improvement in physical security.

But partial compensation, in whatever form, is no guarantee of acquiescence. Two contrasting experiences suggest the limits of compensation and offer clues on how to maximize its political benefits. In Ghana in December 1971, a massive devaluation was announced simultaneously with several "sweeteners"—including a minimum-wage increase exceeding the expected impact of devaluation on the cost of living; abolition of recently imposed and widely resented import surcharges and development taxes; and increases in the producer price of cocoa. But the devaluation was drastic. It took the public by surprise and was poorly explained and defended. It also coincided with widespread political alienation and became the catalyst of the military coup that followed in January 1972. The Jamaican experience in 1978 offers an interesting contrast, although that effort also failed. A sizable devaluation and associated stabilization measures were announced in July 1978, implying cuts in real wages of 25 per cent or more. No significant sweeteners were offered. But Prime Minister Manley and the moderates in his cabinet made strenuous efforts to explain unavoidable stabilization measures to union leaders. The unions grumbled, but they posed no real opposition for almost eight months. Only as the effort was clearly crumbling due to other pressures did the unions join the attack.

Jamaica as well as some other cases suggest that frank and vigorous *explanation and persuasion* can be quite effective in winning temporary public acquiescence to austerity measures, and perhaps especially in gaining union acceptance of wage restraint.

Unions have bowed to persuasion not only in Jamaica but also in Portugal in 1978 and Venezuela in the 1960s; union cooperation was successfully elicited in Italy as well in 1977.[3] In all of these cases, interestingly, the government had strong ties with major segments of organized labor. More generally, governments with good channels of communication to the groups most likely to oppose stabilization are in a better position to use persuasion—challenging the conventional wisdom that authoritarian governments are better placed to enforce unpopular reforms. The phasing of tactics may also be important: A serious campaign of explanation may be more helpful than sweeteners in avoiding initial outbursts, while partial compensation may be most appropriate later in the process, used selectively to dampen growing opposition and to extend the period of acceptance until broader economic benefits begin to become evident.

Persuasion may be less effective in eliciting desired cooperation from the business community. This is partly because the responses desired from labor and the public are not the same as those sought from business. The former groups are basically asked to tighten their belts and continue their work, while investors and entrepreneurs are asked to consider new options, take new risks, write off (at least in part) old investments, and generally change their ways of doing business. Large- and medium-scale businessmen may also have good connections in the government—especially in smaller countries, where political and economic elites often constitute small and overlapping circles. It is tempting to use these connections to try to win exceptions, delays, and modifications in the application of reforms, instead of accepting the changes and considering how best to adjust constructively. In short, somewhat paradoxically, the very fact that business circles are often close to political circles may make persuasion less effective in altering their behavior than it is with groups somewhat more distanced from the government.

As with any unpopular issue, politicians often try to soften opposition to stabilization by *diverting attention*, or by obfuscating or hiding aspects of their policies. The IMF is of course a frequent scapegoat. Recent steps in Egypt and Sudan to reduce the size of loaves of bread rather than increase the price are examples of obfuscation; so was Jamaica's two-step legalization of the "parallel" (black) market for foreign exchange under the Seaga government in 1981 and 1982, which established a *de facto* dual exchange rate but avoided unpopular devaluation.

Regardless of how skillfully governments use these various tactics, stabilization is likely to provoke some open opposition, which may or may not take violent forms. Government efforts to *contain* such protest can be handled well or awkwardly. In Sri Lanka, for example, the government established clear boundaries for acceptable union protest in a series of white papers and statements in late 1977 and subsequently. When opposition unions nonetheless attempted a general strike in mid-1980, public-sector strikers were promptly fired and were not quickly reinstated (contrary to previous regimes' handling of such strikes). There was little further protest from unions, even during the period of stringency during 1981. (The later communal riots in Sri Lanka, in mid-1983, were fundamentally different in causation, government handling, and consequences, but they are not part of the topic addressed here.)

Political Sustainability: What Outsiders Can Do

No government measure, and none of the more specific steps suggested below for outside agencies, is more important for political sustainability than adequate arrangements for international financial liquidity. A government's skill in persuasion can be consummate, its administration energetic, and its allocation of partial compensations well calculated within the limits of available resources, yet in most countries, the urban public—and sometimes the rural too—will not passively accept long-term austerity. Protests, in turn, absorb scarce governmental resources and energies, and the deteriorating public mood saps the effectiveness of stabilization measures. This chapter does not try to address the changes needed in the broader international financial system, but such changes are the essential context for the more specific measures sketched below.

Orderly Debt Rescheduling

One aspect of reform in international financial arrangements warrants mention here because of its direct relevance to internal politics in many developing countries. Ghana's experience in 1969-72 should be kept in mind in the 1980s. When the Nkrumah regime was deposed, Ghanaians nearly unanimously attributed their country's economic hardships to that regime's ill-conceived and sometimes shady debts. Nkrumah's successors sought to honor these debts, but also to reschedule them. Ghana's creditors agreed to this only reluctantly, on fairly short terms and at high costs. The anger that this response prompted within Ghana diverted attention from the need for internal reforms. Moreover, this earlier bitterness also fed the reaction that exploded when the government finally did take stabilization measures. One of the first acts of the military government that overthrew the Busia regime after the latter's December 1971 devaluation was to repudiate most of the Nkrumah debts. In Brazil and elsewhere currently, debts swollen by unanticipated interest-rate increases are similarly viewed as profoundly unfair—indeed as rapacious—and politicians are under intense pressure to abrogate those debts.

In many countries, orderly debt relief thus may be more than an essential economic ingredient of realistic stabilization and adjustment in many developing nations. It may be *politically* crucial to winning public acquiescence to needed reforms and austerity measures. The current haphazard, year-to-year pattern of rescheduling should be replaced by a more long-term and orderly approach. This should be done not only to facilitate orderly economic management but also for its political benefits—to indicate the willingness of outside agencies to share the burdens caused by unanticipated trends that cannot fairly be "blamed" either on governments or on banks. The commercial banks themselves have proved incapable of generating the necessary leadership and collaboration. There is an urgent need for more vigorous intervention by the U.S. government, probably acting in collaboration with the IMF, to encourage and guide a coordinated and enlightened response from the commercial banks.

Adequate Assistance for Medium-Term Programs

The earlier conclusion that political as well as economic factors point toward combined stabilization/adjustment programs, especially in the poorer and less flexible economies, also carries implications for the level and content of external support. A range of instruments is needed: non-project bridging assistance, project finance, and technical assistance to aid in the analyses and institutional development essential to plan and implement adjustment. For U.S. policy, this means both a more forthcoming approach to non-project stabilization assistance and continued attention to development projects and assistance. The cut in the U.S. contribution to IDA VII—the seventh replenishment of the International Development Association—threatens the World Bank's ability to finance an expanded program of structural adjustment loans; the U.S. decision should be reconsidered.

The "Insurance" Role of Aid

Another implication of the need for longer programs concerns the increased risks of unpredictable problems with weather, international prices, or other key factors beyond a government's control. If a stabilization program is designed to cut imports and consumption to the limits of political acceptability, bad weather or bad prices can push domestic hardship over that fuzzy boundary. A prudent leader—even one convinced of the economic rationale for stabilization—will seek more generous initial financing or more gradual measures, unless there is some assurance that plain bad luck will be countered by compensating external support.

The IMF's Compensatory Financing Facility serves this purpose to some degree, by providing low-conditionality loans to help cover export shortfalls due to conditions largely beyond a country's control or to temporary excesses in the cost of imported cereals. In compelling cases, the Fund is also sometimes willing to waive or modify one or more performance requirements on high-conditionality stand-by agreements. But often the institution's response to new problems is to insist on more austerity. Particularly in the cases of highly vulnerable economies, where relatively small changes in external conditions can have major repercussions, it would be politically as well as economically helpful if stand-by agreements explicitly stated the assumptions about major economic variables on which the agreed levels of assistance were based. Appropriate adjustments should then be considered if factors beyond a country's control cause significant departures from the assumed values.[4] The understanding might extend to downward revisions in assistance if events should provide an unexpected windfall. Such a device could simultaneously provide insurance against bad luck and increase the credibility of the effort in the public view, while also emphasizing the need for *sustained* adjustment efforts and countering false hopes that external events may obviate the need for adjustment.

Easing Specific Political Risks

Outside donors also may be able to address directly some kinds of political risks of stabilization, and they should be flexible in allowing politicians to cope with other risks. This is nothing new. For instance, the IMF has not been rigid in its stance toward dual exchange rates and other devices designed to postpone or to ease into devaluation. The United States and other bilateral donors have stepped up relief for the very poor (usually through U.S. Public Law 480, Title II) in support of some stabilization programs, as in Peru in the late 1970s. The issue of urban food prices and supply is particularly touchy in many countries. The economic case for reduced food imports and subsidies is powerful, but so are the political risks. There is probably a role here for further experimentation with carefully designed and temporary food aid (perhaps through P.L. 480, Title III), *even* if this means the temporary dilution of incentives for domestic production increases.

Buttressing Persuasion and Commitment

Outside donors can also help governments do a better job of persuading their own officials and citizens of the need for stabilization measures and can be more imaginative and energetic in promoting stronger commitment among leaders. IMF negotiating teams typically work almost exclusively with a narrow circle of economic officials. If the government is willing, after main outlines have been agreed, Fund teams might meet with a somewhat broader circle of officials (or possibly, at the government's invitation, even with representatives of key interest groups), to discuss and explain the rationale for the measures. This was in fact done in Jamaica in 1978, producing grudging union acquiescence for about eight months of grueling austerity; the effort collapsed for other reasons. At the very least, negotiating teams should view as part of their standard responsibilities the preparation of briefing papers that lay out in clear, non-technical language the reasons for the agreed program and that relate the rationale concretely to the conditions in the country.

Lack of confidence in the economic rationale for stabilization and adjustment measures should be recognized as a major obstacle to commitment and addressed not only in the boiler-room atmosphere of crisis aid negotiations, but also in a longer-term, less tense setting. In many developing countries, responsible and sophisticated economic officials are convinced that the IMF, and to some extent the World Bank, tend to apply standard remedies without a close examination of country-specific conditions. Where areas of persistent skepticism can be identified—for example, with respect to exchange rate management or rigidities in export expansion—this should be a signal for joint analysis in which the country's own staff would participate. The World Bank is already moving in this direction. But the IMF does very little along such lines, and the terms of reference and operating style of its missions are not compatible with such efforts. Any move toward joint analyses would be a new departure for the Fund. Joint studies consume staff time and may raise delicate questions, but they can also be highly educational—usually for both groups involved. The United States should encourage more efforts of this kind, especially in Sub-Saharan Africa. The international financial institutions should also actively seek other ways to bolster understanding and commitment, possibly including small, high-level conferences where officials from countries that have had some degree of success share their experience with others.

The U.S. Agency for International Development (AID) may wish to rely on the international financial institutions to conduct the main thrust of macro-economic policy in most countries. But it could make an important contribution by engaging in dialogue on implications of stabilization and adjustment for those sectors in which AID is active and has credible expertise. For instance, even high-level agricultural officials and ministers often are not aware of links between overvalued exchange rates and agricultural disincentives. AID staff might need some bolstering in order to address competently the links between macro-economic policies and sectoral action.

A major stabilization effort is very difficult politically, and no combination of strategy, tactics, and support measures by governments and outside agencies can do more than somewhat reduce the risks. Clearly, too, approaches must be tailored to the conditions of each case; there are no standard formulas. But the disappointing record of most stabilization programs is a powerful argument for more attention to political sustainability.

Notes

[1] "Stabilization" is used in this discussion to mean the short-term process of correcting a serious and persistent balance-of-payments deficit, typically involving a large foreign debt, and often accompanied by large and growing fiscal deficits and moderate-to-serious inflation. Stabilization programs almost always call for reduced government spending and private consumption (including wage freezes or cuts), to bring resource use into closer line with resource availabilities.

[2] Thomas Reichmann and Richard Stillson, "How Successful Are Programs Supported by Stand-By Arrangements?," *Finance and Development*, Vol. 14, No. 1 (March 1977), pp. 22-25.

[3] See Luigi Spaventa, "Two Letters of Intent: External Crises and Stabilization Policy, Italy 1973-77," in John Williamson, ed., *IMF Conditionality* (Washington, D.C.: Institute for International Economics, 1983), pp. 441-73.

[4] This follows John Williamson's suggestion for contingency conditions. See Williamson, *IMF Conditionality*, op. cit., p. 638.

Chapter 5

The NICs: Confronting U.S. "Autonomy"

Colin I. Bradford, Jr.

In the 1970s a growing number of developing countries began to play a major role in world trade in manufactures and in global economic adjustment. In Latin America, the ranks of these "newly industrializing countries" (or NICs, as they came to be known) included three large, highly industrialized countries—Brazil, Mexico, and Argentina—in the forefront, and Colombia, Peru, and Chile in the next tier. The East Asian NICs that emerged as exporters of manufactured goods on a global scale numbered several highly dynamic, smaller economies—the Republic of Korea, Taiwan, Hong Kong, and Singapore, known as the "gang of four"—followed by Thailand, Malaysia, and the Philippines. By the end of the decade, these countries had also become significant borrowers on international capital markets.

Two points of international tension arose from the new role of this group of nations. The first was the adjustment challenge that the surge in their manufactured exports posed for import markets in the United States and other advanced countries. The second was concern that the NICs' increased international borrowing (of the recycled OPEC surplus) was financing their increased consumption growth while postponing rather than facilitating their adjustment, endangering their creditworthiness.

There was some evidence that the NICs were able to use their high export growth to shield themselves from needed internal structural adjustments in their use of energy. But there was also evidence that, in the aggregate, their investment growth outpaced their consumption growth during the 1970s.[1] The pressure on industrial-country consumer-goods markets generated by the NICs' exports came to be seen as offset by these countries' capital-goods imports from the major industrialized countries.[2] Hence, in a global perspective, by the 1980s these countries were playing a key role in the world economy in both trade and finance. Moreover, the patterns of NIC-OPEC-OECD interaction resulting from their participation were perceived to be mutually reinforcing and quite favorable. From the standpoints of their strong export performance and their accelerated investment growth, financed by external debt, the NICs appeared to be good credit risks.

The negative turning point in these promising patterns of adjustment was not only the second oil price rise but also the shift in U.S. monetary policy in late 1979 from a focus on interest rates to a focus on the growth in monetary aggregates.[3] The subsequent interest-rate shock that affected interest rates worldwide had a massive effect on the global growth outlook and the world debt problem. The NICs found themselves facing two crises simultaneously: an explosion in their debt-service payments (since a high proportion of their debt was at variable interest rates or of a short-term nature) and a collapse in the markets for their exports as high interest rates triggered recession in advanced countries.

Beginning in 1981, therefore, the NICs and other debtor countries faced an adjustment problem that was fundamentally different in scope and character from those posed by the oil price hikes of the 1970s. Because of these dramatic changes in the world economic context, a major problem for the 1980s is the economic survival of many of the NICs and the threat that these countries may pose to the international financial system if their efforts to manage the new adjustment problems fail. For the world community, the global adjustment problem posed by the NICs thus has shifted from a predominant preoccupation with the trade pressures that these nations exerted on import markets to concern about the serious strain on the international financial system posed by their weakened capacity to maintain debt-service payments. For the NICs themselves, the central economic adjustment problem has changed from one of responding to the oil-price increases in the 1970s to one of managing the effects of external interest-rate changes in the 1980s.

As a result of these shifts, NIC adjustment and OECD adjustment have become increasingly intertwined, sparking an important debate on what policies should be followed by the United States and other OECD countries, by the NICs, and by the international institutions. This chapter attempts to elucidate and contribute to séveral aspects of this debate. First, the "outward-oriented" development strategies of the NICs and their economic performance are examined in light of the "new orthodoxy" that views these strategies as consistent with internal liberalization and "getting prices right." This examination attempts to ascertain the general validity of the new orthodoxy in order to evaluate its relevance for developing-country adjustment policies in the 1980s. If the new orthodoxy is universally applicable, it raises the second major issue discussed: Are the NICs "the tip of the iceberg"—that is, merely the first wave of developing-world industrialization and manufactures export, posing a still larger challenge to industrial structures in advanced countries in the future than they have in the past?

These two issues yield a sense of the importance of the individual policy mix to successful export strategies. The chapter then analyzes four aspects of global macro-economic trends and policies in relation to the surge in NIC exports and the rise of developing-country debt: the economic policy of the United States, the coordination of economic policy among the OECD countries, the outward orientation of development strategies, and the stabilization programs of the IMF.

Outward-Oriented Growth Strategies: Some Cautions

The success of the newly industrializing countries in the 1970s in achieving dynamic export expansion, accelerated investment and industrialization, and higher-than-average rates of economic growth elevated their adoption of outward-oriented growth strategies to the category of a "new orthodoxy." The policies followed by these countries that seemed successful in implementing such a strategy were unification and devaluation of the exchange rate, liberalization of imports, and export promotion measures. In the mid-1970s, there was a mistaken tendency to identify export-oriented growth strategies with free market policies—and some fears of the "Hong-Kong-ization" of the Third World with the diffusion of the "new orthodoxy," based on the perceived preeminence of the Asian NICs. More detailed case studies of the Asian NICs and more thoughtful reflection subsequently revealed the actual heterogeneity of the policy mix pursued by the successful exporters of manufactures.[4] In fact, a considerable amount of government intervention had taken place in the successful NICs. Public policy is now understood by most observers to play a fundamental role in achieving an outward-oriented economic thrust, quite apart from the degree of reliance on the market involved in each instance.

Nevertheless debate continues over the degree of bias involved in export promotion and import substitution. Furthermore, as the debt adjustment problems of the newly industrializing countries in the 1980s have overshadowed the trade adjustment problems posed by them in the 1970s, there has been a resurgence of the view that government intervention is inimical to achieving adequate adjustment. In addition, the stereotypical contrast between Latin American "interventionist" import substitution biases and the Asian economies' export orientation and "freedom from price distortion" has been reasserted.

These stylized visions were crisply characterized by *The Economist* in an article drawing on the World Bank's 1983 *World Development Report*: "Increasingly, [the IMF and the World Bank] have found themselves embroiled in the same set of policy issues: how can economies grow even when the international climate is unfavorable? The answer that the fund and bank give can be summed up in four words: get the prices right." The Latin American countries were described as having fallen into an interventionist, price distortion "trap" by adopting import substitution policies and overvalued exchange rates, borrowing too much while exporting too little—and contrasted with most of the Asian countries, which had instead chosen an export-led growth strategy, getting the prices right through more realistic exchange rates.[5]

The widely read Morgan Guaranty newsletter has drawn a similar basic picture, suggesting that "a profound reordering of priorities" is necessary, especially in Latin America, requiring "a basic reassessment of the role of the state." The newsletter states that: "Strategies based on import substitution alone, which entail an anti-export bias, do not deliver enduring economic dynamism— as can be seen in the contrasting records of Asia and Latin America." It also finds a directly related divergence in economic adjustment performance in observing that protectionist trends in Latin America "contrast with the adjustment strategies of most Asian economies, where liberalization (as in Korea, the Philippines, and Thailand) has continued even in the face of balance-of-payments pressures."[6]

Some of the professional economic literature on inward- versus outward-oriented development strategies and adjustment in developing countries tends to establish the same consistency between internal policies of liberalization relying on market signals and outward orientation on the one hand, and price distortion and inward orientation on the other. This idealization of outward-oriented strategies and their efficacy has contributed to its status as the "new orthodoxy." For example, in his summary work on the subject, based on the 1974-78 period, Bela Balassa concludes:

> Outward-oriented economies provided, on the average, similar incentives to exports and import-substitution and to primary production and manufacturing, while inward-oriented economies discriminated against exports and favored manufacturing over primary activities. Outward-oriented economies also placed less reliance on price controls and on interest rate ceilings than did inward-oriented economies. More generally, they gave greater scope to the market mechanism.[7]

Without meaning to caricature serious attempts to make sense of complex problems, it should be noted that there is a tendency in the literature to overstate the contrasts not only regionally but in terms of the kinds of policy approaches and packages that lead to success. The linkage of strategies, policies, and politics tends to emerge from the analysis in somewhat purer form than it takes in actuality. Export-oriented growth strategies are seen to be linked to realistic policies on exchange rates and a reduced role for the state, thereby getting prices right and letting markets work. Import substitution strategies are seen to lead to a larger role for the state and more intervention in markets, thereby distorting prices and generating more severe external imbalances. In fact the coherence of the different elements of a policy package is rarely so clear-cut. Reality is more mixed.

Bringing together the research work underlying both the World Bank's 1983 *World Development Report* and Balassa's conclusions yields some surprises.[8] Table 1 pairs up the NICs and several other developing countries identified as outward- and inward-oriented in the Balassa work with the data from the Bank's research work on price distortions in these same countries in order to examine the actual degrees of linkage between outward- and inward-oriented strategies and the pricing policies pursued. The basic conclusion of the World Bank price distortion research is that the countries with high price distortions are found to have low growth rates and that countries with low price distortions have had high growth rates. Yet the last column of Table 1 shows a surprisingly small difference between the average price distortion index of the six outward-oriented developing economies (1.83) and that of the eight inward-oriented countries (1.95). Indeed, this small difference contrasts sharply with the average price distortion index for those developing countries in the Bank study found to have high price distortion (2.44) and those with low price distortion (1.56). These

Table 1. Price Distortions in Outward- and Inward-Oriented Economies in 1970s

	Exchange Rate[a]	Interest Rate[b]	Price Distortion Index[c]
Outward-Oriented Economies			
NICs			
Korea (Repulic of)	95	−5.0	1.57
Chile	n.a.	−38.6	2.43
Uruguay	106	−20.6	2.29
Others			
Kenya	101	−4.1	1.71
Thailand	92	0.5	1.43
Tunisia	88	−2.7	1.57
Average:	**96.4**	**−11.8**	**1.83**
Inward-Oriented Economies			
NICs			
Brazil	89	−8.0	1.86
Yugoslavia	122	−8.5	1.71
Argentina[d]	128	−31.2	2.43
Mexico[d]	101	−10.7	1.86
Turkey	104	−14.5	2.14
Others			
Egypt	89	−4.4	2.14
India	81	−0.3	1.86
Philippines	99	−4.9	1.57
Average:	**101.6**	**−10.3**	**1.95**

[a] The exchange rate is the annual average appreciation of the real exchange rate during 1974-80 from the base exchange rate in 1972-73 (=100).

[b] The interest rate is the average real interest rate for the 1970-80 period.

[c] The price distortion index is a composite index including seven indicators of distortion: protection of manufacturing, underpricing of agriculture, the exchange rate, the cost of credit, the cost of labor, the pricing of infrastructural services, and inflation.

[d] Internal shocks greater than external shocks.

Source: Table developed by pairing outward- and inward-oriented classifications from Bela Balassa, *Structural Adjustment Policies in Developing Economies*, World Bank Staff Working Paper No. 464 (Washington, D.C.: World Bank, 1981) with data from Ramgopal Agarwala, *Price Distortion and Growth in Developing Countries*, World Bank Staff Working Paper No. 575 (Washington, D.C.: World Bank, 1983), pp. 20, 23, and 40.

averages show that while there is wide variation in price distortion across the countries in the study, there is not much difference between those countries identified as inward-oriented and those that are outward-oriented.

Second, in the World Bank study there is a strong correlation—stronger than that for any other price distortion in the study—between exchange-rate appreciation and economic growth performance. But the averages for groups of countries in the first column of Table 1 indicate that there is not a similarly strong association between the annual average appreciation of the real exchange rate on the one hand, and inward versus outward orientation on the other (96.4 versus 101.6). The proximity of these averages contrasts with the divergence of averages for the three groups of countries (twenty-seven in all) in the World Bank study designated as having low, medium, and high exchange-rate appreciation of 94.3, 110, and 142, respectively.

Third, the World Bank research anticipates and finds that countries with too low a ceiling on interest rates tend to have slower growth rates in gross domestic product (GDP)—and in exports—due to the resulting inefficiencies in the allocation of investment, biases in factor proportions, and reductions in savings. However, the second column of Table 1 shows that the inward-oriented countries in fact have a slightly *less* negative average real interest rate (−10.3 per cent) than the outward-oriented countries (−11.8 per cent). In addition to being in the opposite direction, this difference pales in comparison with the difference in the averages for the twenty-seven countries in the World Bank study between medium and high interest-rate distortions of −3.4 per cent and −14.8 per cent respectively. Thus grouping the countries according to inward and outward orientation in fact narrows the difference in interest-rate distortions among the sample of countries instead of highlighting a causal relationship.

It can be said, therefore, that on average there is not any association between outward versus inward orientation and a general measure of price distortion or distortion in the two key variables (the exchange rate and the real interest rate). To be sure, there are countries for which there is such association: the Republic of Korea, Tunisia, and Thailand in the outward-oriented group show relatively low indexes for all three price distortion variables—but then India, the Philippines, and Brazil in the inward-oriented group show roughly the same low order of magnitude for these three measures.

For those who seek to substantiate the "new orthodoxy," it is regrettable that the Bank's price distortion research did not include

Hong Kong, Singapore, and Taiwan, as this undoubtedly would have strengthened their argument. Nevertheless, even if the addition of these countries did change the overall averages substantially, this would only further prove the unusual character of the three countries and not enhance the generality of the claim. The conclusions from Table 1 would still stand: There is a great deal of heterogeneity and complexity in the real world, and the stylized version of the dichotomy between inward- and outward-oriented strategies should be drawn more cautiously.

It is important, however, not to overstate either these conclusions or those of the World Bank's study. The World Bank research states: "The findings reported here are a case for 'getting the prices right' and should not necessarily be interpreted as an argument for a laissez faire approach."[9] Similarly, the findings reported in this chapter should not be interpreted as an argument either for price distortions or against getting prices right. The argument here does assert that getting prices right is not the *sine qua non* of economic growth and that the identification of correct prices with outward-oriented growth strategies is misleading. Part of the business of getting *policies* right is to provide ample scope for prices and markets to work. But it is surely not the *only* business of public policy. The desire for consistency in policy advocacy does not mean that it has been or will be realized in country experience.

Global Shifts in Industrial Structure

The tendency to enshrine the export-oriented growth strategy of the newly industrializing countries into a "new orthodoxy" capable of replication in other developing countries manifests itself in yet another set of ideas that affects perceptions of the role of these nations in global economic adjustment. The labor movement and others in the United States see the rapid industrialization of the Third World as a primary cause of the current economic malaise in the West. According to this view, the NICs are but "the tip of the iceberg," the first wave of developing countries capable of producing and exporting manufactures on a global scale. The rapid industrialization of these nations is portrayed as having shifted the global industrial advantage toward developing countries and as a major change in the world balance of economic power. These trends are perceived to have put pressure on employment and output of the manufacturing sectors in advanced countries, causing the economic slowdown in the West in the 1970s. The patterns of global adjustment mentioned earlier—whereby the OPEC surplus financed the capital-goods imports and current-account deficits in developing

countries—are perceived by these observers to have aided this
process of global structural change.

This view has been most fully expressed in a book by Michael
Beenstock, who argues that "an important global factor in the
OECD slowdown is the changing balance of world economic power,
which has moved in favour of developing countries."[10] Drawing on
Beenstock's work, Samuel Brittan has written in *Foreign Affairs*: "A
major force behind all these changes and the economic obsolescence
of so much capital equipment in the West has been the emergence of
developing countries as major manufacturing centers. . .the Third
World competition so far seen is only the tip of the iceberg."[11] And a
recent congressional report states:

> Japan is merely the first non-Anglo Saxon, non-European
> "newly industrializing country" to reach maturity. The prob-
> lems the developed world is experiencing with Japan (and with
> each other) are symptomatic of what will be faced again and
> again as more and more "NICs" arrive at and demand entry to
> modern industrial society.[12]

These ideas are important in fueling the advocacy of a deliber-
ate industrial policy for the United States as a means of coping with
the global industrial challenge. Whether or not industrial policies
are an appropriate, necessary, or desirable response to economic
problems facing the United States is a subject of considerable professional and political debate. The Beenstock-Brittan view—which
holds that there has *already* been a shift in global industrial production of sufficient magnitude to contribute significantly to the
economic problems of advanced countries and that this shift is a
mere harbinger of future trends—is highly relevant to the discussion of the future policy direction of the United States.

A number of fallacies should be noted in this approach. First,
the surge in growth in industrial output and exports of manufactures from developing countries, while highly significant, does constitute a bulge, but *not* a linear trend that extrapolates inexorably
into the future and necessarily implies a continuous decline in the
position of advanced countries in the world economy. The NICs have
become new players in world trade but the old actors still have the
upper hand. With 90 per cent of world trade in manufactures and 85
per cent of world output of manufactures originating in the major
industrial countries in 1980, it is difficult to conclude, as Beenstock
does, that the balance of world economic power "has moved in
favour of developing countries."

The shift in the nature of the adjustment problem facing the
NICs in the 1980s is symptomatic, as noted earlier, of a massive

reversal in the trade and financial patterns of the 1970s. The outward-oriented developing countries of the 1970s are now threatened with an era of closed-economy growth. The more constrained availability of external lending and mushrooming debt-service payments massively constrict the developing world's import capacity. The pattern of high investment growth, foreign debt, capital goods imports, rapid industrialization, and high growth in manufactured exports has been broken, making linear extrapolation of global industrial trends implausible.

Second, the "tip of the iceberg" argument is itself a highly questionable proposition. The story of the emergence of the NICs as major world exporters of manufactures is the story of those few countries that have been able to generate a political consensus and national commitment to export-oriented growth. The export surge in these countries did not result from evolutionary economic change. It was made possible by political consolidation that arose from special historical circumstances—and that is not an easily generalized phenomenon. The "tip of the iceberg" is a vivid image that fails to capture the selectivity of the process of rapid industrialization.[13]

Third, the world economic context clearly has a crucial influence on economic policy and performance of developing countries, especially in those seeking to implement outward-oriented policies. It is doubtful that the NIC "model" could have been universally replicated by other developing countries even in *favorable* world economic growth conditions. Given the present adverse world economic outlook, it seems even more unlikely that another group of nations will be able to follow the same model with anything like the same pace in the 1980s.

Fourth, the Beenstock-Brittan view argues that the problem in industrial countries is one of a mismatch of the supply of labor and capital in old industrial sectors with the demand for output in capital-goods industries, high-tech industries, and the service sector: "The basic problem is the sluggishness of factor markets."[14] Yet a number of studies indicate that, at least in the United States, factor mobility within manufacturing in the 1970s has been relatively high and that internal adjustment has been reasonably rapid; data prepared by Grossman, for example, reveal that increased labor absorption by high-growth industrial sectors in the United States exceeded labor shedding by slower-growth industrial sectors between 1974 and 1980. This clearly shows that internal adjustment is occurring in U.S. manufacturing.[15]

Finally, and most important, the Beenstock-Brittan view seriously underestimates the degree to which macro-economic mismanagement in the West has been a key determinant of the economic slowdown. High inflation, high unemployment, low investment, and low rates of economic growth seem to be more fundamentally determined by the conflict of monetary and fiscal policies than by shifts in global industrial structures. As Charles Schultze has recently stated: "Getting America's monetary and fiscal policies in order is far more important for the health of the nation's industrial structure than any conceivable set of new industrial policies."[16]

To see the rise of the NICs in the 1970s as the central cause of the global economic slowdown and the economic problems of the West is to misunderstand the source of world economic problems. This misperception leads to misconceived proposals and solutions for the world of the 1980s.

The Global Policy Stalemate

The global economic crisis is fundamentally rooted in *global* macro-economic mismanagement. The NICs are now a vital piece of the puzzle. Global macro-economic mismanagement has four interrelated dimensions: the economic policy of the United States, inadequate economic policy coordination among the OECD countries, the outward orientation of the development strategies of many developing countries, and the stabilization programs of the IMF. Taken together, these add up to a global policy stalemate in which an interdependent world economy is moving along a very sub-optimal path because of an intellectual and political failure to generate viable alternatives.

U.S. Economic Policy

U.S. economic policy remains a preeminent force in the world economy today. After a decade of anxiety about the decline of its influence in world economic affairs, the United States has imposed on the world the higher priority it assigns to reducing inflation over the competing priority of economic growth and increasing employment. This was achieved through the collision of an expansionary fiscal policy with a contractionary monetary policy that resulted from the refocusing of monetary policy on the growth in the money supply beginning in late 1979. Interest rates rose worldwide, the dollar appreciated, and OECD demand slowed down. As a consequence, the terms of trade shifted massively against the outward-oriented economies, generating a real income loss for a given amount of output growth at the same time that growth in export markets plummeted.

What was going on in part was a realignment between the real and the financial dimensions of the world economy. Briefly, the 1974-79 period was one of gradual global adjustment in which employment and output levels worldwide were not overly compressed to compensate for the change in real relative prices brought on by the 1973 oil shock. International financial and trade patterns enabled moderate global growth and adjustment. The real side of the world economy—output and employment levels—was sustained by the new financial flows arising from the OPEC current-account surplus. However, rates of inflation ran ahead of nomimal interest rates, by and large resulting in negative real rates of interest that were not sustainable over the long run. Successful positive adjustment on the real side was achieved at the cost of disequilibrium on the financial side. In sum, macro-economic management efforts failed to maintain a balanced global strategy between growth and stability. The switch in monetary policy by the United States in 1979, brought partly by pressure from OPEC members who feared the erosion of their financial assets, was designed to correct this imbalance.

The result, however, has been the flip side of the earlier disequilibrium. Excessively high real interest rates have caused a global recession and record-high unemployment levels worldwide, placing particularly acute pressures on the outward-oriented economies. The low levels of output and export growth possible for those economies in the context of this global compression now threaten the financial flows and indeed the very sustainability of the basic outward-oriented strategy. Global macro-economic mismanagement continues—having merely reversed the nature of the imbalance rather than corrected it.

The U.S. economic policy process remains both economically and politically stymied. U.S. monetary policy is stuck on the horns of a dilemma: Although increasing the money supply would normally lead to lower interest rates, inflationary expectations now mean that monetary expansion, paradoxically, immediately generates higher interest rates; tighter monetary policy, however, would also bring higher interest rates through the normal supply-demand mechanism. This shifts the burden of macro-economic policy balance from monetary to fiscal policy. To bring down interest rates, the fiscal deficit has to be reduced; taxes have to be raised, spending has to be reduced, or both. There is no other alternative for U.S. policy for the moment.

But U.S. fiscal policy, too, is stymied politically—both within the Reagan administration and in the Congress. One manifestation of this stalemate is the controversy surrounding the views of Martin Feldstein, outgoing chairman of the Council of Economic Advisers, on the need for tax increases and cuts in defense spending to reduce the fiscal deficit. Other signs are the failure of the modest tax increase bill in the House of Representatives (by a vote of 214 to 204) in the last days of the 1983 Congress and the May 1984 defeat in the Senate (by a vote of 49 to 49) of the tax-increase and spending-cut package proposed by Senator Lawton Chiles for the Senate Democrats. As Senator Chiles privately summed up the situation on the last day of the 1983 Congress: "Unemployment is high but not as high as it used to be, inflation is high but not as high as it used to be, and interest rates are high but not as high as they used to be. There just isn't the push out there to change things."[17] The lack of adequate pressure for change allows U.S. economic policy to hew to its present suboptimal path, with enormously negative spillover effects on the world economy.

Economic Policy Coordination

The problems of recession, unemployment, and exchange-rate misalignment in the advanced industrial countries can be addressed by greater coordination of economic policies among these countries. Despite the logic in favor of coordination and appeals by Chancellor Helmut Schmidt, President Giscard d'Estaing, and others,[18] policy coordination remains an element of the ideal rather than the real world. The Reagan administration has developed a counter-logic of its own, against "concerted action," as policy coordination has come to be called. Martin Feldstein has asserted that "a program of concerted action is not really applicable to the situation in the United States."[19] He has argued that the United States, unlike smaller or weaker economies, is able to run sustained current-account deficits with offsetting capital inflows. Whereas other economies would experience pressure to correct recurrent balance-of-payments deficits through exchange-rate adjustments, the United States has greater policy autonomy and consequently can keep interest rates high through tight monetary policy, attracting foreign capital, while simultaneously having an expansionary fiscal policy, providing a stimulus to the world economy.

This reasoning is politically useful in attempting to insulate U.S. economic policy from external pressures to change the macro mix, but it is economically faulty in two respects. First, the most important stimulus to global growth is not the size of the U.S. current-account deficit but the magnitude of U.S. imports, which depend on the growth of the domestic economy. Second, the U.S. current-account deficit was compensated for by capital outflows from other OECD economies, which constrained their own current-account deficits. From the point of view of the outward-oriented developing economies, the variables critical for adjustment and growth are the size of the overall OECD current-account deficit, and in particular OECD import growth—not the size of the U.S. current-account deficit alone.

The Reagan administration advances several other erroneous arguments for global belt-tightening, stressing the need for economic policy autonomy. It is said that whereas one country can control its exchange rate, interest rates are not within the control of the policymakers of individual governments. Interest rates will decline, it is argued, only if worldwide public-sector borrowing declines—that is, only if there is global recourse to Reaganomics. The argument concerning interest-rate autonomy may be true for most other economies, but it is certainly not true for the United States. The United States controls its interest rate through its own monetary and fiscal policy mix, and world interest rates follow the U.S. lead.

Another Reagan administration argument for global belt-tightening rather than global recovery is that, with the decline in the OPEC current-account surplus, global savings have declined. But the OPEC surplus is not necessarily an *increment* to global savings, although it clearly acts as their channel. Shifts in the channeling of savings do not necessarily affect the magnitude of global savings, and certainly do not constitute a persuasive case for global contraction.

Finally, it is argued that the U.S. ratio of taxes as a share of GNP has remained constant between 1980 and 1983 while the share of government spending as a share of GNP has gone up by 25 per cent in the same three-year period. This is an effort to put the onus of the U.S. fiscal imbalance on spending approved by Congress rather than on the administration's tax cut. The real problem, however, is not just a mismatch in the numerator variables of taxes and spending but also in the declining value of the denominator— the GNP—as recession has worsened due to the clash in the fiscal-monetary policy mix.

None of these arguments provides a basis for U.S. economic policy autonomy nor a reasonable rationale for global contraction rather than global recovery. All are assertions of policy preferences and policy priorities about which there can be, and is, lively debate. The Reagan administration's arguments for policy autonomy and price stability have the effect of deepening the policy stalemate. They tend to obscure the interactive multiplier effects that follow from macro-economic policy interdependence and they exclude from consideration the potential benefits to be derived from international coordination. The fact that the United States can still set its macro-economic policy independently does not necessarily mean that the optimal path for the United States itself is the one made possible by autonomy.

The quest for autonomy in economic policymaking in the United States—whether in the Reagan version of imposing hegemonic policy preferences or in the alternative version of advocating an industrial policy for the country—seems to be more rooted in politics than in economics. Both the Republican administration and the Democratic candidates are responding to a perceived need to reassert the authority of the presidency in American political life and to reassert the leadership of the United States in world affairs in the wake of Watergate, Vietnam, the oil price shocks, and rising Soviet militarism. As much political sense as this "reassertionism" may make domestically, it conflicts directly with the striking and indeed unique accomplishment of the NICs, which achieved policy autonomy in the different economic context of the 1970s while becoming exporters of manufactures on a global scale. The issue for the United States is how to accommodate the rise of new economic powers so as to achieve positive global adjustment rather than how to reassert American preeminence. This action-reaction politics, unfortunately, worsens rather than redresses the imbalance in global policy management. Instead of facilitating adjustment globally or domestically, "reassertionism" drives the world economy from one disequilibrium solution to another.

The Outlook for Outward-Oriented Strategies

Without resumed growth in world trade, increased flows of external capital, and lower interest rates, the prospect for successful trade- or debt-financed economic growth is seriously restricted for both the established and the aspiring NICs. After thirty years of encouraging developing countries to adopt outward-oriented growth strategies and to become more closely integrated into the world economy, the United States has contributed to creating a context that threatens to usher in an era of closed-economy growth for the Third World.[20]

Advocacy of the new orthodoxy may have been somewhat overstated in earlier periods of more promising growth. Its viability and relevance for developing countries in the world economy of the 1980s is unfortunately still more limited. Nevertheless, the universal call to export more is sounded as the solution to the world debt problem. But export market growth is seriously dampened by the deflationary policies required in Europe to prevent even more capital flight to the United States and further exchange-rate depreciation. The total value of the imports of industrial countries was less in 1983—and is projected by the IMF to be less also in 1984—than it was in 1980, despite the record U.S. trade deficit.[21]

The greater openness of the oil-importing, middle-income countries and their greater integration into the world economy make them significantly more sensitive than other developing countries to growth in the OECD countries. Recent World Bank figures show that the decline in growth in the middle-income nations was twice as sensitive to the drop in growth rates in advanced countries in the recession from 1980 to 1982 than it was to the modest drop in advanced-country growth rates after 1973, as well as twice as sensitive as the growth rates of all developing countries to advanced-country growth rates over these same periods. Similarly, if a substantial recovery were to take place in the advanced industrial countries in the 1985-95 period—if, for example, they were to achieve an average annual growth rate of 5 per cent (the World Bank's high-growth projection) rather than 2.5 per cent (the Bank's low projection)—this again would stimulate a recovery in the middle-income countries twice as great as that in all developing countries.[22] Not surprisingly, these figures illustrate the greater openness of the oil-importing, middle-income countries and their significantly greater sensitivity to growth in the OECD due to their greater integration into the world economy. Therefore the call to export more must carry with it higher growth in OECD import markets to have an effect on the growth and debt outlook of the more industrialized developing world.

With the OECD economic outlook less than promising, another solution proposed for developing-country problems is the encouragement of South-South trade. Yet there are limits to the "export more" enjoinder in this dimension, as developing countries cannot simultaneously achieve surpluses in their trade with each other. Hence the prospect for export growth is less than good. Since new foreign borrowing by developing countries is now used chiefly to meet debt-service payments, it appears that neither trade nor debt can alleviate the difficulties of these nations. This leaves no alternative but drastic cuts in imports. Developing counties are being forced by the global economic climate to adopt inward-oriented, closed-economy growth strategies. Unless the OECD economic outlook changes, the new orthodoxy is dead as a practical economic policy alternative for most developing countries.

IMF Stabilization Programs

In this context, the widespread application of the conventional IMF approach to economic stabilization appears to be inevitable. The fact that classical demand-management stabilization programs— such as budget reductions, tight monetary policy, devaluation, and wage restraints—are being summoned to the fore as a major element in the current global strategy is yet another sign of the policy stalemate. It is based on the continuing priority given to inflation over growth in the IMF outlook. Despite serious doubts in the international economic community about the traditional IMF approach and the development of a "counter-culture viewpoint" among economists, bankers, and public policy officials, the traditional precepts prevail.[23] The IMF's most recent *World Economic Outlook* states: "What is certain, however, is that disinflation is a prerequisite to returning to a path of satisfactory economic growth."[24]

Some economists propose a "more balanced" concept of stabilization, placing more emphasis on increasing investment, facilitating structural change, and promoting higher employment and faster economic growth. These ideas influenced both the 1979 revision of the guidelines on IMF conditionality and the World Bank's relatively new program of structural adjustment lending. Serious problems nevertheless remain. Tony Killick, a prominent sympathetic participant in the debate (see Chapter 2), has observed that "it is doubtful whether structuralism contains within it a coherent approach to short-term economic management. . . . The apparent absence of a viable alternative set of policies means that the debate about least-cost methods of short-run adjustment is not one between orthodoxy and structuralism but rather concerns a range of options within orthodoxy." He writes of the "dilemma of the missing alternative."[25]

A key element is the time period in which adjustment is attempted. The 1979 revisions in the IMF conditionality guidelines not only urged more balance in the approach but also, importantly, pressed for *medium-term* adjustment programs of three to five years. Nevertheless, current Reagan administration policy and IMF practice is to use IMF stand-by resources for one-year stabilization programs. The fundamental role envisioned for and by the Fund now is providing resources for short-run stabilization efforts. This time horizon leaves little opportunity for supply-side policies to be integrated into the traditional monetary model to achieve a balanced approach. As a result, the world is left with a lopsided macro-economic approach in this dimension of global economic management as well.

Conclusions

World economic management makes it acutely evident that we are less than we could be as a global community. Policy stalemate reigns in the U.S. economic policy process, in international economic coordination, in the salience of outward-oriented strategies, and in the IMF approach to stabilization programs. Each dimension has its own economic and political rationale for the status quo. Realism suggests we should accept the resultant outcomes as the most probable.

But these outcomes are politically unacceptable and economically unnecessary. The United States should not settle for a suboptimal growth path for its economy based on an intellectual and political failure to exploit fully the benefits of an interactive relationship with the world economy. Debtor countries should not have to accept the repressive consequences of the global policy stalemate. The reversal of three decades of global integration is not inevitable. And there is no imperative that requires massive imbalances in growth and employment to be the price for financial stability, especially when those real imbalances in fact threaten to undermine the world financial system.

The global policy stalemate also does not create an acceptable context for developing-country political processes to work in an open and democratic fashion. This is particularly crucial to a number of key developing countries that are in the midst of rapid political change: Brazil, Mexico, the Republic of Korea, the Philippines, Poland, Chile, Argentina, and Peru, to name several.

More important, the involvement of the United States in the world economy now subjects it to forces and pressures that require greater balance between the real and financial dimensions of U.S. economic policy. It was the OPEC countries that found the erosion of their financial assets due to negative real interest rates to be a reason to push the United States toward an abrupt change in its monetary policy in 1979. In the current circumstances, it is the overvalued dollar, rising U.S. interest rates, and the enormous U.S. trade deficit that add instability to the world economy and point toward still another sudden adjustment and over-correction. The international repercussions of U.S. economic policy have had destabilizing effects on the world economy over the last decade. The issue now is: Will the U.S. role in the world economy be a source of balance or instability in the future? The political challenge for the United States is to fashion a domestic economic policy that is consistent with the new world economy and the power of the United States within it.

Notes

[1] Colin I. Bradford, Jr., "The NICs and World Economic Adjustment" (Chapter 11) in Louis Turner and Neil McMullen, eds., *The Newly Industrializing Countries: Trade and Adjustment* (London: George Allen & Unwin in cooperation with the Royal Institute of International Affairs, 1982).

[2] William H. Branson, "The OPEC Surplus and U.S.-LDC Trade," Working Paper No. 791, National Bureau of Economic Research, Cambridge, Mass., 1981.

[3] Nicely shown by John Lewis in "Can We Escape the Path of Mutual Injury?" (Overview), in John P. Lewis and Valeriana Kallab, eds., *U.S. Foreign Policy and the Third World: Agenda 1983* (New York: Praeger Publishers for the Overseas Development Council, 1983), pp. 17-22.

[4] For case studies of Asian NICs, see Wontack Hong and Lawrence B. Krause, eds., *Trade and Growth of the Advanced Developing Countries in the Pacific Basin* (Seoul: Korean Development Institute, 1981), and Fernando Fajnzylber, "Some Reflections on South-East Asian Export Industrialization," *CEPAL Review*, December 1981, pp. 111-32.

[5] *The Economist*, September 24, 1983, p. 39.

[6] Morgan Guaranty Trust Company, *World Financial Markets*, September 1983.

[7] Bela Balassa, "The Adjustment Experience of Developing Economies After 1983," in John Williamson, ed., *IMF Conditionality* (Washington, D.C.: Institute for International Economics, 1982), p. 172.

[8] For these fuller research results, see, respectively, Ramgopal Agarwala, *Price Distortions and Growth in Developing Countries*, World Bank Staff Working Paper No. 575 (Washington, D.C.: World Bank, 1983) and Bela Balassa, *Structural Adjustment Policies in Developing Economies*, World Bank Staff Working Paper No. 464 (Washington, D.C.: World Bank, 1981).

[9] Agarwala, *Price Distortions*, op. cit., p. 46.

[10] Michael Beenstock, *The World Economy in Transition* (London: George Allen & Unwin, 1983), p. 12.

[11] Samuel Brittan, "A Very Painful World Adjustment," *Foreign Affairs*, "America and the World 1982," Vol. 61, No. 3 (1983), pp. 562-64.

[12] U.S. House of Representatives, Committee on Energy and Commerce, Staff Report, *The United States in a Changing World Economy: The Case for an Integrated Domestic and International Commercial Policy* (Washington, D.C.: U.S. Government Printing Office, September 1983), p. 12.

[13] See Colin I. Bradford, Jr., "Rise of the NICs and Exporters on a Global Scale" (Chapter 2), in Turner and McMullen, *The Newly Industrializing Countries*, op. cit.

[14] Beenstock, *World Economy in Transition*, op. cit., p. 90.

[15] Robert Lawrence, "Is Trade De-Industrializing America? A Medium-term Prospective," *Brookings Papers on Economic Activity*, Washington, D.C., September 1983; Colin I. Bradford, Jr., "U.S. Adjustment to the Global Industrial Challenge" and appendix data by Gene Grossman, in Robert Thornton, Richard Arenson, and Attiat Ott, eds., *Reindustrialization: Implications for Industrial Policy* (Greenwich, Conn.: JAI Press, forthcoming in 1984).

[16] Charles Schultze, "Industrial Policy: A Dissent," *The Brookings Review*, Fall 1983, pp. 3-12.

[17] In a conversation with the author.

[18] For another major appeal, see *Promoting World Recovery: A Statement on Global Economic Strategy by Twenty-six Economists from Fourteen Countries* (Washington, D.C.: Institute for International Economics, 1982).

[19] *The Economist*, June 11, 1983, p. 43.

[20] Colin I. Bradford, Jr., "International Debt and the World Economy: Global Integration on Trial," Subcommittee on International Trade, Investment and Monetary

Policy, Committee on Banking, Finance and Urban Affairs, U.S. House of Representatives, Hearings, May 3, 1983, pp. 666-98.

[21] International Monetary Fund, *World Economic Outlook*, Occasional Paper No. 27 (Washington, D.C.: 1984), p. 178.

[22] Calculated by the author from Tables 2.1 and 3.1 in World Bank, *World Development Report, 1983* (New York: Oxford University Press, 1983), pp. 7 and 27, respectively.

[23] *New York Times*, October 2, 1983.

[24] International Monetary Fund, *World Economic Outlook*, op. cit, p. 23.

[25] Tony Killick, ed., *Adjustment and Financing in the Developing World* (Washington, D.C.: International Monetary Fund, in cooperation with the Overseas Development Institute, London, 1982), pp. 65-66 and 35, respectively.

Chapter 6

Brazil's Debt Crisis and U.S. Policy

Riordan Roett

Brazil has come to symbolize a basic dilemma in Latin America and the Third World: How can governments deal with economic recession and widespread social malaise and simultaneously continue with the process of political democratization? With more than 120 million inhabitants, Brazil is the fifth largest country in the world. It also has the largest debt in the Third World—amounting to more than $90 billion at the end of 1983. Brazil's torturous negotiations with the International Monetary Fund and the private commercial banks are taken as a sign of the financial dependence of the Latin American states on the "money-center" banks and the international monetary authorities. Many argue that Brazil also illustrates Latin America's growing loss of political autonomy in structuring its ties with the industrial states of the North.

The "cost" to Brazil, in human terms, of accepting and implementing an austerity package is obvious. For millions of Brazilians, deprivation is no longer "relative" but absolute. Moreover, the social decay of Brazilian society has placed a heavy strain on a fledgling political system that is in uneasy transition from an authoritarian military regime to a competitive democratic government. What happens in Brazil will be watched carefully by other Latin American democratic states that are expected to follow similar adjustment programs. At some point, one or more of these countries may determine that the cost is too high. The implications of such a possible decision for U.S. policy in the Western Hemisphere, and for the international financial system, are serious.

The Situation in Brazil

1984 has begun for Brazil as 1983 ended: with bitter economic news. Last year inflation reached a historic high of 211 per cent. Retail food prices increased 227.5 per cent. The gross domestic product (GDP) fell by 3.9 per cent. The decrease in industrial production was 7.9 per cent—a staggering figure, given that industry represents 37 per cent of the total GDP. In the city of São Paulo, employment figures were 44 per cent below those of 1965-67 and falling. There is no hope of creating in 1984 the 1.6-1.8 million jobs required for new entrants into the work force. Many estimate the combined unemployment and underemployment figure (admittedly difficult to calculate) reached at least 40 per cent of the working population.

Although the government has agreed with the IMF and the private commercial banks to hold the 1984 inflation rate to 75 per cent, it is widely predicted that the rate will in fact reach 150 per cent. The buying power of the once comfortable Brazilian middle class is expected to fall by at least 30 per cent in 1984.

Brazil reached, indeed surpassed, its target of a $6-billion trade surplus last year. The goal for 1984, part of Brazil's agreement with the IMF, is $9 billion. But the 1983 figure was attained only at the high cost of a drastic cut in imports, a move that has had a deadening impact on the productive capacity of the once robust industrial plant. Rapidly decreasing buying power at home has reduced internal demand for domestic goods, and the continuing global recession has depressed markets, particularly in the Third World and in Western Europe, driving Brazil toward the U.S. market. There are also increasing signs that the rapid growth of Brazilian exports to the United States is intensifying protectionist pressures from U.S. producers. In an election year, it may be difficult for the administration to resist responding to domestic calls for protection from Third World products.

The down side of the inability of Brazil and other Third World countries to import goods from the industrial countries is a loss of jobs in the United States and Western Europe. A depressed Brazilian economy, with inadequate foreign exchange, is in no position to buy very much from its traditional trading partners. Brazil is further handicapped by the short-term costs of paying "cash on the barrel" for its vital petroleum imports and the need to finance its foreign debt of more than $90 billion.

The social implications of the economic crisis have become grave. Crime has risen dramatically in Brazil's urban centers. Hunger and malnutrition are common in both the rural and urban areas of the country. The number of street children, homeless or abandoned youths, is one very noticeable sign of the crisis. The drought in the Brazilian Northeast is now in its fifth year, and the shortage of food and health care, recognized to have reached crisis proportions, has aroused public clamor for action.

With belt-tightening economic measures to continue in 1984, there is no possibility of the government reallocating scarce resources from debt management and the purchase of critical imports to the funding of needed social programs. Brazil does not have a "social net" for its unemployed, and the continuing and deepening economic crisis represents painful hardship for millions of poor and unemployed Brazilians. Of those employed, the majority earn an average of $150 per month, and the sharp increases in food costs, rent, and transportation have seriously eroded their standard of living.

The Political Impact of the Crisis

The worst economic crisis in Brazil's history, and the most widespread social malaise in any Brazilian's memory, has made the work of the Brazilian government extremely difficult. In the best of circumstances, the combined socio-economic crisis would pose a severe test for the country's political institutions. In the present worst of circumstances, the political system is demonstrating signs of severe strain.

Brazil's elaborate and successful process of political liberalization was initiated in the late 1970s. Just at that time, unfortunately, the second oil shock made it clear that even Brazil was not immune to world economic conditions. Nevertheless the nation's political elite decided to move ahead with the restoration of democratic rule. A political amnesty was promulgated. *Habeas corpus* was restored. New political parties were organized. Press freedom was confirmed. And in November 1982, nationwide elections were held for Congress, governorships, and municipal offices. The next scheduled step in this ongoing process is the election of a new president in January 1985 by an electoral college, with the inauguration to take place in March 1985.

The precipitous decline in Brazil's economic fortunes in 1982 forced the government to go to the IMF for assistance. Private commercial banks waited for the Fund's approval before releasing promised funds or agreeing to negotiate new loans. A late-1982 package of agreements came apart early in 1983; the remainder of the year was spent in renegotiating the terms of a new agreement and building domestic political support for the imposition of very tough stabilization measures.

The new government quickly discovered that the political landscape had changed dramatically after the elections. Growing social discontent had risen to a level that could no longer be ignored. The credibility of the government's economic team, led by Planning Minister Antonio Delfim Netto, plummeted as the group lurched from one unworkable agreement to another with the Fund and the private commercial banks. President João Baptista Figueiredo's physical health deteriorated badly in July 1983, necessitating a leave of absence; his political position had already eroded seriously during the first half of the year.

At the beginning of the transition from an authoritarian political system in the late 1970s, it was assumed that the pace of change would be carefully controlled by President Figueiredo, a retired general, and his immediate staff. But the President appeared to lose interest in politics as the country became increasingly politicized. A growing outcry against the economic team seemed only to strengthen his conviction that the group should remain in place. As he began to "coordinate" the procedures for a search for his successor, the system began to unravel.

New political leaders with a popular mandate raised serious questions about the sacrifices required of Brazilians as a result of the austerity measures negotiated with the IMF. President Figueiredo's seeming lack of interest in day-to-day politics led to growing dissension within his own party. The succession debate produced a number of possible candidates in the government party, but the front-runner, former São Paulo Governor Paulo Maluf, was unacceptable to President Figueiredo. Opposition party chieftains and a strong dissident wing of the government party called for direct elections to give the next president a popular mandate to deal with the nation's mounting problems. President Figueiredo at one point appeared to welcome direct elections, then changed his mind to support the indirect procedures of the electoral college. In late December 1983, the President dramatically withdrew from the position of coordinator and returned the succession process to the government party.

By March 1984, President Figueiredo decided to strongly support an indirect election and did so in a nationwide television address. Even with indirect voting, it is not impossible that some segment of the government party will vote for an opposition candidate—for a figure of "consensus"—to avoid having to vote in the electoral college for an unacceptable government party candidate. The government may seek its own consensus candidate, of course, bypassing the current crop of declared contenders in favor of a more neutral figure, either civilian or military. Although such maneuvers are a healthy part of any political system, in Brazil they are interpreted as signs of instability by the more conservative circles, both civilian and military; a similar "instability" in the early 1960s led to the military coup d'etat of 1964. Other observers believe that the main beneficiary of the current drift in Brazil would be a nationalist from the right—one able to mobilize support both among the parties and within the armed forces. The program of such a nationalist undoubtedly would take a confrontational stance on the claims of the private commercial banks and the demands of the IMF.

U.S. Policy Choices

The situation in Brazil should be cause for concern on the part of the private commercial banks and the international monetary authorities as well as the U.S. government. A prolonged economic crisis will further increase social pressure on the government of Brazil. Precipitous action against the banks and the adjustment measures of the IMF may increasingly appeal to beleaguered political leaders. Although default by Brazil might not destabilize the international financial system, it would be a signal to other states that there are limits to tolerance in Latin America of the degree of sacrifice that can be expected from the middle classes as well as the poor.

The rhetoric of Brazil's leaders on the debt issue has recently hardened and now parallels the tone used by many civilian political and business leaders. Speaking at the January 1984 Conference on the Latin American Economy in Quito, Ecuador, Brazilian Foreign Minister Ramiro Saraiva Guerreiro said that the commercial banks must understand that their long-term interests are more important than short-term profits. He called for a rescheduling of Latin America's debt—both interest payments and principal. The sentiments of Saraiva Guerreiro were enthusiastically shared by the heads of state and other foreign ministers participating in the meeting.

In the realm of commercial policy, it makes good sense to seek measures that will stimulate economic recovery in Brazil specifically and in Latin America generally.[1] An upturn in Brazil will produce immediate demand for imports that will have a favorable impact on the economies of the industrial countries by stimulating production and creating new jobs. Trade is key to any recovery in Brazil. And the United States must take the strongest possible stand against protectionism by encouraging Brazilian exports to the markets of the United States as well as Western Europe and Japan. The United States should also take the lead in seeking export credit facilities for Brazil and its neighbors. A U.S. export development fund has been proposed as one possible mechanism for fostering trade. The fund would mobilize support from the export sectors of the industrial countries through joint financing by national export credit organizations, private commercial banks, and the World Bank. This mechanism is doubly attractive because it would include the participation of both private entities and the World Bank, functioning in an expanded capacity.[2]

The debt held by the private commercial banks has become a major political issue in Latin America. To forestall Brazil and other states from being driven in desperation to consider default or a unilateral moratorium, the U.S. government needs to actively encourage private banks to reconsider immediately the structure of the debt. If it is apparent that, even with its $9-billion trade surplus in 1984, Brazil will not be able to finance both needed imports and interest payments, then a new policy is required. Why does the United States appear to be a prisoner of the private banks in formulating its policy for the Hemisphere generally and for Brazil specifically? With widespread malnutrition and even starvation very visible in Brazil, continued emphasis on adjustment and stabilization in the fourth year of a severe recession simply is not constructive policy. Moreover, U.S. official indifference to the situation runs a risk of the private banks becoming the scapegoats of the current crisis, making them far less willing in the future to provide the new lending that will be needed.

If the Reagan administration finds it difficult to "interfere" in the marketplace and to pressure the private banks to change their policy, an alternative may be to reverse current administration policy and rely more heavily on the World Bank and other international lending agencies to alleviate Brazil's dangerous predicament. Supplementing the role of the IMF in balance-of-payments financing makes good sense—even if not to the Reagan administration. The United States should support the proposal to create a new subsidiary of the Bank to provide loans to Third World countries at less burdensome rates than those applied to regular loans. Moreover, the new entity would not have to limit its total lending, dollar for dollar, to the level of its assets—as does the World Bank. It is estimated that within a year or two at the most, the IMF will require new resources. The United States should take the lead in providing those funds now and forestall an acrimonious debate in a crisis atmosphere in the future.

There is a good deal to be said for the suggestion that the leverage of the World Bank be increased. Currently the Bank borrows and lends an amount roughly equal to its paid-in and callable capital. U.S. endorsement of an increase in the Bank's borrowing capacity would signal its support both for the Bank and for the concept of increased credit for the debtor states.

Others have suggested that the World Bank and/or the IMF establish a comprehensive credit insurance facility in cooperation with individual export credit agencies in the industrial states. Measures to stimulate an inflow of equity capital through multinational investment need to be encouraged. A return to an emphasis on equity investment is a key element in any comprehensive strategy for rekindling long-term growth in countries such as Brazil.

Another set of proposals suggest the creation of an IMF-administered political-risk guarantee that would be available (presumably for a fee) to commercial banks in case of new lending to Third World countries. Such an approach should persuade the smaller private commercial banks of the need to continue participating in the syndication of new loans and in rolling over old credits, as well as provide a substantial cushion for the money-center banks that carry the burden of debt financing.

None of these proposals can be considered "radical." All offer points of departure for a careful examination of alternative mechanisms for avoiding further politicization of the debt and for generating growth in the Third World. The current policy of the United States appears to be "wait and see." The waiting period may be shorter than the Reagan administration realizes, and what they ultimately "see" may prove both unmanageable and contrary to U.S. interests in the Hemisphere.[3]

Conclusion

Brazil is an excellent test case of U.S. policy in the Hemisphere with regard to debt management. It is a major actor in the Americas. Its debt burden is mammoth. Its resource base is very promising. And most important, it is deeply committed to the restoration of democratic government, which should be a key element in the Reagan administration's foreign policy in the region. Giving Brazil sufficient space to maneuver—both economically and politically— makes good sense; it is not charity. A compelling case can be made for such a policy. It would offer Brazil an opportunity to again become economically active and to carefully identify the resources it needs to reorganize its debt and meet its financial commitments. It would allow the Brazilian government to take action to alleviate the most horrendous social implications of the economic crisis. And it would offer needed support for political democracy.

Wishful thinking will not produce the desired results. It is escapism, not policy, to hope that oil prices will not rise, that interest rates will remain stable, that the expected recovery in Western Europe will occur, and that U.S. markets will somehow remain open to Brazilian products. The Reagan administration needs to consider one of two, if not both, alternatives: direct action to provide relief for Brazil and vigorous support for the World Bank and other international organizations to do likewise.

It is of course possible that the wishful-thinking scenario will occur. Why take the chance? A well-formulated policy now would alleviate further human suffering in Brazil and demonstrate substantive U.S. support for Brazil's *abertura*—its political liberalization process. A U.S. response *now* would also serve U.S. economic needs, in that exports to Latin America would increase, creating jobs in the factories of the U.S. export sector. Everyone involved in or watching Brazil's plight agrees that the country's economic and social recovery is essential—for Brazil, and for the world. But the United States appears sluggishly unwilling to take the leads that offer the best chance of producing such a recovery. The issue needs to be widely discussed and should become a major component of the U.S. electoral debate in 1984. Surely an administration that will do anything to save El Salvador can find a rationale for saving Brazil.

Notes

[1] Pedro-Pablo Kuczynski, "Latin American Debt," *Foreign Affairs*, Vol. 61, No. 2 (Winter 1982/83), pp. 344-64, and "Latin American Debt: Act Two," *Foreign Affairs*, Vol. 62, No.1 (Fall 1983), pp. 17-38.

[2] William H. Bolin and Jorge Del Canto, "LDC Debt: Beyond Crisis Management," *Foreign Affairs*, Vol. 61, No. 5 (Summer 1983), pp. 1099-1113.

[3] Riordan Roett, "Democracy and Debt in South America: A Continent's Dilemma," *Foreign Affairs*, "America and the World 1983," Vol. 62, No. 3 (1984), pp. 695-719.

Chapter 7

Mexico's Adjustment in the 1980s: Look Back Before Leaping Ahead

Lance Taylor

In Mexico's history, public policy and national experience tend to repeat themselves with the cycles of *sexenio,* the six-year presidential term. The initial economic policies of President Miguel de la Madrid, who took office in December 1982, were based on restraint and the economist's vision of rationality. The policy offered by his administration emphasized demand contraction along the lines generally urged by the International Monetary Fund together with economy-wide attempts to "get prices right."

In content as in rhetoric, the initial de la Madrid approach bore a striking resemblance to those of his two predecessors. Luis Echeverria (1970-76) and José López Portillo (1976-82) reversed course sharply in the second and third years of their terms, shifting from contraction to expansion and from price rationalization to attempts to redistribute income through trade policy and public subsidies. The de la Madrid administration now confronts the very same mix of economic and political forces that made its predecessors change policy direction. How Mexican policy will move and how the United States will react are key economic questions for the next few years. Given the close linkages that now exist between the two countries, the actions of one are bound to have a significant effect on the other.

Mexico's current policy package responds to the crisis of 1982, when four years of growth stimulated by public investment and oil exports fell apart in financial collapse. During the growth period, public-sector spending rose from 23 per cent of gross domestic product (GDP) in 1978 to 32 per cent in 1981, while the public deficit rose to 8 per cent in 1980 and 15 per cent in 1981. Since Mexico's "oil dividend"—its petroleum profits less investment expenditures for extraction and refining—reached 4-5 per cent of GDP only in 1982 (it was small or negative before), the country spent too much too fast. That excess of imprudence prompts the cautious policy of today.[1]

Although their inheritances were different, Mexico's previous two presidents were also prudent and price-conscious for a time. Why did they not—and why may President de la Madrid not—continue such policies in the medium run?

Price Rationalization and the Exchange Rate

The rationale for correcting relative prices was the same in the first years of all three presidents. It is a rationale that borrows heavily from doctrine ruling at the World Bank and American "supply-siders."[2] Stated crudely, the argument is that the aggregate supply of goods can be increased by getting myriad micro-prices "right." The extra productive capacity is supposed to come from the elimination of price "distortions" of the type emphasized in textbook neoclassical economics. The outcome should be faster growth at lower rates of inflation. An important Mexican official tells us that: "if goods whose relative prices have suffered serious deterioration because of price controls in recent years acquire reasonable [price] levels, there might also be new investment to expand their production."[3]

News from the North and Mexico's own past both suggest that only part of a successful policy is being described here. Such simple tinkering with prices and regulatory rules did little to stimulate the U.S. economy under the Carter administration. Aggressive deficit spending by the Reagan administration did finally break the recession, but neither U.S. president had much success in raising private investment. In Mexico, investment was also stagnant during the early years of the two previous *sexenios*. This is one reason why policy may now again shift toward demand expansion. Supply-side miracle cures have been few and far between, and there is no good reason to expect one in Mexico today.

Ineffectiveness of Supply-Side Pricing

Even if the problems of manipulating aggregate demand under price reform are ignored, further difficulties remain. One is that it is not always clear just which relationships among prices are "right." And even if "correct" prices can be guessed at, they may not be attainable. The exchange rate is a key price that illustrates both problems. Both export and import trade prospects are usually judged in terms of the "real exchange rate"—that is, the nominal rate corrected for relative inflation rates in Mexico and in the economies of its trading partners. In the wake of the financial crisis, Mexico devalued sharply, raising the nominal exchange rate from 25 pesos per dollar in 1981 to about 150 pesos at the end of 1983.[4] As a result the real rate is now also high, or (in the usual confusing terminology) "undervalued."

Presidents Echeverria and López Portillo both chose to devalue early in their terms, but then allowed the real exchange rate to fall (or tend toward overvaluation) as Mexican inflation rates outran those of major trading partners. Under López Portillo, at least, it is not clear that the initial devaluation gave Mexico a real exchange rate that was "right." The country suddenly became oil-rich, and the increase in national income came in the form of dollars, not all of which could be spent abroad. Internal demand for essentially non-tradable goods such as services, transport, electricity, and commerce went up. The resultant price increases at first took the form of higher markups or profits. But these were soon passed along into higher wages, rising costs of production, and a generalized inflation. As a consequence, the real exchange rate fell.

As this process became established during the second and third years of President López Portillo's *sexenio*, his economic team chose not to increase (or devalue) the nominal exchange rate for at least two reasons. The first is that devaluation is itself inflationary, since it drives up costs of imported intermediate inputs to production. Higher costs push up the prices of final goods and accelerate the inflationary process just described. Generally, a year or so after a "maxi" devaluation, the percentage increase in the real exchange rate may be half or less the percentage increase in the nominal rate resulting from the devaluation; the rest of the change has been inflated away. Given that Mexico had newfound export possibilities anyway, the technicians no doubt questioned the merits of devaluing and thereby generating more inflation for modest real exchange-rate gains.

The second reason is that the financial system was built around "Mexdollars." These were not the "genuine article" from the U.S. Treasury, but dollar-denominated accounts (with a good rate of interest) extended by Mexican banks and ultimately backed by the Bank of Mexico's foreign-exchange reserves. Golden Mexdollars were transmuted into leaden pesos when, in the wake of the 1982 crisis, foreign reserves vanished and Mexican banks were forced to honor their dollar-denominated obligations in the devalued local currency. Before then, however, it was deemed useful to delude Mexdollar holders into believing that they could switch between currencies without risk. A stable nominal exchange rate was the tool Mexican authorities used to that end.

The fundamental reason that the real exchange rate was allowed to appreciate was the first one. A weak peso seen from the outside is equivalent to a low real wage seen from within. Based on inference from trends in the minimum wage, it seems likely that real wages rose a bit under President Echeverria and declined under President López Portillo. In the latter's *sexenio*, however, there was very rapid output growth, so that expansion of employment in effect compensated for falling wages. Had the López Portillo team pursued an aggressive exchange-rate policy, inflation would have been higher and the wage decrease even sharper.

The dilemma today is that President de la Madrid is stuck with both devaluation and unemployment. The real wage has fallen by at least a quarter since 1981, and the real GDP growth rate for 1983 will be negative—about minus 5 per cent. It is not clear how long the marriage of an undervalued exchange rate and a low real wage can last in these circumstances.

Demand Contraction: The IMF Package

On the demand side, Mexico is now operating under a Letter of Intent with the International Monetary Fund, calling for reductions in the public-sector deficit along with a high (undervalued) exchange rate and a low real wage. When agreed upon late in 1982, the package was supposed to cut the current-account trade deficit from 2.2 per cent of GDP in 1983 to 1.2 per cent in 1985; to result in GDP growth rates of zero in 1983, 3 per cent in 1984, and 6 per cent in 1985; and to reduce inflation from 100 per cent in 1982 to 55 per cent in 1984 and 18 per cent in 1985.[5]

As of late 1983, the current-account target looked likely to be overfulfilled, with perhaps a small surplus over the calendar year. Oil exports remained strong, but non-oil exports were flat, presumably due to the normal lag response to real devaluation. The reason for the current-account improvement was a sharp fall in all types of imports except food (as 1982 was another in a series of bad crop years). Drawing on stocks of importables built up before the 1982 crisis was no doubt involved in the current-account improvement, but the main cause was the unprecedented decrease in real GDP. The IMF "medicine" was working in the usual way: improving the current account by creating massive economic contraction.

The public-sector deficit was in the target range—interest payments were higher but investment lower than anticipated. The inflation target seemed likely not to be met, as firms that had been hit by the crisis sought to recover profit margins. Nominal minimum wages increased by less than half the price inflation during the first half of the year. With such a decline in the real income of wage-earners, consumption demand declined.

Without a full macro model of the economy, it is impossible to say whether the targets for the years after 1983 can be fulfilled. There is, however, room for reasonable doubt on this score. If the public sector expects its deficit targets and interest payments to remain high, then demand injection from investment and current spending must be strictly curtailed. Contractionary effects from a reduced fiscal presence will only be made worse if inflation is underestimated, since the planned nominal levels of current spending amount to less in real terms.

Other components of final demand are unlikely to demonstrate rapid growth. The price control effort will continue to hold down real wages and consumption demand, making non-oil exports the only possibly dynamic element. Here, the real devaluation will no doubt help performance, by stimulating demand for relatively cheap Mexican exports. But overall export growth will depend on the strength of the recovery in the United States. The whole program dangles on the very insecure thread of U.S. growth and low interest rates.

With regard to inflation, much will depend on the degree of wage repression that can be sustained. Simple computations can be based on a breakdown of the growth rate of prices into growth rates of wages, profits, and import costs. Assume that the profit rate is allowed to rise at 5 per cent per year to stimulate the private sector. Import costs under the IMF package are to be held constant in real terms by a "crawling peg" exchange rate policy under which gradual, small, nominal devaluations compensate for the differential between the internal and external rates of inflation. Now suppose that wages increase once a year by a fraction (the "pass-through coefficient") of last year's inflation rate. For example, the inflation rate in 1982 was about 100 per cent, and the pass-through coefficient was a bit more than one half. Because of reduced wage pressure, the 1983 inflation rate was somewhat over 80 per cent.

Running such calculations forward in time shows that even with a pass-through coefficient of 0.6 the annual inflation rate will still be about 30 per cent in 1986, well above the target. A pass-through of 80 per cent leaves inflation above 60 per cent in 1986. Eighty-per cent wage indexing has proved controversial in several countries; 60-per cent indexing may be politically *impossible* in the medium run. The conclusion is that effective control of inflation may well require profit cuts or abandonment of the crawling peg— and consequent exchange appreciation. The prospects are not promising.

Need for Financial Reform

Under both Echeverria and López Portillo, Mexdollars were viewed as an important stabilizing element in the financial system. The Mexdollar scheme was perfected in 1977, when the interest rate on dollar-denominated deposits was raised to international levels. Under Mexico's traditionally open capital market, Mexdollar and peso deposits were freely interchangeable, but the former gained in importance. In an article written in 1980, two important Mexican officials tell us, with some justification, that as Mexdollars waxed:

> capacity for managing monetary policy improved, with the reduction of capital movements across frontiers and their conversion. . .into portfolio changes between pesos and dollars within the country. In this way the financial market is more integrated with movements in the international rate of interest, but more isolated from brusque changes in capital flows.[6]

At one level, this justification for the Mexdollar system was undoubtedly correct. At another, it was dreadfully mistaken: Mexico was operating as open a capital market as any country has ever had with negligible reserve cover. For example, in 1980, net foreign assets of the financial system were 2.9 per cent of GDP, compared with an import share of 13.5 per cent. Reserves were on hand to finance between two and three months' imports—a low level for transaction purposes. There was no cover for Mexdollar deposits amounting to 4.5 per cent of GDP, let alone for the financial system's foreign liabilities of 11.4 per cent of GDP. When confidence collapsed in the crisis of 1982, two runs on deposits virtually wiped out dollar reserves, and the system fell apart.

A moral can readily be drawn from this experience: Small economies like Mexico risk great financial distress if they maintain open international commodity and capital markets without deep reserves—no matter how many sensitive but limited financial buffers like Mexdollars happen to exist.[7] The present administration in Mexico has not faced up to the choice between institutionalizing capital controls or building up reserves. With luck, it might "escape" by not deciding. But then the next president and the Mexican people might again suffer financial crisis.

Some Problems with Trade Liberalization

Policies (other than the exchange rate) that affect the current trade account are yet another divisive issue in Mexico. Under the tutelage of the IMF, President López Portillo early in this term undertook trade liberalization, de-emphasizing export subsidies and taking down the quotas and restrictions Mexico traditionally used to control imports. The most notable change brought about by this and other factors was the deterioration of non-oil exports—the result of slow U.S. growth, exchange appreciation, and the elimination of policies aimed at export stimulation. Capital-goods imports rose along with the investment increase of 5.4 per cent of GDP over the period, and interest payments also grew rapidly. The increase in consumer-goods imports accounted for one third of the change in the current account. In contrast to imports of intermediate and capital goods, rapidly rising consumer imports cannot solely be attributed to fast growth; the main causes were liberalization and taste shifts toward foreign products.

Policies for the Future

The contradictions inherent in the current policy package that have been discussed—real wages versus the real exchange rate, ineffectiveness of micro supply-side price policy, slow growth, inflation, the need for financial reform in the wake of Mexdollars, and problems with trade liberalization—all suggest changes will soon be made. What can be learned from recent Mexican history to help make the new policies productive?

Since the financial crisis is so recent, maintaining *external stability* will be a key policy concern in Mexico. The current repression of wages suggests that *distributional issues* will be politically important in the latter years of the de la Madrid term. Finally, there will be pressure from industrialists for the creation of conditions more favorable to *economic growth* and profits.

The most difficult choices relate to the exchange rate and other commercial policy tools, since these bear heavily on all of the objectives just mentioned. Any recovery in the price of oil or greater access to foreign borrowing will create pressure for exchange appreciation and a higher real wage. The outcomes might be an official decision to slow the current crawling devaluation or an increase in the rate of inflation. Either way, the stimulus for non-oil exports would be reduced. It would make sense to put into place mechanisms by which exports could be supported while overall inflationary pressures were held down. A directed export subsidy scheme is

one possibility; multiple exchange rates are another. Unlike devaluation, such policies do not generate economy-wide cost pressures toward higher prices, but act more selectively. Use of such
measures on a large scale presupposes a centrally directed industrial policy and reluctance to allow market forces alone to determine
patterns of production and trade. The historical record suggests
that this will be the policy trend during the remaining years of
President de la Madrid. *Dirigismo* has always been strong in Mexico. The challenge is to aim it at the right targets.

There is also scant reason to dismantle import protection.
Although liberalization did not star in the 1982 crisis, it was an
important supporting player. Making essentially non-competitive
consumer imports very expensive or banning them outright is an
approach that should be retained. These measures can bring immediate balance-of-payments benefits and stimulate further import
substitution in the long run. Policy choices relating to capital-goods
and intermediate imports are more difficult, since decision-makers
must balance possible inducement of import substitution against
high costs for domestic users. Sensible decision-making here involves weighing the trade-offs between the current costs of, and
possible long-term gains from, technology appropriation and the
achievement of economies of scale. The decisions reached now in
Mexico's ministries of commerce and industry will not all prove
correct when viewed in hindsight. But they will continue to be
made, and import protection will be a key ingredient.

One reason that export stimulation and import protection have
long been practiced in Mexico has been the country's wide-open
capital market; with no influence whatsoever over the capital account of the balance of payments, governments (regardless of ideological color) naturally sought to control what they could on the
current-account side. The crisis demonstrates that in the future it
will also be necessary to make it harder for finance capital to flee.
One possible corrective might simply be to maintain domestic confidence by holding far higher reserves than in the past, supplemented by appropriate "swap" arrangements between the Bank of
Mexico and other central banks. Since Mexico is now a major player
in world capital markets, it should be included in the network of
mutual support agreements that now exist among the central
banks of the advanced countries. The United States should consider
assisting Mexico in converting its current bilateral swap arrangements into a more fully international cooperative mechanism.

A second group of measures might make holding foreign assets
more difficult and non-monetized domestic assets more attractive.
The "carrot" here would be a sizable market in peso-denominated
bills and bonds, to be established beginning at the short end of the

maturity spectrum. The "pay-off" would be a market to smooth short-run portfolio shifts (as Mexdollars used to do); an additional advantage would be that the monetary authorities could break away from their antiquated reliance on changes in reserve requirements to regulate the money supply. Setting up such a market calls for confidence at home (deep reserves) and some difficulty in consummating foreign transactions (capital controls). It also requires a plausible financial instrument, such as Brazil's successful use of Treasury paper or Colombia's *certificados de abonos tributarios,* which are tied to export finance. Mexican financial experts should not be hard-pressed to invent something similar, if their attention can be directed within.

The "stick" in the capital-market policy would be wide-ranging controls over capital movements. There is no dearth of instruments that have been effective in other economies—prior deposits with the banking system in exchange for access to loans, prior permits, and total prohibition of certain types of transactions, such as very short-term loans. At the same time, the state could build up long-run dollar balances apart from monetized reserves. Partial immobilization of oil reserves in a "National Stabilization Fund" held abroad would be an appropriate policy when the next market recovery comes; letting all the dollars into the country would simply set the stage for the sort of speculation that took place in 1981 and 1982. Finally, steps should be taken to dissuade Mexican nationals from holding large accounts in foreign currencies. Mexico is virtually the only developing country that extends such open capital market privileges to its wealthy citizens. Legal sanctions against abuses can only be effective if attitudes within the country support them. If the de la Madrid campaign for moral renovation is to be effective at any level of Mexican society, it must begin with addressing the issue of capital flight.

To control inflation, an internal incomes policy has to be coordinated with demand pressures (or the lack of same) coming from oil sales abroad. Under both Echeverria and López Portillo, inflation reacted to the overall level of aggregate demand. However, the process of inflation was itself intimately linked to foreign price increases (reduced in impact by exchange appreciation) and internal cost pressures. In such circumstances, inflation can be slowed by four types of incomes policy: wage repression, nominal exchange-rate appreciation (or slower depreciation in a crawling peg), reductions in indirect tax rates, and policies aimed at reducing markup rates.

All these policies restrain inflation, but each has undesirable side effects. Again, the economic team must balance favorable and unfavorable consequences. For example, wage repression faces obvious ethical objections and is fraught with political risk if pursued too aggressively. Exchange appreciation creates loss of competitiveness—a particularly difficult problem in a developing country afflicted with the oil syndrome. Markups may be reduced by effective trade liberalization, which may also retard the process of import substitution. Price controls are difficult to apply administratively, and always create the danger of company owners abandoning the economy through capital flight. Under present circumstances, wage repression seems likely to prove increasingly difficult, and trade liberalization will not be pursued if the Mexican growth rate comes back up and import demand rises. This leaves only the options of exchange appreciation and some version of price controls. But these, in turn, require the interventions in trade and capital markets discussed above to be effective. A policy package of the type described here is best pursued in an integrated fashion, since each intervention is dependent on the others for success.

The final area of concern is the internal distribution of income. Part of the problem of chronically lagging agricultural supply, for example, stems from the low incomes received by traditional producers of key crops, including maize and beans. Under López Portillo, an attempt was made to rectify this through an expanded program of food subsidies to both producers and consumers. But the program was abandoned under de la Madrid as part of the governmental reshuffling that occurs with each new *sexenio*. The usual resistance by the IMF to any kind of food-subsidy scheme also played a role in the program's demise. Interestingly enough, poor agricultural performance and political pressures led to renewed interest in both producer and consumer subsidy schemes during 1983, and administrative organs duplicating some functions of the earlier program of subsidies began to appear. How rapidly they grow will provide one basis for judging overall shifts in economic policy.

Migration is also intimately linked to the income distribution issue. Labor flows to and from the United States have eased adjustment on both sides of the border. In the long run, however, the distributional changes necessary to moderate pressure for migration must come from Mexico. Bold tax and transfer policies designed to help poor people will ultimately become essential. At the same time, such moves may undermine the business class's faith in the system.

If successfully implemented as a package, the policy measures proposed above might provide sufficient incentives to rentiers and entrepreneurs (not to mention bureaucrats and politicians) to direct their investment and energies inward by discouraging the accumulation of foreign bank accounts and consumer luxuries. If this redirection of economic energies fails, not much hope can be retained for the autonomous development of Mexico.

Alternatives for the United States

The political and economic patterns that drive each *sexenio* cycle are well established in Mexico, and there is little that outsiders can do to influence their course. Movement toward a more inward-oriented strategy, with more of a governmental role in industrial policy and more emphasis on income redistribution, may be inevitable over the next few years. If such a shift does take place, the born-again or newly arisen policy makers in charge of implementing it will not be avidly pro-American.

For the United States—faced with such attitudes—the best profile is likely to be a low one. In particular, tranquility should be maintained on the financial front. Mexican external liabilities are to a large extent assets of American banks, and confrontation between debtors and creditors will do no one any good. Rather, American policy should be directed toward completing the integration of Mexico into the world financial system.

Beyond that, the policies likely to contribute the most to steady relationships with Mexico are forbearance as export subsidy schemes start to appear, an open mind about migration, and an open purse at the IMF. Rigid U.S. opposition to the likely direction of Mexican policy in the period ahead—or aggresssive attempts to web Mexico into a grand North American economic system—will only bring grief to both sides.

Notes

[1] For more detailed and quantitative analysis of most topics in this paper, see Lance Taylor, "The Crisis and Thereafter: Macroeconomic Policy Problems in Mexico," paper presented to the Conference on Economic Problems of Common Concern to Mexico and the United States, University of California at Santa Cruz, November 10-12, 1983.

[2] See World Bank, *World Development Report, 1983* (New York: Oxford University Press, 1983), especially Chapter 6. Formal justification for American supply-side ideas is given by Victor A. Canto, Douglas H. Jones, and Arthur B. Laffer, *Foundations of Supply-Side Economics* (New York: Academic Press, 1983).

[3] Francisco Gil Diaz, "Investment and Debt: A Perspective for the Next Decade," paper presented to the Conference on Economic Problems of Common Concern to Mexico and the United States, University of California at Santa Cruz, November 10-12, 1983.

[4] In 1983, dual exchange rates ruled throughout the year. The quoted rate is an average.

[5] Several descriptions of the IMF/de la Madrid policy package have circulated in

Mexico. The one here follows Jaime Ros, "La Política de Estabilización: Problemas y Perspectivas," paper presented to the Seminar on the Mexican Economy: Current Situation and Macroeconomic Perspectives, El Colegio de México, August 8-10, 1983.

[6] Leopoldo Solis and Socrates Rizzo, "Excedentes Petroleros y Apertura Externa," in Ricardo Ffrench-Davis, ed., *Las Relaciones Financieras Externas: Su Efecto en la Economía Latinoamericana* (Mexico City: Fondo de Cultura Económica, 1983), p. 375.

[7] Further substantiation of this point is provided by the case of Thailand, another economy that has traditionally maintained open capital markets. There, commercial banks obtain 10-20 per cent of their resources abroad, but lend only in local currency. Nationals cannot hold foreign-denominated deposits and, most important, the Central Bank retains reserves substantially larger than the commercial banks' foreign liabilities. When faced with severe external pressure after the oil shocks, Thailand did not have a run on local foreign exchange deposits and a financial crisis. Deep dollar cover frightens off speculators.

Chapter 8

Central America and the Caribbean: Adjustment in Small, Open Economies

DeLisle Worrell

Notable similarities exist between the economies of Caribbean and Central American states, even though history, language, commerce, and intellectual tradition have distanced the English-speaking Caribbean from Latin America. Recent U.S. policy toward the region has, if nothing more, turned a spotlight on the middle Americas as a whole. Countries of the region are becoming more aware of neighbors who speak different languages and more interested in their economies. By comparing the economic fortunes and the economic policies of two countries of the English-speaking Caribbean and two countries of the Spanish-speaking isthmus, we may gain insights about the way small, open economies adjust to external shocks. This chapter explores the impact on these four economies of the policies of multinational institutions and industrialized countries and the effectiveness of their domestic policy instruments.

The countries considered in this chapter—Barbados, Costa Rica, Jamaica, and Nicaragua—are all small, developing, and highly trade-oriented (see Table 1). Their shares of tradable goods in total production are high, as are their ratios of exports and imports to national income. The countries produce a limited range of goods for export, relying on imports to provide variety in domestic consumption. Imports provide most raw material inputs for production, almost all fuels, and all machinery. Bank credit is the most important source of working capital and must be considered a vital factor of production. Labor costs are below those of newly

Table 1. Statistical Profiles, 1981

	Barbados	Costa Rica	Jamaica	Nicaragua
GNP per capita (US$)	3,500	1,430	1,180	860
Ratio of exports to GDP	0.67	0.37	0.33	0.20
Ratio of imports to GDP	0.80	0.46	0.50	0.50[a]
Import classification (percentages)				
Consumer goods	0.35	21	13	29[a]
Intermediates	0.29	40	34	38[a]
Fuels	0.14	17	33	20[a]
Capital Goods	0.22	21	20	12[a]
Employment by sector, 1980 (percentages)				
Agriculture	8	29	21	49
Industry	26	23	25	20
Services	66	48	53	30
Average per capita wages per month (US$)	300	84	216	200[a]
Ratio of investment in GDP	0.29	0.18	0.19	0.16[a]

[a] 1979.

Sources: For Barbados: Central Bank of Barbados, *Annual Statistical Digest 1982* and *Balance of Payments 1982* and Government of Barbados, *Economic Report 1982*. For other countries: World Bank, *World Development Report*; IMF, *International Financial Statistics*; IDB, *Economic and Social Progress in Latin America* (various years).

industrializing countries, because of a reserve of unemployed labor, but they are considerably higher than in the low-income developing countries. Most of the labor force remains in agriculture and services, with only small proportions in manufacturing and mining. In all of the four countries, banking services are widely used by households as well as firms; until recently all of these countries featured a mix of indigenous and foreign banks, with one or two large institutions dominating and leading the market.

In the 1950s and 1960s, the economies of all these countries grew at annual rates of 5 to 10 per cent, largely as a result of new lines of production. In all cases, significant light manufacturing emerged during this period, mainly in response to regional market opportunities, but with some industries exporting to the United States as well. In Nicaragua and Costa Rica, new agricultural staples were introduced and expanded rapidly; in Barbados and Jamaica, tourism became an important economic activity. The exploitation of bauxite substantially improved the performance of the Jamaican economy.

Inflation rates remained moderate during these years, although they tended to accelerate in the last half of the 1960s. Countries suffered balance-of-payments turbulence from time to time, but there were no prolonged crises. In part this reflected the unwillingness or inability of monetary authorities to finance counter-cyclical government spending. Commercial banks were never very forthcoming with finance for governments, which were forced to curb outlays when the economies, and in particular the export sectors, sagged. Foreign-exchange losses quickly became self-correcting in the absence of sources of funds from central as well as commercial banks to sustain expenditure in excess of national income.

However, three of the four countries continued to have a residue of chronic unemployment as economic growth failed to generate sufficient jobs. In Jamaica and Nicaragua, rapidly rising population exacerbated the problem; in Barbados, where a low birth rate slowed the growth of the labor force, unemployment was less severe. Internal migration created further imbalance in the labor force in Jamaica, with urban population growth reaching unmanageable proportions and an inevitable increase in social and political tension.

Political development in these countries in the post-World War II period presented many contrasts. Jamaica and Barbados became constitutionally independent at the end of a gradual process of increasing self-rule; like Costa Rica, they featured a parliamentary system with regular electoral competition between political parties. Nicaragua remained under authoritarian rule throughout the 1950s and 1960s.

The concentration of income varied widely among the four countries. Nicaragua featured a glaring dichotomy between ownership and privilege on the one hand, and the need to work and deprivation on the other. Jamaica possessed great extremes of wealth and poverty, but the country also boasted a substantial and increasingly affluent middle class with growing economic and political influence. In Barbados and Costa Rica, economic development during the 1950s and 1960s contributed to narrowing the income distribution range. Although neither country had succeeded in eliminating destitution by the end of the 1960s, obvious deprivation was less common there than in Jamaica or Nicaragua.

The Seventies (1970-79)

The economic fortunes of the four countries began to diverge in the 1970s, when they, like all developing nations, were hit with a series of unsettling world economic events. It was then that the industrial countries began their long bout with inflation. The prices of their exports to the region started to rise, soon to be followed by the sudden oil price increase. The prices of agricultural exports (especially important for Costa Rica and Nicaragua) fluctuated widely at the same time that demand for minerals and tourism contracted in the wake of widespread recession, with particularly serious implications for Jamaica and Barbados.

In Nicaragua and Jamaica, natural and political disasters exacerbated the negative external economic trends, resulting in economic contraction on a devastating scale. In Nicaragua, one of the most destructive earthquakes of recent times demolished the capital, Managua, in 1972. The civil war that broke out only six years later, in 1978, virtually halted economic production. In Jamaica, the government that came to power in 1972, under the leadership of Michael Manley, embarked on a program of nationalization and collective ownership in the mid-1970s. Major sugar farms were converted to workers' co-operatives, many large hotels were bought by the government, and the state took significant shares in the mining and financial sectors. These initiatives proved disastrous, failing to reduce inequities in income distribution and undermining output and productivity in agriculture. The country entered a period of decline in 1974 that continued without interruption until the end of the decade. The adverse effects of external disequilibria were aggravated by ill-judged domestic policies and by the vacillation of policymakers.[1] Jamaica's economy was dealt a further blow when the disastrous hurricane of 1976 brought on floods that decimated agricultural output.

In contrast, the economies of Barbados and Costa Rica remained in reasonable shape for most of the 1970s. Both countries experienced slower real output growth and episodes of high inflation and foreign-exchange loss, yet generally remained on an expansion path. In Barbados, however, that expansion was based narrowly on tourism growth for most of the decade and therefore seemed always to be at risk.

The Second Oil Shock and Aftermath (1979-82)

The second oil crisis of 1979 and the severe world economic recession that accompanied it found Nicaragua at an economic standstill, the Jamaican economy contracting, Barbados on a tenuous path of economic expansion, and Costa Rica alone in reasonably good health. In the ensuing years, however, all four countries found themselves in serious economic difficulty. The principal external sources of disequilibrium were continued inflation in the industrial world (affecting developing-country imports), the oil price increase, a deep recession in the industrial world, further instability in the prices of developing-country exports, and the high cost of capital.

In Nicaragua, falling export prices in 1979 added to the losses caused by the rising price of oil. The Sandinista government managed to get the economy going again, and output briefly rose in 1980 and 1981. Prices recovered enough to cover additional oil costs in 1980, but this gain lasted only for that year. The terms of trade worsened with the decline in export prices in 1981 and 1982 (despite the slight decline in the price of oil in 1982). A combination of severe drought in some areas and extensive floods in others caused heavy losses in output. Inflation rates fluctuated between 20 per cent and 50 per cent. Foreign-reserve losses outweighed the modest accumulation of 1981. In 1982, efforts to sustain the growth momentum of 1980 and 1981 failed, and production declined.

In Jamaica, the economy continued to falter for multiple reasons, including increases in the prices of oil and other imports, failure to attract the investment inflows that were expected after the change of government in 1981, and the decline in sugar prices in 1981. The change in government also failed to arrest the flight of capital, and few of the skilled personnel who had left in large numbers in the 1970s were induced to return. The recession in North America—particularly the closure of aluminum plants in the southern United States due to significant increases in energy costs—had an especially severe impact on Jamaica's exports of bauxite and alumina. Moreover, Jamaica's substantial inflows from multinational lending agencies (the Inter-American Development Bank and the World Bank) and from governments (Canada and the United States) were largely neutralized by the country's heavy burden of repayment on earlier loans. Thus net inflows for projects during the 1979-81 period were only 37 per cent of the gross. The shortages of foreign exchange, the uncertain investment climate, and the large-scale emigration of skills in the 1970s had so "decapitalized" Jamaican industry and agriculture that supply could not be quickly increased. In theory, spare capacity existed, but in practice, the neglect of maintenance and the failure to keep up with new technology meant that little of this capacity could be activated without new investment. Output fell each year except for 1981, when production just managed to match the previous year's level; unemployment, already in excess of 25 per cent, rose still further; inflation rates remained at double-digit levels.

In Barbados, the oil price rise did not have immediate consequences, since demand for the country's tourist services remained strong for a while and the price of sugar, the main agricultural product, rose sharply in 1979. Barbados also was able to maintain sizable capital inflows for improvements in infrastructure and for the expansion of tourist accommodation. Foreign-exchange receipts were sufficient to finance quite substantial import growth in 1979 and 1980. Output continued to rise until 1980, when the rate of growth reached 7 per cent. But 1981 and 1982 were years of contraction. The terms of trade turned against the country in 1981 and 1982, with a fall in sugar prices that greatly outweighed gains from earlier sugar price peaks, and with further pressure on import prices. Recession in North America also slowed the demand for manufactured exports and tourist services. Employment fell, prices rose more quickly, and the balance of payments deteriorated badly—further aggravated by domestic supply problems, particularly in the sugar industry. A switch from local to foreign financial asset-holding followed the dramatic rise in interest rates in major financial markets in 1981, until Barbadian rates were forced up in response. Capital inflows stayed high up to 1982.

In Costa Rica, the growth rate dropped from 9 per cent in 1979 to 1 per cent in 1980, with output contracting thereafter. Inflation rates exploded from 20 per cent in 1979 to 90 per cent in 1982. A massive drain of foreign-exchange reserves in 1979 marked the onset of a continuing balance-of-payments crisis. The economy first suffered a collapse in coffee prices, soon followed by the oil price rise. Direct investment fell by over 50 per cent in 1981, partly because of the global slowdown in foreign private investment, but largely because the Central American Common Market became moribund, eliminating the strongest incentive to potential investors to produce in the region. Although Costa Rica itself suffered no political dislocation, the political instability of its neighbors also may have helped to discourage foreign investors. Massive short-term capital outflows intensified the country's problems. Despite efforts to contain expenditure on foreign commodities, the authorities ran out of foreign exchange, and unpaid foreign arrears built up rapidly in 1981 and 1982.

Governmental Responses to the Crisis

In all four countries, the governments recognized that a slowdown in national expenditures was inevitable because of foreign-exchange stringency. There was no leeway in national budgets to boost incomes to keep up with accelerating costs of living and no way to compensate for effective loss of foreign purchasing power. The hope was that sufficient foreign financing could be secured to cushion the shock of contraction and to allow time to establish new activities that could earn foreign exchange. For the short run, governments adopted a range of fiscal and monetary curbs, interest-rate and exchange-rate adjustments, and controls on foreign currency use. The timing of implementation, the comparative importance placed on each of these instruments, the combinations in which the techniques were used, and their overall effectiveness varied considerably from country to country.

The Nicaraguan government opted for a combination of controls on foreign transactions, fiscal expansion, and external finance. Austerity measures introduced in January 1980 included import restrictions and exchange controls. In September 1980, US$582 million of Nicaragua's foreign debt was rescheduled, while about US$100 million in lending commitments was secured from socialist countries and the United States. The U.S. aid was suspended by the Reagan administration, however, after US$50 million of an agreed $65 million had been disbursed. The government announced its intention to activate idle capacity and promote exports, but efforts in this direction were largely stymied by import and exchange controls, which created bottlenecks in the flow of essential supplies. An expansionist fiscal stance resulted in part from efforts to cope with recent insurrection and disastrous floods. The budget deficit widened from 7 per cent of gross domestic product (GDP) in 1979 to

12 per cent in 1982, and the government's share of credit in 1981 was about 35 per cent.

Jamaica made extensive use of IMF facilities in 1979, 1981, and 1982, although the country had repeated difficulty in meeting program targets (which accounted for the lack of drawings in 1980). In 1980, Jamaica also secured accommodation from commercial banks. Real imports were cut back very severely, as a result of the decline in economic output, particularly in 1979 and 1980. But foreign-payments arrears mounted nonetheless. Although the authorities maintained strict import and foreign-exchange controls, with national foreign-exchange budgets prepared each year, the controls were never fully effective; the import targets were always exceeded and a substantial unofficial market in foreign exchange circumvented the officially monitored system. As a result of black market activities, the authorities failed to attract sufficient foreign currencies into the official system to defend the exchange rate, and a multiple exchange-rate system was introduced in January 1983. The government deficit remained near 15 per cent of GDP, with current spending exceeding revenue and nothing left to help finance capital works. The ratio of government expenditures to GDP kept on expanding, largely because government services were not cut severely enough to match the contraction of the overall economy. The cost of borrowing from the banking system was driven up by a combination of rising foreign interest rates and heavy public-sector borrowing, which pushed up local borrowing rates.

To finance its balance-of-payments deficit and to shore up foreign-exchange reserves, the Barbados government borrowed from commercial banks in 1981 and subsequently also from the International Monetary Fund, under a two-year stand-by arrangement that came into force in October 1982. Projected foreign debt-service ratios remained comparatively low—in the region of 10 per cent for 1982-87—but the relatively short maturities of this balance-of-payments support meant that their effect on the debt-service ratio was disproportionately large. Severe import compression was needed in spite of the external borrowing, and real imports were cut back in 1982. The government kept a tight rein on its budget—except in 1981, which was an election year. The ratio of the budget deficit to GDP was 5 per cent or less (except in 1981, when it was 8 per cent), the share of government activity in national product was shrinking ever so slightly, and savings on the current account provided the equivalent of over 10 per cent of gross capital formation (again, except in 1981). The Central Bank maintained restrictions on consumer credit to inhibit imports of durables, but made provision for working capital for firms at moderate cost.

Domestic interest rates nevertheless were forced upward by the rise in rates abroad and by the consequent outflows of investment income and trade-related finance.

In Costa Rica, budget-tightening measures and exchange rate adjustment were introduced in the hope of securing sufficient IMF finance to maintain external payments balance; by 1981, however, it was clear that these efforts were meeting with little success. A series of fiscal austerity measures introduced in 1980, 1981, and 1982 reduced the deficit from a ratio of 8 per cent of GDP in 1980 to less than 4 per cent in 1982. Current-account dissaving of nearly 4 per cent in 1980 was converted to a small surplus in 1982. Yet the government's demand for credit remained high, absorbing about one third of the total. The balance of payments deteriorated despite these fiscal measures and the 1979 and 1981 borrowing from the IMF. Substantial foreign-payments arrears built up in 1980 and 1981. The colon (Costa Rica's currency) was allowed to float in December 1980 and its value fell by one third during the next year—with the unofficial rate for U.S. dollars reportedly three times as high as the official. The fiscal and exchange-rate measures undertaken in 1981 were not sufficient to satisfy IMF requirements, resulting in the suspension in August 1981 of the IMF extended facility arrangement agreed to three months earlier. Import controls were tightened in September, and the government secured a moratorium on US$1.8 billion of external debt in that same month. The balance-of-payments crisis remained unresolved, and a new stand-by arrangement with the IMF was agreed to only in January 1983.

Challenges and Responses: An Evaluation

Deteriorating terms of trade constituted a problem for all four countries. The prices of coffee, sugar, and bauxite and alumina were extremely unstable and failed to match the pace of general inflation over the period as a whole. All four countries suffered marked increases in import prices; for most, the cumulative effects of inflation in their imports from industrial countries added a much heavier charge on foreign-exchange earnings than did the oil increases. Recession cut the demand for some commodities more than for others. Tourism, bauxite and alumina, and some lines of manufacturing for the U.S. market proved most susceptible. The demand for food products and cotton (an important Nicaraguan export) was rather more resilient.

All the countries had difficulty in raising the level of supply to exploit fully the potential export demand in markets to which they had access. The reasons varied. In Barbados, for example, sugar production fell because the industry failed to adequately manage the transition from outmoded technologies that yielded low productivity (especially in harvesting) to modern methods needed to maintain competitiveness. Poorly developed marketing skills hampered the export of manufactured goods in all cases. The elements also contributed to the problem, with flood and drought reducing agricultural output in Jamaica and Nicaragua. Domestic policies sometimes added to producers' difficulties. Faced with a shortage of foreign exchange for the purchase of raw materials, Jamaica and Nicaragua tried administrative rationing. The resulting inefficiencies caused further losses. In times of economic difficulty, the managements of enterprises proved largely incapable of coping with the situation effectively, resulting in low utilization of capacity, poor quality control, wasteful inventory practices, and poor industrial relations. Increases in the cost of bank finance in Barbados, Costa Rica, and Jamaica were a further inhibition to raising the level of output.

Investment slowed everywhere due to growing uncertainty about markets and costs. The slowdown in world trade growth dampened export prospects, and the contraction in domestic and regional economies reduced the size of the most easily accessible markets. The enormous variation in interest rates and the instability of exchange rates in Jamaica and Costa Rica complicated investment planning; most firms decided to postpone investment until economic conditions stabilized. Unsuccessful stabilization programs in Jamaica and Costa Rica aggravated the situation, while civil war and increasing isolation from the North American mainstream made Nicaragua unappealing to investors. Governments generally lacked sufficient finance to allow them to compensate for low private-sector investment. Where additional project finance could have been supported without increasing debt servicing to intolerable levels, as in Barbados, projects could not be brought on stream any more quickly.

A decline in foreign investment was particularly noticeable in all of the countries. Multinational companies cut back on investment in developing countries during the global recession, and high rates of interest and variable exchange rates strongly discouraged fixed capital formation. Unfriendly economic and political strategies, war, social unrest, and increasing bureaucratization in some countries made the situation even less inviting. As a result, productive capacity failed to expand at all in Nicaragua and Jamaica, while Barbados and Costa Rica suffered drastic slowdowns. Low investment also diminished the speed with which the countries were able to embody new technology so as to maintain international competitiveness (although the adoption of new techniques varied considerably among countries—from slow in Barbados to negligible in Nicaragua).

The amount of balance-of-payments financing made available to these countries never came close to offsetting cyclical terms-of-trade swings and sudden demand shocks. As John Williamson has argued, access to balance-of-payments financing should be sufficient to cover reversible foreign-exchange losses and to allow adequate time to engineer changes in production and consumption in response to more fundamental changes in foreign demand and prices.[2] Reversible losses (resulting from a self-correcting, one-shot market failure) should be covered because very erratic foreign-exchange flows are damaging for investment; this forms the rationale for IMF support in cases of export shortfalls through the Fund's Compensatory Financing Facility (CFF). Unexpected foreign-exchange shocks may require fundamental adjustment, which involves not only foreign exchange but also time; if foreign exchange is not forthcoming in the short run in quantities sufficient to avert an immediate crisis, the prospects for orderly adjustment quickly recede.

If needs are estimated to amount to the sum of terms-of-trade losses and reductions in external demand, balance-of-payments support loans covered no more than 65 per cent of such requirements in Barbados, Costa Rica, and Nicaragua during the 1979-82 period; Jamaica borrowed considerably in excess of its needs as here defined (see Table 2). Moreover, much of the debt accumulated during the 1970s carried maturities of no more than five years, making the recent burden of repayment very heavy. Interest rates sharply increased the real cost of borrowing: in 1981 and 1982, loans raised by Barbados, Jamaica, and Costa Rica bore interest charges that exceeded the annual increases in these countries' export prices by three to four percentage points. With financing both expensive and inadequate, domestic adjustment had to be very abrupt, as evidenced by the many sharp contractions of imports.

Financing to make up for short-run variations in the terms of trade is offered only under the IMF's Compensatory Financing Facility. The formula used to compute eligibility assumes that the losses are entirely due to export effects; no allowance is made for fluctuations in the prices of imports. Furthermore, calculations are made for the value of exports, rather than export prices, so that the recipient country gets no credit for aggressive export marketing or for successful supply policies pursued in the face of declining prices. The limit for drawings under the CFF is one quarter of the coun-

Table 2. Balance-of-Payments Financing and Needs

	Years[a]	Overall Need[b]	Terms of Trade Loss	Financing As % of Need	As % of TOT[c]	CFF[d] as % of Need
Barbados	1981	BDS$ 89.8mil	BDS$ 62.1mil	32.7	54.6	
	1982	BDS$112.8mil	BDS$196.8mil	42.0	24.1	23.9
Costa Rica	1980	Cor. 0.2bil	Cor. 0.3bil	65	43	
Jamaica	1979	J$ 210.2mil	J$ 234.6mil	—[e]	—[e]	20.6
	1980	J$ −20.6mil	J$ 53.9mil	144.0	364.2	203.3
	1981	J$ 21.2mil	J$ 53.6mil	⋯	18.1	⋯
Nicaragua	1979	Col.-0.66bil	Col. 0.11bil	⋯	—	⋯
	1980	Col.-0.46bil	Col. 0.14bil	⋯	—	⋯
	1982	Col. 0.99bil	Col. 0.14bil	—	—	—

[a] Year when either a terms-of-trade loss or a "balance-of-payments need" has been identified.
[b] Defined as terms-of-trade losses plus exogenous falls in export demand; an exogenous *increase* in export demand has a negative sign.
[c] Terms of trade.
[d] Export compensatory financing facility of IMF.
[e] Net financing; repayments cancelled CFF receipts.

Sources: IMF, *International Financial Statistics* (various years); IMF *Surveys* of May 14, 1979; October 29, 1979; April 14, 1981; June 17, 1981; and August 26, 1982; Central Bank of Barbados, *Balance of Payments 1982*.

try's quota. Because of these strictures, CFF drawings for Barbados, Costa Rica, and Nicaragua covered as much as 27 per cent of financing needs (as defined above) only once (in the case of Barbados in 1982). Jamaica's CFF drawings covered between 21 and 43 per cent of its requirements.

The IMF's experience in the Caribbean and Central America cannot be a source of satisfaction to the Fund's directors. Jamaica, which has used Fund resources to the limit, has yet to resolve its adjustment problems, which date from 1976. The controversial nature of Fund conditionality as applied to Jamaica has made the institution a *bête noire* to Jamaicans from the entire range of the country's political spectrum. In Costa Rica, the IMF conditions were associated with another political imbroglio, and they failed to secure the objectives set down by the Fund. The Sandinista government in Nicaragua has stayed shy of the Fund. In Barbados, a modest IMF stand-by arrangement provoked intense domestic political controversy, even though the Fund's conditions were nothing more than a rubber-stamping of a program worked out and monitored by the Barbadian authorities themselves. Management of the adjustment process would have been far less problematic without the necessity of a formal IMF imprimatur for actions that depended entirely on the abilities of local economic management.

Lines of credit from commercial banks may also be used to cover random variations in the terms of trade and reversible terms-of-trade shocks. But the commercial banks, which provided over 50 per cent of the financing extended to Barbados, Jamaica, and Costa Rica, were expensive sources; use of their resources was limited if countries wished to avoid insupportable debt-service burdens. Moreover, the banks have a kind of herd instinct and a few questionable risk cases can cause loan funds to dry up quite suddenly; reactions to the difficulties of Mexico and of Brazil graphically illustrate the point.

The flight of capital added greatly to the difficulties experienced by all four countries, although Barbados, which did not experience prolonged or extreme disequilibrium, suffered less foreign-capital loss than did the other countries. Contrary to the expectations of their advocates, aggressive exchange controls—especially if adopted only when the external payments situation is clearly out of control—simply accelerate capital flight. Provocative differentials between domestic and foreign interest rates may act as an incentive to transfer financial assets abroad, although it is doubtful that interest rates on financial assets have much to do with real investment, which varies with expected rates of return on the perceived investment opportunities. Capital outflows become uncontrollable when a country is racked by war and civil strife; Nicaragua remained subject to random disturbances even after it had emerged from the worst ravages of war, and spasmodic political violence continued in Jamaica until 1980. These countries also suffered a simultaneous exodus of skilled personnel. Since it takes many years to build up indigenous human resources, this probably was more damaging to long-term growth prospects than the outflow of finance.

None of the four governments deliberately attempted to spend its way out of disequilibrium in the 1979-82 period; instead, all tried to cut budget deficits, with varying success. Where economic contraction was severe, as in Jamaica, it proved difficult to cut government expenditures fast enough to bring the budget into better balance. A smaller fiscal gap is of course easier to close: There are more chances to cut spending without reducing employment, and a significant impact may be achieved by postponing or shelving some government investment programs. However, exogenous factors such as floods and insurrection can prejudice the chances of closing the budget deficit.

The results of the exchange-rate policies pursued by these four countries during 1979-82 will not resolve the debate between those who suspect that devaluation is destabilizing and those who regard it as an effective tool of adjustment. Advocates of devaluation argue that inflation is a reason for devaluation: A country experiencing more rapid inflation than its competitors must devalue or suffer economic decline. Skeptics point out that devaluation in open economies exacerbates inflation. In Costa Rica and Jamaica, sharp devaluation was associated with virulent inflation. Barbados, which maintained an unchanged nominal exchange rate, had the lowest inflation rates; had its currency been devalued significantly, it undoubtedly would have lost this distinction. Nicaragua did not devalue despite its high inflation rates. If it is true that exchange rates determine competitiveness, then Nicaragua should have fared much worse than the others. Yet it is not clear that it did fare worse, although it started with a very depressed production level in 1979.

Devaluation by itself rarely secures substantial improvements in the balance of external payments. Imports do not decline quickly in response to increases in their local currency costs because a large proportion of them are producer goods and because the affluent upper class's capacity to import is not immediately affected to any extent. Exports do not respond readily to the higher local currency returns because of productive capacity limits and low operating efficiencies. Devaluation may, to some extent, shift resources out of non-tradable activities and into the production of exports or import substitutes; in practice, such shifts usually take a long time to appear, and it is often hard to demonstrate that they depend crucially on the exchange rate. The inflation associated with devaluation provokes domestic cost increases, so that increases in the relative price of tradables may be short-lived. Moreover, the crucial resources for the expansion of tradable production are human skills, which are not particularly responsive to aggregate relative-price relationships.

All four countries used controls on foreign-exchange spending—both exchange controls and import restriction—but with varying intensity. Very few items were subject to detailed scrutiny in Barbados, but in Jamaica and Nicaragua, controls were pervasive. Nicaragua seems to have controlled foreign-exchange usage effectively, but at the cost of severe inflation and industrial dislocation. In Jamaica, the controls system was decidedly destabilizing. Imports and foreign-exchange spending targets were always exceeded, and by substantial amounts. The controls induced excess demand for foreign exchange, leading to extensive black markets in imports, exports, tourism services, and foreign exchange. The attempt to push controls beyond the limits of the government's administrative capacity, the capability of information systems, and the tolerance of citizens resulted in an effective loss of control. In both Jamaica and Nicaragua, pervasive controls created distortions in the allocation of resources and in relative prices, which helped erode productive capacity and heightened anxieties that contributed to capital flight.

The alternative to foreign-exchange controls is more severe domestic deflation, which usually appears to be an unacceptably harsh strategy for adjustment, but is generally preferable. When a country has insufficient foreign exchange, expenditures abroad must be cut. Control mechanisms attempt to do this without reducing overall domestic spending; to be effective, the controls must direct the "excess" spending power to home goods. Inevitably a great deal of this excess must be used to pay the cost of circumventing the exchange control system, by influence peddling and purchase of foreign currency at highly inflated black-market exchange rates. Domestic production of goods is heavily import-using in any case, and so cannot be expanded to meet any increased demand, given the foreign-exchange shortage. To the extent that controls succeed in arresting a hemorrhage of foreign exchange in the open economy, they do so by reducing overall expenditure, not by switching demand to domestic products. It is better to secure the contraction directly by fiscal measures, for example. The costs of fiscal contraction—inflation, and perhaps a small addition to unemployment—are nowhere as high as the costs of control: shortages, disruptions of production, antipathy between government and citizenry, loss of confidence in economic management, and a decline in private investment.

Jamaica and Costa Rica were among a number of developing countries that raised interest rates in response to pressure from the revisionists who dominate the multilateral lending institutions. For many years, conventional wisdom suggested that low interest rates promoted the growth of less developed countries by lowering the costs of capital. The governments of some developing countries helped discredit this view by financing profligate spending with cheap local borrowing, using the excuse that fiscal spending was "developmental." In the early 1970s came the radically opposing view that low interest retarded development by reducing the accumulation of bank deposits and encouraging loans to the "wrong sectors" (that is, those that were very capital-intensive). The revisionist position, which is now a tenet of World Bank-IMF orthodoxy, holds that countries may raise the real savings rate by increasing nominal interest rates to create as large a gap between the nominal rate and the rate of domestic inflation as exists between interest rates in major financial markets and world inflation. The assumptions underlying this view cannot be sustained in the Caribbean.[3]

The cost of borrowing to finance production overheads is far more influential than the return on bank deposits. In the circumstances of 1981 and 1982, attempts to lift interest rates well clear of the rate of inflation led to high and variable domestic interest rates. Finance costs rose to levels prohibitive for some firms, boosting production costs and adding to inflationary pressures, and discouraging fixed capital formation. At Costa Rican inflation rates, real interest rates proved elusive, even at ruinous nominal interest rates. Caribbean experience suggests that there is a good case for maintaining close correspondence between *nominal* rates at home and rates in financial markets (compared with the World Bank view that *real* rates should be equal at home and abroad). However, attempts to keep nominal interest rates ahead of inflation are costly; rising finance costs will fuel inflation and reduce the profitability of export firms and import-competing firms that cannot manipulate the prices of the products they sell.

Recommendations

In small, open developing economies such as the Caribbean and Central American countries examined in this chapter, successful adjustment with growth requires actions on both the domestic and international fronts. Poorly conceived domestic economic policies can exacerbate external shocks and drive an economy into deepening recession, and shortsightedness leaves the country with few adjustment options. However, many of the policies of industrial countries, multinational agencies, and international commercial banks make it difficult for even the most intelligent and carefully executed domestic strategy to succeed. Specific recommendations offered here relate to both short-run and long-run domestic strategies, as well as to the policies of foreign governments and multilateral institutions.

Domestic adjustment strategies. The primary objective of domestic economic policy should be to avoid sharp discontinuities. The art of adjustment is to make changes in ways that do not cause a decay of productive capability. Economic expansion depends on confidence, which develops as people come to accept certain givens about the economic adjustment process. Investment takes place when people feel sufficiently confident in the predictability of behavior patterns and are able to base their plans on them. Radical policy changes—such as big devaluations, once-and-for-all liberalization of trade and finance, wholesale nationalization, or the imposition of comprehensive administrative controls—call the accepted norms into question, increase uncertainty, and destroy confidence in the orderly processes of economic interaction. They increase the probability of industrial unrest, social conflict, and political instability. The invariable consequence is a sharp fall in investment and a reduction in the economy's long-run growth potential.

To avoid "shock treatment" policies and their harmful aftermath, economic managers must plan thoughtfully, exercise foresight, prepare economic projections, and map out strategies for a number of contingencies. Policymakers will then be primed to meet difficulties as they arise, even if problems are not always fully anticipated. The results will show in a more effective choice among the range of policy options. Furthermore, such planning may increase the flexibility of policy response: More options are available if potential threats are identified well in advance and suitable precautions taken.

Small, open economies have limited scope for short-run adjustment; the most important lesson their managers have yet to learn is how to stay within these limits. Their only powerful tool for adjusting expenditure is a government's budget. If it appears that an expenditure slowdown may be necessary, fiscal cutbacks should be introduced early, when modest contraction can be effective and is relatively painless. Fiscal restraint becomes increasingly difficult as the economy deteriorates, government revenues lag, and growing unemployment increases pressures for government spending. Governments of open economies must avoid any temptation to spend their way out of a downturn, even one that is thought to be temporary. The resulting demand for foreign exchange carries a risk of an external payments crisis that can seldom be justified.

The contemporary emphasis on policies to alter relative prices in the adjustment process is greatly overdone. No doubt authorities should be concerned about providing incentives for the production of tradable goods in countries where foreign-exchange scarcity may limit the pace of economic expansion. Where domestic factors cost the same to producers in all sectors, where factor use does vary with product prices or the relative prices of the factors, and where low profitability rather than managerial capability, resources, or market size is limiting production of tradables, an increase in the relative price of tradables will encourage additional output in that sector. But these conditions do not hold for much of the potential output of most small, open developing economies, leaving little "corrective" leeway for the recommended approach of "getting prices right."

In any case, there is precious little the authorities can do to affect relative prices. If they devalue, they must find ways of suppressing wages. If they raise interest rates, they are likely to depress tradable output and to fuel inflation by increasing the cost of financing. If they impose controls, they not only harm production and push up prices but also generate relative price changes quite different from what they intended as wasteful new activities emerge. The only useful tools for modifying relative prices are indirect taxation and subsidies (if a government's budget can support them), used sparingly so as not to provoke hostile reaction.

Exchange and import controls should be implemented with a light hand. Any wholesale controls will mean loss of efficiency, since governmental administrative capacity is generally limited. If controls are extensive, they provide fertile ground for influence peddling—promoting the growth of a "control-evasion industry." Selective controls are therefore recommended only for areas where administration is straightforward—for example, control of large discrete items like motor cars.

A shortage of foreign exchange may force a country to change its buying and selling price, but devaluation by itself will secure little by way of adjustment or growth. Without devaluation in these circumstances, much economic activity goes underground, where it cannot be affected by official policy. Devaluation allows the authorities to retain supervision of foreign transactions, which may then be influenced by taxes and incentives designed to affect relative prices of goods and factors of production. Monetary authorities should not wait until reserves dry up to introduce exchange-rate changes, as ample reserves will be needed to defend the new rate. They must act early to arrest any dangerous slide in reserves—before the market perceives a threat to their ability to maintain the value of the currency. It is also a good idea to raise nominal domestic interest rates well above foreign rates at the same time. Those who speculate against the currency should pay in terms of yield foregone.

Longer-term domestic policy should focus on developing human skills, diversifying the production and marketing of tradable goods, and raising productivity levels throughout the economy. The human resource is most critical to development. Countries thrive on their citizens' capacity for good management, inventiveness, and self-confidence, and on the available variety of specialized skills. With sufficient endowment in these areas, very limited physical resources and capital go a long way indeed. These capabilities may be enhanced by intensifying formal and informal personnel interchanges at all levels between industrial and developing countries. This is a relatively inexpensive investment with a potentially large payoff—even with allowances for a "brain drain." Restrictions on foreign travel to "save" foreign exchange is a short-sighted policy. Of course, an appropriate domestic educational strategy is a necessary prerequisite; it is not emphasized here only because the necessity is widely accepted, to the neglect of the qualities stressed above.

There is not much that developing countries can do to improve their terms of trade in the short run, but in the medium term they may seek to promote new exports that have brighter prospects than those currently produced. Success requires careful selection and the intensive pursuit of a few activities. There are not enough human resources to support export initiatives over a broad front; unless policymakers discipline themselves to focus on selected items, their efforts will dissipate ineffectually. The need for action is urgent and results will take time to materialize, so policies must be implemented now to create the potential for flexibility in three to five years.

Increasing productivity is essential for economic growth. As Arthur Lewis has pointed out, productivity must increase in all sectors, especially the sectors that absorb labor, if gains made in the leading sectors are to be retained.[4] If wages in the tradable sector are determined by the supply of labor available from a low-productivity sector producing for the home market, then the productivity gains achieved in the tradables sector will not be received at home in the form of higher wages paid to domestic labor; instead, via product price reductions, they will flow to the tradable sector's customers overseas.

Developing countries need not operate on the frontiers of new technology, but they should ensure that all investment contributes to raising productivity. Technological developments have opened at least two areas where developing countries may move quickly to secure productivity gains with minimum lag time. Low initial costs and ease of computer use offer developing countries with a good educational infrastructure (such as Barbados and Costa Rica) the opportunity to march smartly into the age of information. The rising cost of energy should be used as an incentive for introducing energy-efficient devices and energy conservation; developing countries will often possess an advantage in not having to convert or dispose of any wasteful, "older-generation" systems.

International policies. Industrial nations and multinational institutions must take seriously the need for adequate financing of buffer stocks and other commodity price stabilization schemes. There is no economic argument against the need for price stabilization; wild fluctuations in commodity prices are bad for developing countries because they create a bias against investment, but they also slow down world demand, to the detriment of all. The industrial countries' lack of enthusiasm for price stabilization is short-sighted, as is their support of uncompetitive agricultural activities at the expense of developing-country producers. Because the problem is political, developing countries can do the world a favor by intensifying pressure for a change of heart rather than abandoning the struggle in the face of stubborn sectoral interests in the industrial world.

The procedures of multinational lending institutions should be modified to provide rather more unconditional finance. The IMF's Compensatory Financing Facility—designed to compensate for export and other shortfalls—has worked well, but the Fund's rules have often not permitted it to cover the full amount of the shortfall. Moreover, because the export shortfall is averaged over all export commodities, the scheme needs to be supplemented with price support mechanisms for specific commodities.

The Williamson argument for financing sufficient to provide for orderly adjustment to an external disturbance seems convincing. It requires a medium-term adjustment facility linked to measures of the magnitude of external demand losses that require an extended period of adjustment. Failure to provide adequate financing to cover the effects of the second oil shock has been the international community's most conspicuous dereliction in recent years. Countries were left to cope with dramatic terms-of-trade losses on their own, with global consequences that remain with us still. Arguably, the contraction in the world economy has been far more severe than the relative price changes warranted; unquestionably, the destabilization of international financial markets has inhibited the international flow of an important factor of production (finance) to the detriment of near-term growth prospects. The financing from such a facility would be conditional, but countries would be eligible for some initial drawing if they had suffered terms-of-trade or other exogenous losses.

IMF conditionality could be made more effective by being limited to the foreign-exchange target—the target that is critical to the Fund's mission as a lending agency. Moreover, a country that meets the foreign-exchange target is in a position to service IMF credit, guaranteeing the Fund's continuing solvency. The Fund's interventions in countries' domestic policies have probably reduced its effective influence. This aspect of conditionality has given the institution a bad name, making countries shy away from use of its facilities; it has exacerbated domestic political tensions in borrowing countries because of the IMF's notoriety, prejudicing the chances of sensible adjustment programs; and it has exposed conflicts among the Fund's own staff that cannot have done much for the institution's morale. Although it is now too late to repair much of this damage, limiting conditionality to the most relevant variable might serve to remove Fund officials somewhat from the thick of conflict.

This suggestion is not very far from how things often turn out in practice; a country that violates the IMF targets but accumulates reserves has no qualms about allowing an IMF lending program to lapse. The IMF is able to exercise leverage only when reserve targets are breached. There is a misconception that targets give the IMF some control over national policy. In fact, control resides with the national authorities. If they are competent and influential, adjustment will succeed; if they are ineffectual, adjustment will fail—whether or not there are IMF targets. IMF target-setting for variables other than foreign exchange is probably counterproductive; in its zeal to obtain "realistic" targets, the Fund routinely declaims on public utility rates, bus fares, subsidies, and transfers—in effect pressing for political decisions. The ire such interventions arouse can obscure the real economic issues.

Moreover, the theory on which IMF analysis rests is controversial, and, like all economic theory, value-laden. The controversy centers on the assumptions that underlie the theory and the relationships its embodies.[5] For example, it is assumed that changes in monetary liabilities affect expenditures directly through some form of portfolio adjustment and that this adjustment process is complete within the period of analysis. There is presumed to be a correlation between financial saving (deposits) and real saving (which finances investments) and between financial accumulation and investment. These assumptions fail to acknowledge the pervasive influence of oligopoly and the inadequacies of private-sector information systems.

It is possible for a national economy to effect a balance of real output and expenditure at varying levels of output, each associated with a different distribution of income and power. At one extreme is a regime of complete "liberalization": If it works, the poorest citizens suffer enormous hardship, at least for some time. At the other extreme is the command economy: Making it work is enormously difficult, and if it does, everybody is relatively poor, but nobody is destitute. The IMF is not morally qualified to judge between these and the range of alternatives in between. Nor is it intellectually justified in applying universally a useful but nevertheless questionable economic model.

The international commercial banks must become more efficient in their lending procedures. They have not devoted adequate resources to evaluating potential clients, and they are short of expertise for such evaluations. Their assessments place too much emphasis on legal safeguards, wide margins on their cost of funds, and government guarantees. They place too little emphasis on their own hardheaded judgments of a country's ability to repay. The banks' reactions to the current international debt crisis shirk the real task of financial intermediation; by seeking cover behind an IMF shield they may obtain free of charge those very services they exist to provide.

It is hard to understand why the commercial banks so stubbornly resist the notion of long-term lending for periods approaching twenty years. It may well be argued that no one has much idea what the world will be like in twenty years, but the same may be said for the state of the world economy five or seven years hence. The margin of safety gained by limiting maturities to seven years or so cannot be of much consequence. Long-term credit would enhance clients' ability to pay and relieve the bank of the headache of redeploying maturing loans. New forms of credit insurance might be devised to cover part of the risk of lending to developing countries. Banks might seek cover from brokers offering this novel insurance for a portion of their lending, passing on the cost of premiums to their clients. Just as many central banks provide local commercial banks with forms of credit insurance, the IMF might consider selling credit insurance to banks. For prudent customers, an enhanced debt-servicing capability (for a given level of borrowing) would still make the insured long-term loan an attractive possibility.

High interest rates in international markets continue to impoverish developing countries. But only wiser economic management in the industrialized world can relieve this situation. Meanwhile, open economies must be careful not to induce capital outflows and foreign-exchange shortages by allowing a wide gap between these rates and their own.

Notes

[1] For a spectrum of opinion on the Jamaican experience of the 1970s, see Norman Girvan, Richard Bernal, and Wesley Hughes, "The IMF and the Third World: The Case of Jamaica, 1974-80," *Development Dialogue*, No. 2 (1980); Jennifer Sharpley, "Economic Management and IMF Conditionality in Jamaica," in John Williamson, ed., *IMF Conditionality* (Washington, D.C.: Institute for International Economics, 1983), pp. 233-62; Russell Kincaid, "The Fund's Assistance to Jamaica Has Sought to Check Decline. . .," *IMF Survey*, December 15, 1980; Adlith Browne, "Economic Policy and the IMF in Jamaica," *Social and Economic Studies* (University of the West Indies), December 1981; and DeLisle Worrell, "External Influences and Domestic Policies: The Economies of Barbados and Jamaica in the 1970s," *Social and Economic Studies* (University of the West Indies), December 1981.

[2] Williamson believes that a facility such as the IMF's Oil Facility of 1974 should be one of the Fund's regular lending windows. It would provide medium-term loans, with maturities that allowed for well-planned national structural adjustment rather than hasty, shock-reaction measures. The amount of the advance would presumably be linked to the estimated magnitude of the shock that generates the need for structural change. Apart from oil, other transitions resulting from technological developments (such as the serious erosion in the competitiveness of Jamaican bauxite) might be accommodated in this way to allow countries time to switch production capability elsewhere. See John Williamson, "The Lending Policies of the International Monetary Fund," in Williamson, *IMF Conditionality*, op. cit., pp. 605-60.

[3] One must assume that financial liabilities and real saving are correlated and that local and foreign liabilities are substitutes for one another. See DeLisle Worrell and Ronald Prescod, "The Development of the Financial Sector in Barbados, 1946-82," *Economic Review*, Central Bank of Barbados, September 1983.

[4] See W. Arthur Lewis, *The Evolution of the International Economic Order* (Princeton: Princeton University Press, 1977).

[5] Gerald Helleiner, "Conclusions and Policy Implications," in Williamson, *IMF Conditionality*, op. cit., pp. 581-88.

About the Overseas Development Council and the Contributors

The Overseas Development Council is an independent, nonprofit organization established in 1969 to increase American understanding of the economic and social problems confronting the developing countries and to promote awareness of the importance of these countries to the United States in an increasingly interdependent international system.

In pursuit of these goals, ODC functions as a center for political analysis, a forum for the exchange of ideas, and a resource for public education. Current projects fall within four broad areas of policy concern: trade and industrial policy, international financial issues, development strategies and development cooperation, and political and strategic aspects of U.S. economic relations with the Third World.

ODC's program is funded by foundations, corporations, and private individuals; its policies are determined by a governing Board and Council. In the selection and coverage of issues addressed by the current ODC program, including the new U.S.-Third World Policy Perspectives series that this volume initiates, the ODC staff and Board also benefit from the advice of members of the ODC Program Advisory Committee.

John W. Sewell is president of the Overseas Development Council.

The Editors

Adjustment Crisis in the Third World is the first volume in the Overseas Development Council's new series, *U.S.-Third World Policy Perspectives*. The editors of the series, Richard E. Feinberg and Valeriana Kallab, are both with the Council.

Richard E. Feinberg has been vice president of the Overseas Development Council since 1983. After coming to the Council in 1981 as a visiting fellow, he became an ODC senior fellow and director of the foreign policy program. From 1977 to 1979, Feinberg was Latin American specialist on the policy planning staff of the U.S. Department of State, prior to which he served as an international economist in the U.S. Treasury Department and with the House Banking Committee. He is currently also adjunct professor of international finance at the Georgetown University School of Foreign Service. Feinberg is the author of numerous books as well as journal and newspaper articles on U.S. foreign policy, Latin American politics, and international economics. His most recent book is *The Intemperate Zone: The Third World Challenge to U.S. Foreign Policy* (1983).

Valeriana Kallab is the Council's director of publications and senior editor. Before joining ODC in 1972 to head its publications program, she was a research editor and writer on international economic issues with the Carnegie Endowment for International Peace in New York. She was co-editor (with John P. Lewis) of *U.S. Foreign Policy and the Third World: Agenda 1983* and (with Guy F. Erb) of *Beyond Dependency: The Third World Speaks Out* (1975). She is a member of the U.S. National Commission for UNESCO.

Contributing Authors

Albert Fishlow is professor of economics at the University of California, Berkeley. From 1978 to 1983, he taught at Yale University, where he also directed the Concilium on International and Area Studies. Fishlow served as U.S. deputy assistant secretary in the U.S. Department of State in 1975-76, prior to which he taught for many years at the University of California, Berkeley. In 1972-73, he was a visiting fellow at All Souls College, Oxford. His many publications include "Making Liberal Trade Policies Work in the 1980s," in Roger D. Hansen and contributors, *U.S. Foreign Policy and the Third World: Agenda 1982;* (with Sueo Sekiguchi and Jean Carrieri) *Trade in Manufactured Products with Developing Countries: Reinforcing North-South Partnership* (Trilateral Commission, 1981); (with Abraham Lowenthal), *Latin America's Emergence* (1979); and "A New International Economic Order: What Kind?" in Albert Fishlow, Carlos Diaz-Alejandro, Richard R. Fagen, and Roger D. Hansen, *Rich and Poor Nations in the World Economy* (1978).

Tony Killick became director of the Overseas Development Institute (ODI) in London in 1982. From 1980 to 1982, he headed a major ODI research project on the IMF and stabilization in developing countries—a project that resulted in the publication of the two-volume study, *The IMF and the Third World: The Quest for Economic Stabilisation* and *The IMF and Stabilisation: Developing Country Experiences* (1984), which he co-authored with the ODI colleagues identified below. Prior to joining ODI in 1979, Killick was Ford Foundation visiting professor at the University of Nairobi (1973-1979); research fellow at Harvard University (1972-73); economic advisor to the government of Ghana (1969-72); and senior economic advisor to the U.K. Ministry for Overseas Development (1967-69). **Graham Bird** is a senior lecturer at the University of Surrey and a research associate of the Overseas Development Institute. **Jennifer Sharpley** is also an ODI research associate and was formerly a fellow of the Charles Michelson Institute in Bergen. **Mary Sutton,** now research advisor to Trocaire in Dublin, was formerly a research officer at ODI.

Stanley Please is currently a visiting scholar at Nuffield College, Oxford, and a consultant to the World Bank. Until 1983 he was on the staff of the World Bank, successively as chief of the Bank's fiscal division (1963-72) and as program director for its Eastern Africa Region (1972-77) and for its East Asia Region (1978-79). From 1980 to 1983, he was senior advisor to the senior operational vice-president of the World Bank and responsible for developing the Bank's program of structural adjustment lending. Since 1980, he has also been deeply involved in the Bank's work on Sub-Saharan Africa.

Joan M. Nelson is a visiting fellow at the Overseas Development Council. She has long been concerned with various aspects of the politics of development. After serving during the 1960s on the policy planning staff of the U.S. Agency for International Development (AID), she taught at the Massachusetts Institute of Technology and at the Johns Hopkins School of Advanced International Studies. She has also been a consultant to the World Bank and to AID. Joan Nelson's publications include: *Access to Power: Politics and the Urban Poor in Developing Nations* (1979); (with Samuel P. Huntington) *No Easy Choice: Political Participation in Developing Nations* (1976); and *AID, Influence, and Foreign Policy* (1968).

Colin I. Bradford, Jr., teaches international economics at Yale University, where he also directs the Master's Program in International Relations and serves as associate director of the Yale Center for International and Area Studies. He holds a research appointment at the National Bureau of Economic Research, for which he organized a recent conference on the global implications of the trade patterns of Asia. Prior to joining the Yale faculty, Bradford was director of the office of multilateral development banks in the U.S. Treasury Department, economic and foreign policy advisor to U.S. Senator Lawton Chiles, and associate fellow with the Overseas Development Council. Participation in several research projects on the NICs in recent years has taken him to Brazil, Korea, Mexico, the Philippines, Malaysia, and Singapore. His publications include "The Rise of the NICs as Exporters on a Global Scale" and "The NICs and World Economic Adjustment," both in Louis Turner and Neil McMullen, eds., *The Newly Industrializing Countries: Trade and Adjustment* (1982); and "U.S. Adjustment to the Global Industrial Challenge," in *Reindustrialization: Implications for Industrial Policy* (forthcoming, 1984).

Riordan Roett is professor and director of the Latin American Studies Program as well as director of the Center of Brazilian Studies at the Johns Hopkins School of Advanced International Studies in Washington, D.C. In recent years he has served as a consultant to numerous private commercial banks and multinational corporations operating in Latin America. The third edition of his book, *Brazil: Politics of a Patrimonial Society*, will appear in 1984. His article *"Democracy and Debt in South America"* recently appeared in *Foreign Affairs*, in the special issue, "America and the World, 1983."

Lance Taylor is professor of economics and nutrition at the Massachusetts Institute of Technology. Active as a development economist since taking his Ph.D. at Harvard University in 1968, he has worked as a consultant or visiting lecturer in more than twenty countries, including Mexico, Brazil, Egypt, and India. His most recent book is *Structuralist Macroeconomics* (1983). Taylor is a member of the Program Advisory Committee of the Overseas Development Council.

DeLisle Worrell has been director of research of the Central Bank of Barbados since 1973. In recent years he has held visiting fellowships at the Woodrow Wilson School of Public and International Affairs at Princeton University and at the Federal Reserve Board in Washington. He has served as a consultant to the Commonwealth Secretariat on foreign investment in Barbados, to the Caribbean Community Secretariat on industrial policy in the Caribbean, and the U.N. Conference on Trade and Development (UNCTAD) on exchange rates. His recent publications include "The Impact of Fluctuating Exchange Rates on Barbados and Jamaica," in Michael Connolly, ed., *The International Monetary System: Choices for the Future* (1982); and "Industrial Policies and Economic Growth," in the journal *Social and Economic Studies* (University of the West Indies), December 1982.

Overseas Development Council

Board of Directors*

Chairman: Robert S. McNamara
Vice Chairmen: Thornton F. Bradshaw
J. Wayne Fredericks

Marjorie C. Benton
William H. Bolin
Thomas L. Farmer**
Roger Fisher
Orville L. Freeman
John J. Gilligan
Edward K. Hamilton
Frederick Heldring
Susan Herter
Jerome Jacobson
Ruth J. Hinerfeld
Joan Holmes
Robert D. Hormats

William J. Lawless
C. Payne Lucas
Paul F. McCleary
Lawrence C. McQuade
Alfred F. Miossi
Merlin Nelson
Joseph S. Nye
John Petty
Jane Cahill Pfeiffer
John W. Sewell**
Daniel F. Sharp
Barry Zorthian

Council

Robert O. Anderson
Robert E. Asher
William Attwood
Marguerite Ross Barnett
Douglas J. Bennet
Edward G. Biester, Jr.
Jonathan B. Bingham
Eugene R. Black
Robert R. Bowie
Harrison Brown
Lester R. Brown
Ronald B. Brown
John C. Bullitt
Goler T. Butcher
Frank C. Carlucci
Lisle C. Carter, Jr.
Kathryn D. Christopherson
George J. Clark
Harlan Cleveland
Frank M. Coffin
Owen Cooper
John C. Culver
Ralph P. Davidson

Richard H. Demuth
William T. Dentzer, Jr.
Charles S. Dennison
John Diebold
Albert Fishlow
Luther H. Foster
Arvonne Fraser
Stephen J. Friedman
Richard N. Gardner
Peter Goldmark
Katharine Graham
James P. Grant
Arnold C. Harberger
Theodore M. Hesburgh, C.S.C.
Philip Johnston
Vernon E. Jordan
Nicholas deB. Katzenbach
Philip H. Klutznick
J. Burke Knapp
Peter F. Krogh
Geraldine Kunstadter
Walter J. Levy
George N. Lindsay

* Board Members are also members of the Council.
** Ex Officio.

William McSweeny
Harald B. Malmgren
Edwin M. Martin
John Mellor
Robert R. Nathan
Rev. Randolph Nugent
Daniel S. Parker
James A. Perkins
Samuel D. Proctor
Charles W. Robinson
William D. Rogers
J. Robert Schaetzel

David H. Shepard
Eugene Skolnikoff
Davidson Sommers
Joan E. Spero
Stephen Stamas
C.M. van Vlierden
Alan N. Weeden
Clifton R. Wharton, Jr.
Thomas H. Wyman
Andrew Young
George Zeidenstein

ODC Program Advisory Committee

Chairman:
John P. Lewis

Shahid Javed Burki
Albert Fishlow
James Galbraith
Jeffrey Garten
Denis Goulet
Davidson R. Gwatkin
Edward K. Hamilton
G.K. Helleiner
Albert O. Hirschman
Robert D. Hormats
Michael M. Horowitz
Gary Hufbauer
Peter B. Kenen

John Mellor
Theodore H. Moran
Joseph S. Nye
Kenneth A. Oye
Dwight H. Perkins
Gustav Ranis
Ronald K. Shelp
Robert Solomon
Joan E. Spero
Lance Taylor
Norman Uphoff
Nadia Youssef

Overseas Development Council
1717 Massachusetts Ave., N.W.
Washington, D.C. 20036
Tel. (202) 234-8701

A New Series from the Overseas Development Council

U.S.-THIRD WORLD POLICY PERSPECTIVES

Policy issues explored in coming volumes of the series, scheduled for joint publication by Transaction Books and the Overseas Development Council in 1984-85:

UNCERTAIN FUTURE: COMMERCIAL BANKS IN THE THIRD WORLD

Richard E. Feinberg and Valeriana Kallab, editors

The future of international commercial lending to the Third World has become very uncertain just when the stakes are greatest for the banks, the developing countries, and the international financial system. New approaches are needed that take into account the interests of both banks and developing-country borrowers, and that promise to ease the present unstable mix of misperceptions, obligations, needs, and expectations. Having played an essentially creative role in the recent past—how will the banks respond in the period ahead, when financing will be even more urgently needed? The individual chapters of this volume discuss the strategic thinking of the banks; the changing relationship between the commercial banks and the IMF and World Bank; the role official institutions might play in increasing bank lending; case studies of how banks could better gather and process information on creditworthiness; needed reforms relating to bank supervision and regulation; and the politics of international commercial lending.

Contributors: William H. Bolin, Catherine Gwin, Christine Bogdanowicz-Bindert, Karin Lissakers, George J. Clark, and Benjamin J. Cohen.

Richard E. Feinberg is vice president of the Overseas Development Council. He previously served as the Latin American specialist on the policy planning staff of the U.S. Department of State, and as an international economist in the Treasury Department and with the House Banking Committee. His most recent book is *The Intemperate Zone: The Third World Challenge to U.S. Policy* (1983).

Valeriana Kallab is the Overseas Development Council's director of publications and senior editor. Before joining ODC in 1972, she was a research editor and writer on international economic issues with the Carnegie Endowment for International Peace in New York.

ISBN: 0-87855-989-2 (paper) **140 pp.**
No. 2, September 1984 **$12.95**

U.S. FOREIGN POLICY AND THE THIRD WORLD: AGENDA 1985

John W. Sewell and contributors

The U.S. administration that takes office in 1985 will face a set of major challenges in putting U.S.-Third World relations on a positive track. The Overseas Development Council's 1985 *Agenda*—the tenth such U.S. policy assessment produced by the Council—will analyze recent U.S. policy performance and policy options in the areas of trade and industrial policy, international finance, development strategies, and political and strategic aspects of U.S. economic relations with the Third World. Extensive statistical annexes on U.S.-Third World economic transactions and indicators of economic and social development will again be provided.

John W. Sewell has been president of the Overseas Development Council since January 1980. From 1977 to 1979, he was the Council's executive vice president, directing ODC's research and public education programs. His many articles and other publications on international development issues include "Can the North Prosper Without Growth and Progress in the South?" in the ODC's *Agenda 1979*, and *The Ties That Bind: U.S. Interests in Third World Development* (1982).

ISBN: 0-87855-990-6 (paper)   **160 pp.**
No. 3, January 1985   **$12.95**

U.S. TRADE POLICY AND DEVELOPING COUNTRIES

Ernest H. Preeg and contributors

North-South trade relations are deeply troubled. U.S. exports to developing countries declined by $18.2 billion for 1980-83, at the cost of some 1.1 million jobs in the U.S. export sector. Many developing countries face financial crises that can only be resolved over the longer run through resumed expansion of trade. In this volume, distinguished practitioners and academics identify specific policy objectives for the United States on issues that will be prominent in the proposed new round of GATT negotiations: adjustment of U.S. firms and workers to imports from developing countries, including sensitive sectors such as textiles and steel; transition or "graduation" of the newly industrialized countries of East Asia and Latin America to a more reciprocal basis of access to markets; special benefits for the poorest or least developed countries; and preferential trading arrangements.

Ernest H. Preeg, a career foreign service officer and currently visiting fellow at the Overseas Development Council, has had long experience in trade policy and North-South economic relations. He was a member of the U.S. delegation to the GATT Kennedy Round of negotiations and later wrote a history and analysis of those negotiations, *Traders and Diplomats* (The Brookings Institution, 1969). Prior to serving as American ambassador to Haiti (1981-82), he was deputy chief of Mission in Lima, Peru (1977-80), and deputy secretary of state for International Finance and Development (1976-77).

ISBN: 0-87855-987-6 (paper)   **192 pp.**
No. 4, March 1985   **$12.95**

DEVELOPMENT STRATEGIES: A NEW SYNTHESIS

John P. Lewis and contributors

Contrary to the widespread popular view that few development efforts have worked, many Third World national development ventures in fact have been comparatively successful when measured against historical precedents. But growth rates have slowed, and the international economic environment is now much less favorable to growth and development progress than in the 1960s and even the 1970s. What has been learned from past development promotion experiences? And what approaches hold promise for the harsher economic circumstances of the 1980s and 1990s?

In this volume, prominent development practitioners and critics—including some Third World experts—discuss ideas now taking shape on how to pursue development effectively in the future. New syntheses of policy are being proposed which seek, for example, to reconcile equity with growth objectives; to reconcile both of these with developing-country adjustment needs; to strike balances between "inward" and "outward" orientations of strategy in different types of countries; and to tailor agricultural promotion and rural development to particular country circumstances.

John P. Lewis is professor of economics and international affairs at Princeton University's Woodrow Wilson School of Public and International Affairs. He is simultaneously senior advisor to the Overseas Development Council and chairman of its Program Advisory Committee. From 1979 to 1981, Mr. Lewis was Chairman of the OECD's Development Assistance Committee. He has served as a member of the U.N. Committee for Development Planning, of which he was also rapporteur from 1972 to 1978. For many years, he has alternated between academia and government posts (as Member of the Council of Economic Advisors, 1963-64, and Director of the U.S. AID Mission to India. 1964-69), with collateral periods of association with The Brookings Institution and The Ford Foundation. His recent writings have focused on South Asian development and North-South economic relations.

ISBN: 0-87855-991-4 (paper)
No. 5, May 1985

160 pp.
$12.95